DEGREES WITHOUT FREEDOM?

Degrees Without Freedom?

Education, Masculinities,

and Unemployment in North India

CRAIG JEFFREY

PATRICIA JEFFERY

ROGER JEFFERY

STANFORD UNIVERSITY PRESS

Stanford, California

2008

Stanford University Press
Stanford, California
© 2008 by the Board of Trustees of the
Leland Stanford Junior University

Library of Congress Cataloging-in-Publication Data

Jeffrey, Craig.
    Degrees without freedom? : education, masculinities, and
unemployment in North India / Craig Jeffrey, Patricia Jeffery, and
Roger Jeffery.
    "The book draws especially on research conducted in the villages
of Nangal [Bijnor District] and Qaziwala . . . a Muslim-dominated
village closer to Bijnor town"
        p. cm.
    Includes bibliographical references and index.
    ISBN 978-0-8047-5742-3 (cloth : alk. paper) —
    ISBN 978-0-8047-5743-0 (pbk. : alk. paper)
    1. Young men—Employment—India. 2. Education—India.
3. Unemployment—India. 4. Underemployment—India.
5. Masculinity—India. 6. India—Ethnic relations. 7. Equality—
India. I. Jeffery, Patricia. II. Jeffery, Roger. III. Title.

HD6276.I42J44 2008
331.3'40954—dc22

                                               2007016656

Printed in the United States of America

Typeset at Stanford University Press in 10/15 Minion

Contents

Tables

Acknowledgments

The book draws especially on research conducted in the villages of Nangal and Qaziwala and our greatest debt of gratitude is to the people of these villages for their warmth, kindness and generosity. We also thank the Economic and Social Research Council (R000238495), Ford Foundation Overseas Development Administration and Royal Geographical Society for funding our research. We are indebted to our four research assistants, Swaleha Begum, Chhaya Pandey, Shaila Rais and Manjula Sharma, who worked with dedication, cheerfulness and care. For their support and encouragement in India, we also thank Amita Baviskar, OP Bohra, Radhika Chopra, Zoya Hasan, Krishna Kumar, Jagpal Singh, Nandini Sundar, Patricia Uberoi, Satya Vira, Leela Visaria and Pravin Visaria. In Edinburgh and Seattle we thank especially Paul Bennett, Paul Brass, Manuela Ciotti, Markus Daechsel, Hugo Gorringe, Katharyne Mitchell, Heidi Pauwels, Priti Ramamurthy, Kalyanakrishnan Sivaramakrishnan and Matt Sparke. In addition, Mukulika Bannerjee, Harriet Bulkcley, Sharad Chari, Stuart Corbridge and Paul Robbins provided helpful advice; Stuart Aitken, Radhika Chopra, Colin McFarlane, Susan Wadley and Stephen Young read and commented on earlier drafts of the book, Kacy McKinney assisted with the construction of the index, and Muriel Bell and John Feneron at Stanford University Press provided generous editorial assistance. Finally, we thank Jane Dyson for the enormous support and guidance she offered Craig through the writing process.

The Authors

CRAIG JEFFREY is Associate Professor in Geography and International Studies at the University of Washington. His research focuses on youth politics, oppositional masculinities and everyday corruption in South Asia. He is also interested in critical pedagogic practice, particularly around the themes of youth and popular culture. Craig Jeffrey has published over thirty articles on his research including papers in *World Development, Modern Asian Studies, Annals of the Association of American Geographers* and *Development and Change.* He is currently co-editing a book with Jane Dyson on global youth and spatial change entitled *Telling Young Lives: Portraits of Global Youth* (forthcoming from Temple University Press) and writing a research monograph on corruption and the middle classes in India.

PATRICIA JEFFERY is Professor of Sociology at the University of Edinburgh, Scotland, where she has held teaching and research positions since 1973. She has carried out a series of social research projects in rural Bijnor district, north India, since 1982. Her recent books include (with Roger Jeffery) *Don't Marry Me to a Plowman: Women's Everyday Lives in Rural North India* (Westview Press and Vistaar, 1996); (with Amrita Basu, edited) *Resisting the Sacred and the Secular: Women's Activism and Politicised Religion in South Asia* (Routledge, 1998, and Kali for Women, 1999); and (with Radhika Chopra, edited) *Educational Regimes in Contemporary India* (Sage, 2005).

ROGER JEFFERY has taught at the University of Edinburgh, Scotland, since 1972, and is now Professor of Sociology of South Asia. He has carried out a series of social research projects in rural Bijnor district, north India, since 1982. His recent books include (with Patricia Jeffery) *Population, Gender and Politics: Demographic Change in Rural North India* (Cambridge University Press, 1997); (with Nandini Sundar and Neil Thin) *Branching Out: Joint Forest Management in Four Indian States* (Oxford University Press, 2001); and (with Jens Lerche, edited) *Social and Political Change in Uttar Pradesh: European Perspectives* (Manohar, 2003).

DEGREES WITHOUT FREEDOM?

1

Introduction

Chandbir

In March 2001, when we were walking around Nangal, a village in western Uttar Pradesh (UP), India, we met a man named Chandbir.[1] In his mid twenties in 2001, Chandbir came from a family belonging to the middle-ranking Jat caste and owning 4 acres of land. He possessed a high school pass but failed three times to obtain a position in the army. Some of Chandbir's friends teased him by promoting him within the army hierarchy every time he failed the examination, and they called him 'Captain Chandbir' in 2001.

Chandbir was keen to talk, and he led us over to a rope bed in his family's courtyard. We asked him how he regarded education in the light of his failure to obtain a salaried job. Perched on the edge of the rope bed, Chandbir leaned forward eagerly, and told us:

Education provides great benefit. Education allows one to obtain good employment, and, if you don't obtain a service job, you should still certainly study. An educated person can do any work or business. An educated person can also run a shop. In addition, education provides manners. An educated person can talk to anyone. Wherever you go, education provides confidence. Education is very important. . . . When I work in the field in the sun, my mind starts to whirl. I've realized that to get out of the dust and soil [*dhūl mittī*] of the village people need to study. It's only by studying that they will escape.

There are many Chandbirs in Nangal. Growing enthusiasm for education is a marked feature of contemporary India. During fourteen months' ethno-

[1]All names in the book are pseudonyms.

graphic field research in north India in 2000–2002, we heard many parents and young people telling us that prolonged education (*parhāī*) is central to children's futures. Like Chandbir, parents and young people discussed the benefits of education with reference to a range of skills and knowledge offered by schooling. They imagined education to provide a good job, manners and an escape from the 'dust and soil' of the village.

The physical landscape of Nangal village, Bijnor District, also testified to the importance of education in western UP. Driving into the village from the direction of the district town, Bijnor, one first encountered a large private secondary school: several whitewashed buildings clustered around an area of scuffed ground that served as a children's playground. Advertisements for private tutors, coaching institutes and textbooks surrounded the school compound. In the early mornings and late afternoons, children crowded this area dressed in colorful uniforms and clutching bulging school bags. Education also marked the landscape of Qaziwala, a Muslim-dominated village closer to Bijnor town. At the junction between the main road and the track to Qaziwala is a large madrasah, an Islamic educational institution, which in 2001 catered for over 1,200 pupils. Around 7 AM, and again at about noon, children poured in and out of the madrasah. At the same times, buses, cycle rickshaws and three-wheeled motorized vehicles plied the main road carrying richer children south-east to private schools in Bijnor and poorer children north-west to a government-aided secondary school.

Between September 2000 and April 2002, we lived in a middle class colony, Awas Vikas, built mainly in the mid-1990s on the edge of Bijnor. The landscape surrounding our home was also replete with signs of a growing enthusiasm for formal education. A large advertising hoarding opposite the entrance to the colony proclaimed that 'Modern Era Public School,' a new English-Medium school in Bijnor, provides "every facility for the best education in India." From 5 AM every morning, teenaged children streamed into Awas Vikas on bicycles and scooters to start private tutorials before school. By 7 AM, cycle rickshaws, typically carrying ten to fifteen carefully groomed schoolchildren, set off toward the numerous primary schools scattered around the town. Between Bijnor and Delhi, signs for educational institutions offering opulent and successful futures lined the road: schools promising children "the mind of an Athenian and the body of a Spartan," institutions dedicated to "giving your kids a head start in life" and multiple nurseries tailored to "the exceptionally gifted child."

We encountered similar narratives of education as social opportunity in the seminar rooms of Delhi. Scholars often referred to mainstream schooling as a basis for individual 'empowerment' and a wellspring for social and political transformation. Development workers in organizations such as the UK's Department for International Development (DFID) and the World Bank spoke in similar terms.

Such perceptions are part of general understandings of the significance of education in contemporary India. Indeed, more than half of President Abdul Kalam's address to the nation on 14 August 2004 was devoted to emphasizing the importance of the education system "in creating an enlightened, dynamic and prosperous society" and transforming "a human being into a wholesome whole, a noble soul and an asset to the universe."[2] From the sugar cane fields of rural Bijnor district, through the offices of provincial western UP and onwards along the road to Delhi, development planners, businesspeople and parents depicted education as a tool for personal and collective development.

The idea of education as a central 'social good' has a long history in UP (see Kumar 1994). It occupied a prominent place in the imagination of the founders of post-colonial India (Kumar 1994). Nor is it surprising that we encountered, in the seminar rooms of Delhi, development workers and scholars speaking in rich tones of the benefits of education. Not only do these development workers and scholars have a powerful professional stake in education, as teachers or people engaged in introducing educational initiatives, but they have also gained personally from sustained formal schooling and university degrees, as, indeed, we have ourselves.

At a theoretical level, the narratives and landscapes we encountered in north India remind us of Drèze and Sen's (1995) insistence on education as 'social opportunity.' In his work, *Development as Freedom*, Sen (1999) writes of education as a key tool of individual and social transformation intimately connected to people's ability to obtain a range of 'substantive freedoms,' such as employment, political participation and dignity.

This book highlights the potential for education to transform people's lives. But we also show how power and culture mediate people's access to the freedoms that education provides. Rather than assuming that people from margin-

[2]Full details of his address are available at: http://presidentofindia.nic.in/scripts.

groups always benefit from schooling, we highlight the struggles faced by marginalized educated men to acquire work, political leverage and respect. The idea for this book first came from a conversation with a young man called Girish.[3] At least twice a week, Girish would come round to our house in Awas Vikas on his moped. Girish was the son of a Brahmin doctor who had moved from Nangal to a colony on the edge of Bijnor. Holding a BA degree, Girish sold pharmaceuticals for a private company but harbored dreams of capturing a government job. In these respects, he was quite similar to many richer young men in Nangal and Qaziwala. Sitting down during our conversations, Girish exuded a restless energy, his legs swaying from side to side as he spoke. On one occasion, Girish felt moved to comment on our project on schooling and inequality in western UP by noting that "education is nothing, what matters here now is *source* and *force*."[4] '*Source*' referred to social contacts and '*force*' connoted physical might or the combination of money and muscle. A few days later, and preoccupied with the same thought, Girish told us, "What I meant to say is that it is money and *jugār* that matter here." In his Hindi/English dictionary, McGregor (1993: 376) translates *jugār* as 'provisioning' but in western UP it commonly refers to the capacity to improvise shrewdly with available resources.[5] While we were living in Bijnor, Girish went for an interview for a position in the railway service. Reflecting the massive disparity between the demand for government jobs and supply of such positions, over a thousand people appeared for the handful of posts on offer. Each of these thousand people had the requisite educational qualifications. Girish remembered that "those with *jugār* got the jobs."

What we now remember about that meeting with Girish, and what became increasingly clear to us as our research progressed, was the active and energetic

[3]Our overall research project focused on the relationship between rising secondary school education and the reproduction of class, caste, religious and gendered hierarchies.

[4]Where we italicize English words in documenting reported speech, this indicates that these are the precise words that our informants used rather than translations from Hindi.

[5]Throughout the book we have used McGregor's (1993) dictionary for translating Hindi words.

manner in which young men in north India have responded to educated underemployment and the varied ways in which they discussed education. But the broader point we take from Girish is that education rarely acts as some irresistible force propelling young people toward secure employment and respectable futures. Rather, educated young people—in India as in many areas of the world—emerge from school or university into highly competitive fields of social struggle in which the utility and meaning of 'education' and 'modernity' emerge as problematic, and in which *source*, *force* and the need to improvise become paramount concerns.

This chapter seeks to provide a conceptual framework for understanding young people's efforts to negotiate educated un/under-employment. We wish to locate the struggles of young men such as Girish with reference to key scholarly debates on education, youth cultures and social inequality. The next section of this chapter introduces Drèze and Sen's theory of education as social opportunity. We then consider how a focus on youth cultures, the cultural politics of modernity and masculinity might offer additional insights into young men's practices. Finally, we outline our methodology and the argument and structure of the book.

Sen, Education and Freedom

In collaborative research with Jean Drèze (Drèze and Sen 1995), Sen offers a counterpoint to mainstream development's preoccupation with questions of economic growth and governance. Instead, Drèze and Sen propose that international development organizations and national governments in poor countries should pay much greater attention to improving education and health care. The authors advance their argument with reference to how the widespread provision of basic education may improve a country's economic growth, using China as a key example, and by presenting a set of propositions about education's connection to individual and collective well-being.

Drèze and Sen argue that elementary education (Classes 1 to 8) is valuable to the freedom of a person in five distinct ways. First, education has an intrinsic importance in that being educated has a value in itself. Second, education plays 'instrumental personal roles': "Education [is] important for getting a job and more generally for making use of economic opportunities. The resulting expansion in incomes and economic means can, in turn, add to a person's freedom to achieve functionings that he or she values" (Drèze and Sen 1995: 14). Third, Drèze and Sen identify 'instrumental social roles' whereby education facilitates public discussion of social needs and encourages subordinate groups to make informed collective demands. Fourth, they refer to 'instrumental process roles,' understood as benefits aside from the explicitly educational function of schools, such as promoting social interaction and broadening young people's horizons. Finally, education is perceived to play empowerment and distributive roles: "Greater literacy and educational achievements of disadvantaged groups can increase their ability to resist oppression, to organize politically, and to get a fairer deal" (Drèze and Sen 1995: 14–15).

Drèze and Sen's ideas have powerfully shaped how scholars, practitioners and activists think about schooling in poor countries. As Sen (1999; chapter 12) explains in later work, they go beyond human capital approaches[6] by insisting on close links between education and various *social* goods. Moreover, unlike human capital theorists, Drèze and Sen are sensitive to how unequal access to education frequently reproduces inequality within society, a point well made in a volume of regional case studies (Drèze and Sen 1997). Implicit in Sen's work is recognition of the multiple means through which people learn, for example through apprenticeships (Lave and Wenger 1991; Hameed 2005), labor (Breman 1985; Parry 1999) or play (Katz 2004). Moreover, Drèze and Sen have made important empirical contributions to understanding how education works in India.

Nevertheless, a review of critical approaches to education suggests two principal difficulties with Drèze and Sen's (1995) and Sen's (1999) construction. A first problem with Sen's schema is one of emphasis. In laying repeated stress on the importance of schooling in and of itself, he risks downplaying how schooling is differently experienced. The notion that education is intrinsically benefi-

---

[6]Becker was instrumental in promoting the notion that 'human capital', comprised of skills and knowledge learnt in school, improves workers' productivity and generates economic growth. In the wake of this theoretical formulation, numerous studies emerged which purported to demonstrate the close connection between economic growth and people's possession of school knowledge (e.g. Heyneman 1980, 2003).

cial is now widely circulated by governments, non-state actors and local people. Yet these ideas have routinely been the subject of critique: from the radical 'deschoolers' (Illich 1972) to scholars who stress the role of formal education in creating 'failure' as a social label (Willis 1977; Levinson and Holland 1996). Others have pointed to how school education is implicated in the creation or perpetuation of national, religious, gendered, and class identities and beliefs (e.g. Althusser 1971; Bowles and Gintis 1976; Bourdieu and Passeron 1977; Foucault 1980; Giroux 1983, 2001).[7]

The second problem relates to the social and political processes through which marginalized people obtain substantive freedoms. Sen is sometimes slow to explain clearly the mechanisms through which one freedom creates others. Moreover, where he has attempted to do so, other scholars have occasionally challenged his interpretation. Reflecting on the comparative position of China and India, for example, Corbridge (2002) has questioned the idea common in Sen's writing that democratic governments are inevitably more likely than authoritarian regimes to generate economic growth, improve welfare and provide food security for the poor. Corbridge argues that Sen fails to consider the Marxist arguments that democratic governments frequently side with dominant classes and that freedoms are often achieved through social struggle. In relation to schooling, Jeffery and Jeffery (1998) have used empirical work in UP, as well as secondary evidence from other parts of India, to question the notion that formal education within school inevitably improves women's autonomy and lowers fertility. Jeffery and Jeffery show that the correlation between low fertility and women's schooling does not demonstrate a causal link. Moreover, many schools in western UP reproduce highly exclusionary gendered norms. Parents characteristically send their daughters to school to groom them for their future role as wives and mothers and install restrictive notions of femininity (see Jeffery and Basu 1996; Jeffery and Jeffery 1998; see also Agarwal et al. 2006).

The operative word in Drèze and Sen's theoretical schema is 'potential': education *can* improve people's access to multiple freedoms *if* other conditions permit. Questions of whether education is the most effective point of entry in processes of social empowerment and, crucially, what *other initiatives* might

---

[7]For a discussion of different generations of critical educational research, see Levinson and Holland (1996).

need to be taken in tandem with efforts to improve educational access become pressing. As Corbridge (2002) and Seabright (2001) have argued, the implications of Sen's work for policy are not always rendered explicit in his writing.

We are not arguing *against* efforts to expand the educational opportunities of the poor. There is an urgent need to support Drèze and Sen's call for improved school facilities within and outside India. A large number of young people in South Asia, especially girls, still lack access to primary, let alone secondary, education. These young people typically enter household labor or poorly paid manual, service or industrial work outside the home, often in grueling and dangerous conditions (Nieuwenhuys 1994; Dyson 2007). Drèze and Sen's arguments have an important strategic political value in the context of political resistance to improving government education and considerable state apathy around addressing the material and educational needs of working children. It should be equally clear that we do not subscribe to the type of 'post-development' theorizing that might imagine formal education as somehow 'inappropriate' to the strategies of rural north Indians. The example of Chandbir reminds us that many young people in rural India have absorbed notions of schooling as a form of development. Rather, we are concerned that Sen's theoretical emphasis on education as a driver for change might divert attention away from social struggles over the value and uses of education in situations of economic uncertainty. As an alternative strategy, we seek to uncover the importance of post-educational landscapes as *terrains of social and political struggle*. We use geographical terminology wittingly to signal our interest in how young people equipped with very different resources compete for work, security and respect *on the ground*.

Global Youth Cultures

Our attention to the politics of educated young people speaks not only to recent calls for greater attention to 'education in practice' (Chopra and Jeffery 2005) but also to nascent literatures on the changing nature of youth cultures in the face of neoliberalism (Nilan and Feixa 2006). Education has failed to open up expanded employment and other substantive freedoms for young people across large swathes of the world. Rising educational enrollment and a decline in opportunities for salaried employment often have an especially marked impact upon the self-perception and cultural practices of young men, who frequently feel under intense pressure to 'cash in' on their education in the spheres of work and politics.[8] The global spread of images of success based on prolonged participation in schooling and subsequent entry into professional or white-collar work has encouraged parents and young men to invest time, money and effort in extended formal schooling. In the global south especially, but also in many 'northern' contexts, widely different forms of neoliberal economic change have simultaneously undermined the opportunities for educated young men to obtain stable and well-paid work. Thus arises one of the most unsettling paradoxes of contemporary globalization: at almost the precise moment that an increasing number of people formerly excluded from mainstream schooling have come to recognize the empowering possibilities of education, many of the opportunities for these groups to benefit from schooling are disappearing.

'Neoliberal economic change' varies widely from place to place (e.g. Harvey 2005). In some areas, processes of economic restructuring have created new opportunities for secure employment, and rates of un/under-employment are quite low. Even where it has not, some young people in the global south are able to benefit from processes of economic restructuring (Bucholtz 2002). For example, in contemporary India there is a thin upper stratum of young people who acquire high quality education in elite institutions and move smoothly into secure salaried work, often within the professions or business. Contemporary concern in the West over the movement of jobs from Euro-America to India has provoked growing scholarly interest in this English-speaking upper class (Fernandes 2006), who are geographically concentrated in the largest cities in India and comprise a tiny fraction of the overall youth population. Recent research on these young people has shown how processes of global change are opening up new leisure spaces, consumption opportunities and 'identity possibilities' for this elite (Lukose 2005).

[8]This is not to deny the rising numbers of young women seeking paid employment, nor how widespread unemployment negatively affects young women in some parts of the world. Recent work shows that educated women seeking paid employment often suffer from a type of 'double subordination' in poor countries: as young people excluded by economic and political structures from secure salaried work, and as women seeking to challenge entrenched gendered ideas that restrict their access to paid employment outside the home (e.g. Miles 1998; Miles 2002).

Notwithstanding this evidence, the combination of people's expanding participation in school and collapsing opportunities for secure employment *is* creating mounting pressures on young men in a wide array of settings. Within India, Nieuwenhuys' (1994) study of unemployed secondary school matriculates in Kerala, Heuzé's (1996) research on employment markets in central India, and Parry's (2005) discussions of steelworkers in Chhattisgarh, all refer to the rising importance of a set of educated un/under-employed youths. Indeed, unemployment or underemployment is now a growing threat for even some of the most advantaged sections of the youth population in South Asia (Fernandes 2006), East Asia (Louie and Low 2005) and Latin America (Gutmann 1996). Moreover, educated un/under-employment is an increasing feature of many western countries (Brown 1995; Bourgois 1995; McDowell 2003).

Underemployment is often defined as dependence on involuntary part-time work, intermittent unemployment, and/or involvement in poorly remunerated labor (Prause and Dooley 1997: 245). In other cases, scholars use underemployment to denote the under-utilization of skills, especially educational capacities. Distinct from this search for key measures of underemployment, our interest is in understanding how young men themselves come to perceive themselves as 'underemployed' or 'unemployed.' We also examine how a person's social position shapes the process through which they define themselves as un/under-employed.

A central question in this context is how far educated un/under-employed young men are able to respond positively to their predicament. The work of French sociologist Pierre Bourdieu bears centrally on this question of young people's agency. Bourdieu is often credited with having moved beyond Marxist treatments of class and capital by emphasizing the importance of social networks and cultural power in the perpetuation of social hierarchies (Calhoun 1993). These preoccupations with inequality and reproduction color his approach to studying unemployment; Bourdieu (1984) argued that educated un/under-employed young people in 1960s France had found creative means to negotiate their exclusion from secure salaried work, but in ways shaped by the financial resources they received from their parents, their social connections and the nature of the credentials they had acquired in school. Those among the educated un/under-employed from relatively wealthy backgrounds often possessed prestigious school qualifications and were well connected in urban society. Capitalizing on their money, social resources and air of cultural ac-complishment, these men managed to acquire reasonably secure, status-saving work. By contrast, poorer members of the educated un/under-employed lacked the money, connections and credentials required to find acceptable 'fallback employment,' and they often struggled to acquire even poorly paid, temporary, service-type occupations.

Bourdieu therefore imputes the educated un/under-employed with the ca-pacity to respond actively to their predicament. He also provides a set of con-ceptual tools for understanding structures that shape young people's strategies. In particular, Bourdieu stresses the importance of cultural capital—the range of goods, titles and forms of demeanor that are 'misrecognized' as legitimate within arenas of power—and social capital, defined as instrumentally valu-able social bonds, in young people's capacity to devise effective responses to economic exclusion. Individuals' chances of success within the 'field' of em-ployment competition depended crucially on the volume and form of their economic, social and cultural capital. Bourdieu also directed attention toward how various types of capital are inculcated in people's 'habitus': orientations to action 'written in' to a person's movements, reflexes and tastes, and which are both structured by people's experience while also structuring future action. Bourdieu's practical application of the concept of habitus pointed to the ability of young people from dominant backgrounds to negotiate markets for presti-gious qualifications and jobs with confidence and ease. Bourdieu dwelt on the elite's 'feel for the game,' or *sens de placement*, and a corresponding lack of social skill and spatial awareness among marginalized social groups.

Bourdieu's concepts of cultural capital, social capital and habitus offer a valuable means of conceptualizing how structures may enable or constrain dif-ferently positioned young men in their quest to negotiate educated un/under-employment. Significantly, his attention to the social networks and symbolic practices through which dominance is reproduced and contested highlights how inequality is practiced in space (Reed-Danahay 2005). Bourdieu's (1986) notion of social capital also anticipates recent social science critiques of the term by attending to the role of the state and other forces in shaping social capi-tal formation and examining the role of social connections in the reproduction of unequal relations of power (cf. Putnam 1993; Jeffrey 2001; Harriss 2002).

But Bourdieu's schema rather implies that—through their inferior habi-

tus—young people from subordinate groups will inevitably lose out to dominant classes and that they are incapable of meaningful social critique. In addition, as feminist critics have pointed out (Reay 1995), Bourdieu's work partially
obscures the gendered character of cultural, social and economic capital accumulation. Moreover, Bourdieu implies that the competition for wealth, social
contacts and cultural capital determines young people's strategies, and thereby
downplays many other human goals, such as friendship and love (Dreyfuss and
Rabinow 1992).[9]

Scholars associated with the UK's Centre for Contemporary Cultural Studies (CCCS)—the so-called 'Birmingham School'—sought to explore young
people's agency more explicitly (e.g. Willis 1977; Hebdige 1979; McRobbie 1979).
Established in 1963 at Birmingham University, CCCS developed a range of critical approaches to the analysis and interpretation of youth cultural practice
which focused in particular on the styles of dress, speech and behavior—or
'youth subcultures'—employed by young men in public settings to challenge
dominant notions of culture and propriety. CCCS scholars, particularly the
sociologist Paul Willis, saw in culture a means for working class young people
to counteract and reject powerful ideas within society. Drawing especially on
Gramsci, Willis (1982: 112) stressed youth involvement in 'cultural production,'
understood as people's efforts to deploy available symbolic resources in ways
shaped by broader structural forces.[10] More than Bourdieu, Willis was aware of
the potential for young people's cultural production to change society. According to Willis, power struggles between unequal social actors are never predetermined, and subordinate groups often make significant gains in fields of struggle. Willis (1982) thus sought to distance himself from the suggestion implicit in
much of Bourdieu's early work on habitus that people's embodied dispositions
trap them into acting in certain pre-given ways. But Willis was nevertheless suspicious of the potential for young people to transform society. Building on the
work of the French Marxist thinker, Althusser (1971), Willis suggested that, even
where they try to resist dominant structures, young people's cultural produc-

[9]For alternative readings of Bourdieu's work, see Lane (2000), Bourdieu (2001), and
Reed-Danahay (2005).
[10]Willis (1982: 112) defines cultural production as "the active, collective use and explo-
rations of received symbolic, ideological and cultural resources to explain, make sense of
and positively respond to 'inherited' structural and material conditions."

tions are always only 'partial penetrations' of those structures: critiques marked by the ideologies of the powerful.[11]

The influence of the Birmingham School, and Willis in particular, is evident in many subsequent critical ethnographies of educated un/under-employment (e.g. Demerath 1999; Levinson 1999), and has also contributed to a new emphasis on agency and practice within broader geographies (Valentine et al. 1998) and anthropologies (Bucholtz 2002) of young people. At the same time, and informed by the work of Butler (1990), several new anthropologies of youth move beyond Willis and his peers by exposing how people's idea of themselves as subjects (their 'subjectivities') and of their own masculinity or femininity do not simply reflect an underlying 'self,' 'identity' or 'habitus' and still less a particular class position. These studies stress instead how people's notions of themselves as men or women emerge out of how they speak, dress and comport themselves, and how these aspects of their style come together within 'performances.' It follows that, as far as identities cohere, they are always in motion, and liable to be unsettled by future rounds of performance. This provides fertile ground for exploring how young people 'orchestrate' discourses and practices to achieve a notion of selfhood (Levinson and Holland 1996), 'author' their lives (Demerath 2003; cf. Foucault 1988; Bakhtin 1986) or engage in forms of subversion, irony and play (Butler 1990; Katz 2004). As Yon (2000) points out, young people's senses of self emerging through practice may be partial, overlapping or contradictory.

There are parallels between these relatively new anthropologies of youth and accounts in the global north, where researchers have argued that young people's cultural performances are increasingly creative, flexible and mobile (e.g. Furlong and Cartmel 1997). Scholars commonly claim that processes of neoliberal economic restructuring and the emergence of what Giddens (1991) calls 'disorganised capitalism' have blocked many of the familiar channels along which young people historically developed attachments, acquired employment

[11]Hall (1985), a member of CCCS, criticized some CCCS scholars' over-reliance on the Althusserian idea that ideologies form an implacable force moving in a 'top-down' direction to inculcate in the minds of working class people ideas against their long-term interests. Hall stressed that power struggles between differently positioned social groups are never predetermined, but comprised of a fluid process of negotiation. Willis's notion of partial penetrations, and the general tone of his papers in the early 1980s, arguably anticipates Hall's critique.

and negotiated their transition to adulthood. Instead, young people in North America, Australasia and Western Europe are imagined to be negotiating landscapes of risk (Beck and Beck-Gernsheim 2002). The burgeoning literature on youth and risk points to how young people's unstable cultural practices traverse and unsettle sociological boundaries of class, race, gender and ethnicity (e.g. Cieslki and Pollock 2002).

Insistence on the fluid and ambivalent construction of ideas of self in practice nevertheless tends to detract from the wider political economic issues at the heart of Bourdieu's and Willis's work. As Osella and Osella (2000) make clear in their ethnography of ex-untouchable mobility in south India, caste, class, age and other aspects of a person's social position powerfully influence how young people strategize after leaving school. Ferguson (1999) engages with this idea by focusing on the types of 'investment' required in sustaining what he terms 'cultural styles.' Because cultivating a style is expensive, financially and in terms of the time spent learning distinct modes of performance, people tend to make choices between competing stylistic options. Ferguson's analysis also shows how the resources people can command, which are a function of their position in relation to wider structures, influence people's choices about where and how to perform cultural styles. Ferguson's elaboration of the notion of cultural style therefore returns us to something close to Willis's theorization of cultural production, but differs in at least two ways. First, Ferguson, building on Butler, refuses to link cultural practice to underlying 'identities,' class-based or otherwise. Second, Ferguson's account differs from Willis's in stressing the importance of skills quite durably inscribed in bodies, movements and tastes within processes of cultural production. There are strong echoes here of Bourdieu's discussion of habitus. But Ferguson rejects Bourdieu's notion that embodied skills can be delimited from a person's social background and that people are to a large extent 'locked in' to particular forms of action by their habitus.

In sum, we find in Willis's ideas of cultural production a concept that emphasizes structure and agency in roughly equal measure, and, in particular, remains open to the *potential* of young people to respond inventively to educated un/under-employment, even in unpromising circumstances. Willis's work foregrounds the value of a culturally and organizationally inflected political economy approach, one that refuses to reduce questions of cultural practice to the ineluctable working of global capitalism but remains sensitive to durable inequalities which constrain educated young people's 'substantive freedoms.' Drawing on Ferguson's and Bourdieu's work we nonetheless remain alive to weaknesses in Willis's notion of cultural production and to the possibility that ideas of cultural capital, social capital and habitus may also help explain the strategies and trajectories of the educated un/under-employed.

Styles of Appropriation

Emphasis on the fluid and highly unstable nature of young people's cultural performances also risks obscuring how powerful cultural ideas may lend a distinctive character to the stylistic choices and political strategies of young men. In particular, recent accounts of educated un/under-employment in the global south point to the key importance of notions of 'modernity' and 'tradition' in young men's cultural styles. At almost the precise moment when scholars have come to critique concepts such as modern/traditional, urban/rural, developed/undeveloped as frameworks for academic thought, young people in situations of economic threat are often using these very categories to reflect on experiences, express aspirations, and signal social differences (Mosse 2003).

The contemporary salience of self-consciously 'anti-modern' or 'neotraditional' youth cultures exemplify this trend (Bucholtz 2002). In a wide variety of settings, young men have used a vision of 'tradition' or 'indigineity' to rationalize poor occupational outcomes, inure themselves against the threat of exclusion or tap into alternative sources of respect, work and sociability. This possibility is rehearsed in Willis's (1977) classic ethnography of a West Midland school in the UK. Willis described how working class 'lads' learnt through their everyday interactions with each other and their teachers to celebrate local traditions of manual labor above middle class jobs. The lads created a strong counter-culture of young male prowess by cherishing ideas of 'toughness' within their peer group, stigmatizing hard workers at school as 'sissy' and rebelling against school disciplining structures. The lads' cultural practices challenged school discourses that prized educational achievement as a route to 'modern' skilled or white-collar salaried work. At the same time, Willis shows that, in valuing manual labor, the lads reproduced the gendered structures of authority that they had learnt in the home. Moreover, their 'rebellion' served to prevent any genuinely transformative politics; that young men came to value manual labor was extraordinarily convenient for the operation of global and national capitalisms in 1970s Britain, which depended on the supply of willing manual workers.

Willis's work is paralleled in certain respects by more recent ethnographies of young men, which also show how the underemployed may borrow and adapt from their own cultural background to create new youth styles. For example, in his analysis of Latino immigrants' 'search for respect' in Harlem, New York, Bourgois (1995), like Willis, describes how young men often respond to their exclusion from secure salaried employment by embedding themselves within macho cultures of resistance founded on a vision of 'tradition.' Bourgois describes how youth street culture among Puerto Rican men in Harlem builds on some 'modern' idioms, but he also highlights the importance of Puerto Rican styles imagined locally as traditional within oppositional practices. "If anything is extraordinary about the Puerto Rican experience, it is that Puerto Rican cultural forms have continued to expand and reinvent themselves in the lives of second- and third-generation immigrants around a consistent theme of dignity and autonomy" (1995: 11).

Recent research has also extended Willis's insights outside Europe and North America. Contrary to the expectation that youth in the global south are concerned with emulating 'The West' or regionally-articulated versions of 'the modern,' many recent ethnographies have shown how the educated un/underemployed may self-consciously oppose hegemonic visions of modernity. For example, Demerath (2003) has documented how, under conditions of intense competition for white-collar work in Papua New Guinea, young people contested the idea that formal education offers a route to upward mobility. He notes the rise among students of alternative discourses of education in which young people criticized those who succeed in school, whom they perceived as 'acting extra.' Elsewhere, Demerath (1999) argues that un/under-employed young men frequently re-evaluated the usefulness of their education in the face of a shortage of salaried work *after* prolonged successful engagement in formal schooling. Demerath describes educated young men who responded to a lack of secure salaried work by returning to their rural homes where they engaged in subsistence livelihoods and sought to revive histories of rural community. Similarly, Levinson (1999) documents how many young men in urban Mexico had circumvented conditions of economic uncertainty by entering artisanal work and investing in community-based social networks or 'intimate cultures' of convivial relations imagined locally as 'indigenous.'

Demerath and Levinson therefore provide examples of how elements of a heritage or indigenous culture may be selectively appropriated and resignified as a response to demoralizing social change. Young men's use of traditional cultural resources *accords* with scholarly notions of modernity as a cognitive transformation—a greater self-consciousness about how one's life differs from the lives of people in the past (Giddens 1991)—even while it *diverges* from regionally hegemonic notions of modernity as a material process of change centered on acquisition of white-collar employment and expensive consumer goods. By demonstrating that they can be *modern*—in the sense of reflexively engaged in projects of self-making—without being *modernized*—in the sense of invested in Westernized styles of consumption and notions of school education as progress—the educated un/under-employed young men described by Demerath and Levinson are constructing what a number of anthropologists have called 'alternative modernities' (Appadurai 1996; Gaonkar 2001).

Dore's (1976) account of a 'diploma disease' putatively affecting the global south offers a rather different picture of the cultural practices of un/under-employed young men. Reviewing evidence from Japan, Sri Lanka and Kenya, Dore (1976: 231) argued that rather than "settling down to their fate in the traditional sector" young men typically responded to un/under-employment by obtaining more education or seeking temporary clerical work. Similarly, Bourdieu (1984) argued that educated young men in France in the 1960s and 1970s continued to place value on being 'modern educated' even in situations of prolonged unemployment.

The conclusions of Dore and Bourdieu resonate with a range of recent ethnographic accounts of youth cultures. For example, Weiss's (2002) analysis of neoliberal economic change in urban Tanzania focuses on the self-consciously 'modern' strategies of educated un/under-employed youth. Weiss argues that young men have responded to economic uncertainties by entering work within the informal economy, especially businesses as barbershop owners. Weiss notes that many of the barbershops are named after the cities in Europe or North America that young men dream of visiting. By ironically indexing the distance between their ambitions and actual economic position, the barbershops have become symbols of young men's exclusion and modern ambitions: "their sense of expulsion and inadequacy is literally built into the urban landscape" (102). Cole's (2005) work on the cultural practices of young men in contemporary urban Madagascar offers further evidence of a tendency for marginalized urban men to re-establish respect by investing in locally-meaningful visions of 'the modern.' She describes how young men have responded to un/under-employment by adopting a fashionable urban style and cultivating relationships with richer young women, who have made money from transactional sex in the urban economy. Cole stresses young men's close attention to sustaining a cosmopolitan, urban and fashionable image in the competition to please and attract wealthy female partners.

It is therefore possible to distill from the available literature on educated un/under-employed young men two complex and internally heterogeneous 'sets' of stylistic strategies: a first in which young men seek to craft lives in opposition to regionally hegemonic visions of what it is to be 'modern' and by selectively appropriating 'traditional' symbols; and a second in which young men strive to present themselves as 'modern,' often but not inevitably by signaling their affiliation with 'the West.' Attempts to reject or rework locally salient ideas of the modern might be imagined then as forms of what Hirschman (1970) termed 'exit from' or 'loyalty to' locally diverse conceptions of modern development. At the same time, it is important not to overdraw the distinction between these two 'sets' of response, which are better understood as different emphases within cultural strategies subject to constant change rather than radical and fixed distinctions. As Sivaramakrishnan and Agrawal (2003) and Liechty (2004) point out, present-day bricoleurs draw on cultural resources that are coded locally as both 'modern' and 'traditional,' often at the same time. Nor should we fall into the trap of suggesting that different styles are laid out as 'choices' for young men. Young men's investments in particular styles are better understood as *appropriations*, a word which suggests creativity but also directs attention toward the influence of structural and ideological forces over contemporary youth.

Our review of styles of appropriation offers a framework within which to locate the arguments in this book. In particular, we can ask whether the dominant response of young men in Bijnor district to the vicissitudes of un/under-employment has been to reinvent symbolic forms coded as 'traditional'—which would suggest an affinity between our case study and the writing of Willis (1977), Demerath (1999)—or whether the main direction of young men's response has been toward embracing 'modern' identities, based for example on the purchase of newly available consumer goods and a belief in education, strategies that would bear a family resemblance to those pursued by the young men described by Weiss (2002) and Cole (2005).

Gendered Styles

What also emerges powerfully from recent ethnographies of educated un/under-employed young men in situations of economic threat is the central importance of gendered ideas in shaping young people's styles. Discussion of masculinities in the global south has lagged behind analysis of women's position. As Osella and Osella (2007: 7) point out in a review of the South Asian literature, men are present in South Asian ethnography but they are generally not the explicit object of study and the gendered nature of their behavior is rarely problematized. Moreover, where anthropologists have considered issues of masculinity in the South Asian literature, they have tended to present formal models of masculine behavior which were not analyzed as products of gender power (see Osella and Osella, 2007: 8–9 for a review).

Recent books on masculinities in Africa (Lindsay and Miescher 2003), Latin America (Gutmann 2003) and Asia (Chopra et al. 2004) move beyond cultural archetypes by focusing more explicitly on the historical construction of normative masculinities and the relationship between these ideal versions of manhood and 'masculinities in practice' (Gutmann 2003). Much of this research draws on the pioneering work of Connell (1987) on the relationship between distinct forms of masculinity. Connell emphasizes that masculinities are constructed differently in different cultures, and in different time periods as well as across a range of scales. Building on Connell's work, research in South Asia shows how men may align their practices to normative masculinities in certain situations—such as the job interview or schoolroom—but privately act in ways that vary widely from idealized visions of manhood (Osella and Osella 2007).

Another important contribution of Connell's work has been to uncover how masculinities are ordered in relations of hierarchy and dominance, a theoretical move which opens up space for examining power relations among men. Connell suggested that specific types of dominant masculinity characterize gender regimes in particular regional and historical contexts. He then asserts that these 'hegemonic masculinities' are "constructed in relation to various subordinated masculinities as well as in relation to women" (Connell 1987: 183, quoted in McDowell 2003: 11).

Connell insists that the relationship of specific men to notions of hegemonic or subordinate masculinity may change at particular 'crisis moments.' Emerging research on Indian young men offers examples of this process. For example, several commentators have written of a disappearance of male adolescence for the poor in India, where rapid economic change and new health threats propel many impoverished children directly into paid work and the demands of adult masculinity (Nieuwenhuys 1994; Verma and Saraswathi 2002). In these examples, young men are commonly forced to assume responsibilities in the home (Osella and Osella 2007: 40), while at the same time rationalizing and resisting their subordination within local masculine hierarchies.

But Connell's notion of 'crisis moments' can also be applied to an analysis of educated un/under-employed young men, whose experience of youth in India is often increasingly drawn out over time rather than compressed (Parry 2005). Educated un/under-employed young men characteristically occupy an ambivalent position with reference to hegemonic masculinities: they conform by dint of their education to certain visions of successful manhood while being unable to assume male breadwinner roles (Osella and Osella 2007). Some young men have reacted to this ambivalence and its attendant threats to their sense of gendered competence by engaging in forms of hyper-masculine performance or through violence. For example, Hansen (1996) describes how educated un/under-employed young men in Bombay in the early 1990s became involved in Hindu right-wing political organizations as a means to 'recuperate masculinities.' Other research, based primarily in Africa, has pointed to the 'feminization' of un/under-employed young men as a result of their movement into poorly paid 'women's occupations' (Agadjanian 2004; Cole 2005).

In contrast to this literature, we argue in this book that educated young men in rural north India have typically responded to un/under-employment by investing in hegemonic visions of 'educated' and 'civilized' manhood. These fragile identities offer some protection from the threat of 'feminization' and allow men to continue to search for 'respectable work.' But these emerging masculinities are neither straightforwardly 'hegemonic' nor 'oppositional.' We also show how caste, class and religious inequalities shape the capacity of educated un/under-employed young men to sustain styles of educated, 'civilized' manhood, and inflect how young men perform urbane masculinities.

The claim to possess educated knowledge and skills, or the opposite strategy of distancing oneself from education, is frequently a key means of signaling masculinities and femininities in varied global contexts (Levinson and Holland 1996). For example, in historical research on formerly marginalized men from the Munda and Oraon tribes in Chotanagpur, India, Bara (1997) showed that the idea of being Hindi-educated offered a cultural basis for challenging the entrenched masculinities of dominant groups, even if it failed to deliver secure employment, and Klenk (2003) makes parallel points in her work on educated young women's cultural strategies in the Indian Himalayas. As these authors suggest, education is often an attractive basis for young people's gender projects because it offers a relatively novel index of success distinct from older measures of power.

Grounding Un/under-employment

Our discussion of the gendered strategies of educated un/under-employed young men unfolds with reference to a specific region: western UP. But we also want to 'ground' ideas of un/under-employed young men's actions in an understanding of space. This entails recognizing that particular places—such as the village—are constituted through dynamics operating at varied scales, including the trans-national (Massey 1994). Our focus on space also involves analyzing how people create distinctive 'spatial forms,' such as social networks, house styles and bodily comportment. We follow Massey (2005) in emphasizing what she calls 'the heterogeneity of space': the idea that elites and non-elites may be using similar spaces to engage in quite different forms of political practice. For example, 'the local government office' may be an important nodal point within social networks linking elites to government officials, but lower castes may be staging protests within the same office as part of efforts to construct alternative social networks. A larger point is that space is constantly under construction and thoroughly implicated in political life, rather than being a static 'backdrop' or 'container' for social action.

We also stress the importance of narrative representations of space within the strategies of young men. Spatial representations, which can be as diverse as notions of nature, beliefs about the West or ideas of entrapment, are threaded through young people's attempts to manage educated un/under-employment. Indeed, environmental, placed-based or scalar ideas are incorporated—often as a central theme—in young people's search for respect, work and political influence (cf. Lefebvre 1991; Gidwani and Sivaramakrishnan 2003). The quotation with which we began this chapter signals this point in highlighting a young man's preoccupation with escaping the 'dust and soil' of the village (cf. Katz 2004).

A more particular concern with ideas of technological accomplishment animates our interest in space, practice and representation. To be successfully 'modern' in the contemporary global south is often to be adept at utilizing particular everyday 'technologies,' such as a gun, pen or telephone. In these instances, being 'modern' or 'anti-modern' involves a certain form of self-disciplining akin to that described famously by Foucault (1977): the willingness and ability to orient one's body to specific technologies and norms. To accomplish a cultural style coded locally as either 'modern' or 'traditional,' a person often needs to learn to stand in line (Corbridge 2003) or listen well (Hirschkind 2003), for example. As Foucault (1980) argued, these technological capacities require the development of habits and perceptual categories that are durably inscribed in the body. To be 'properly modern' is frequently to be so thoroughly steeped in an approved version of modernity and the accompanying self-regulatory modes of movement, thought and perception that the 'right practices' come as *second nature*. As Foucault (1980) primes us to expect, these self-regulatory norms are productive as well as repressive, emanate from within society as well as from above and are always performed rather than simply possessed. Comparative analysis of these 'small wars' over who is believed to have internalized 'modernity' or 'tradition' most comprehensively and what this means for a person's dignity offers a compelling window into the cultural politics of un/under-employment in the contemporary global south.

At the same time, Foucault's work sometimes underestimates the role of gender in shaping people's attitudes to technological accomplishment. As much feminist work has shown, ideas of what it is to be 'masculine' or 'feminine' mediate the process through which people perform modern technological accomplishment (e.g. Bartky 1988; Sawicki 1994). The iconic force of technological skills—the capacity to hold a gun or pursue an effective dietary regime, for example—is often derived in large part from the link between these self-regulatory acuities and models of masculinity or femininity. Hence, we can grasp why young people pursue particular cultural styles only when we appreciate how gendered models of success and visions of technological achievement cohere in particular settings.

Time is another key theme in our account of educated un/under-employed young men's strategies. In claiming or rejecting a modern image, people are also expressing something significant about their temporal location. Educated un/under-employment may accelerate, slow down or disturb their transition through gendered conceptions of 'the life course.' For example, young men's marriages may be delayed (Heuzé 1996), they may decide to drop out of school (Levinson 1999), or their educational careers may be interspersed with periods of paid work (Roberts et al. 1999). What counts as 'youth' often changes in this context. In many parts of India, delays in young people's marriage and acquisition of waged employment have led to an extension of notions of youth (Heuzé 1996; Parry 2005). In the context of such changes, the educated un/under-employed may experience and vocalize time in new ways. For example, young men may apprehend their youth as a state of constant crisis (see Hansen 1996) or a slowing down, stasis or void (Heuzé 1996).

A temporal frame of reference is also crucial to understanding the political process through which people produce particular cultural styles. An imagined future may be as important as present and past circumstances in shaping young people's styles and associated livelihood strategies (Oxfeld 1993). Indeed, in many contexts, the educated un/under-employed may seek support and approval not for what they *are*, but what they promise to *become* (Heuzé 1996).

At an analytical level, time is important in considering how young men inhabit the images which they create for themselves. A particular cultural style may 'work' for a person during one historical moment and then become unfamiliar or uncomfortable at a later stage. This is well attested in Ferguson's (1999) analysis of underemployed mineworkers in Zambia in the 1980s, who fashioned images of themselves as cosmopolitan people when they could afford to do so—in an economic 'boom'—only to find that this style alienated them from the rural peers upon whom they came to depend during recession. Other work shows that people move in and out of particular styles, according to the resources, mood and context (e.g. Osella and Osella 2007). These insights are germane to our study, which examines the difficulties that young men face in fulfilling visions of transformation based on an educated masculinity which offer, in the short term, a measure of pride and self-respect.

Research Strategy

This book emerges out of field research in Bijnor district conducted between 2000 and 2002. Bijnor district lies to the east of the River Ganges, about 90 miles northeast of Delhi. Our investigations were primarily based in two villages: Qaziwala and Nangal. Qaziwala lies 3 miles northwest of Bijnor and is principally populated by Muslims. Nangal lies about 10 miles southeast of Bijnor town and 90 percent of its inhabitants are Hindus.

Scholars have questioned the notion implicit in many rural studies of India that the village forms a natural political, social and economic unit. As Sharma (1980: 19–21) observed, the coherence of the village in north India is a male construction, since an adult woman usually migrates at the time of marriage to her affines' village, and the strategies of rural men also traverse village boundaries (e.g. Breman 1985). But the village remains an important context for understanding social and political change in India: employment opportunities for most rural people remain limited to the village area, most villagers depend upon services located in the village, and the village remains a powerful imaginative social unit. Indeed, in as far as the village is constituted through broader processes of social, economic and political change (Massey 2005), our research was designed to reflect this point. Distinct from the rather static nature of some village studies in India, we traveled outwards from our core research locations to explore, for example, madrasah and school education in Bijnor and Delhi.

Our fieldwork occurred in two stages: between September 2000 and April 2001, when our research was concentrated in Qaziwala and between September 2001 and April 2002, when we worked mainly in Nangal and Bijnor. In each village, we began by conducting household censuses as an up-date to identical censuses carried out in 1990 by Roger and Patricia. We then selected households with young men or women aged between fifteen and thirty-four. We aimed to interview young people and their parents from three caste/religious communities:[12] Jats and Chamars (a Dalit[13] caste) in Nangal and Muslims in Qaziwala. In each caste/community group, we concentrated on interviewing members of 15 families in particular. We selected families to interview using a purposive sampling method with the overall aim of ensuring that the sample included families in different class positions within each caste/community group and families who had adopted varying educational and employment strategies. We often made multiple visits to these selected households. We conducted a total of approximately 400 village interviews, with roughly 140 people, of whom 45 were young men aged between 20 and 34. We carried out an additional 120 interviews with teachers in schools and madrasahs, government officials and politicians, mainly within Bijnor district.

The tendency for South Asia scholars to place caste at the center of research has been the subject of critique, particularly by postcolonial and Subaltern School scholars. Several authors have claimed that the use of caste as an organizing concept has served to obscure other forms of inequality (Inden 1990), silence subaltern voices (Guha and Spivak 1988) and reinforce colonialist categories employed to oppress the Indian population (Dirks 1992, 2003). In more recent work, however, Dirks (2003) points to the opposite danger of disavowing caste completely. In many parts of rural north India, both caste and religion have been important historically in governing a person's access to power such that different caste/community groups have often followed divergent trajectories. For our work, then, caste/community groups provide a useful starting point for an account of social change in Bijnor district. Distinct from earlier orientalist approaches, we conceptualize caste and community as an ambivalent means of

[12]We use the term 'community' henceforward in this chapter to refer to religious community.

[13]The word 'Dalit' means 'broken' or oppressed and usually refers to those at the bottom of the caste system.

analyzing education, youth and underemployment and show how a person's caste and religion influence but do not determine their strategies.

Our semi-structured interviews in the village related to three key areas of discussion: formal school and madrasah education; families' schooling, employment and marriage strategies; and political affiliations and activity. In practice, we found that parents and young people moved from these topics to discussing a disparate set of concerns, such as the health of family members and quarrels with their neighbors, to much broader issues, including, for example, religious practice, international politics, development, 'the modern' and the state.

Our interviews ranged from thirty minutes to three hours in length and were conducted mainly in Hindi.[14] Our research assistants took detailed notes at the time and wrote up transcripts of our interviews in Hindi or Urdu in Roman script within twenty-four hours of the conversation.[15] We then translated these accounts into English and entered them into a computer alongside our notes on the conversation, including detailed material on people's manner, dress, mood and the setting of the interview. Once back in the UK, we coded the fieldnotes collected using the Atlas.ti data analysis package. We worked with codes dictated by our theoretical approaches as well as ones generated inductively out of our informants' accounts.

Roger and Patricia had nearly twenty years' field experience in Nangal and Qaziwala and Craig had conducted previous social research in Meerut district, western UP. The three of us speak the varieties of Hindi/Urdu spoken locally. This reduced problems of access and allowed us to generate relationships with our informants relatively rapidly. Roger was mainly responsible for interviews with older men, Patricia for interviews with women and Craig for interviewing younger men, although this division of labor was not rigid. We usually worked individually with one research assistant, such that Craig, Roger and Patricia would be interviewing different people on any one day. Our village interviews typically took place in people's homes, but our conversations often attracted the interest of other family members, neighbors and guests. In addition to these

[14]Vocabularies locally often vary from 'standard' or 'school' Hindi toward 'vernacular' dialects, as well as toward what is often defined as 'Urdu'.

[15]In our experience, the presence of an electronic recording device reduces people's willingness to discuss sensitive topics, so we did not use one.

interviews, Craig spent time with young men in public areas of the villages, in the agricultural fields surrounding the villages, in Awas Vikas or cycling between Bijnor and Qaziwala.

We conducted most of our village interviews with three research assistants: Chhaya, Manjula and Shaila. We also worked with another research assistant, Swaleha Begum, who was considerably older than the other three and was principally responsible for assisting Patricia with interviews in madrasahs and translation work. Of the three assistants who worked most closely with us in conducting village fieldwork, Chhaya and Manjula are upper caste Hindu young women who were in their late twenties or early thirties in 2001. Chhaya was brought up in Nangal, lived in Bijnor and was the only one of our research assistants to be married. Manjula was brought up in Mumbai and lived in a town in Bijnor district. Shaila was in her mid-twenties and came from a prominent Muslim family in Bijnor. Reflecting their relatively prosperous and urban upbringing, Manjula and Chhaya had masters degrees and Shaila was studying for a MA in 2001. Manjula, Shaila, Chhaya acted as facilitators as well as note takers in the village interviews: introducing new topics, intervening to clarify points and encouraging bystanders to participate in group discussions.

We rarely sensed that young men felt inhibited by the presence of a young woman, and they sometimes spoke with disarming candor about their lives. But the presence of Chhaya, Shaila and Manjula tended to instill in young men a type of earnestness. We observed a lightening in the mood and speech of young men in situations in which Craig, who is much younger than Roger and Patricia, hung out with them alone. Young men often engaged to a greater extent in horse play, joking and teasing, and they were more willing to discuss their ideas about sex, young women and their bodies. Our accounts of educated un/under-employment are therefore woven together out of information from relatively formal interviews and our records of more opportunistic participant observation with young men.

The young men who are the subjects of this book often acted as our guides and mentors. They helped with logistical issues in Bijnor, acted as intermediaries in our discussions with others and invited us to social events. During interviews, they often introduced new topics relevant to our research, asked about parallel dynamics in the UK or suggested others whom we should meet. Some of the young men and a minority of their parents were familiar with the idea of fieldwork. They sometimes asked us for summaries of our emerging findings and questioned us on our methodology. Many of our informants were keen for our research to proceed smoothly and felt some investment in our project. The energy and interest of many of these men made the process of field research feel more like entering an interpretative community than studying 'research subjects.'

This is not to deny practical, political and ethical difficulties and dilemmas associated with research in rural western UP (see also Jeffery and Jeffery 1997). Many of these difficulties arose out of our position. As middle class British citizens with secure employment in universities, villagers identified us as 'educated' (*parhe likhe*) people as well as outsiders (*videshī*). All three of us are graduates of Cambridge University in the UK and this, combined with our working at another prestigious institution (the University of Edinburgh), meant that we embodied a particular vision of 'educated accomplishment.' We often felt uneasy about directing our conversations toward the politics and nature of education and employment, where we so obviously represented a form of educated power.

Language was one means through which we addressed these difficulties. In addition to speaking in Hindi, during the course of research we became better able to incorporate local idioms into our speech. Our capacity to demonstrate familiarity in Hindi with ideas imagined as 'local' allowed us to draw attention away from our position as 'foreign educated visitors,' at least in some instances and for some of the time. We also addressed these issues by establishing our long-term investment in understanding the conditions of the rural poor in western UP. We frequently drew on our previous research in western UP (e.g. Jeffery and Jeffery 1997; Jeffrey 2001) to generate conversations around such topics as agricultural production, religious communalism, private education and the local state. Our previous field research sensitized us to how our informants varied not only according to education but also with respect to their political opinions, and it allowed us to anticipate some of our own sensitivities around politics, education and gender issues.

We also tried to stress the non-evaluative nature of our research, our openness to different opinions on education, politics and employment and our interest in sharing information about similarities and differences between India and Scotland, where Craig was born and Patricia and Roger had lived for thirty years. The last point is crucial: large sections of our interviews were often given over to our describing Scottish life and these descriptions often provided a basis for lively discussions of education, inequality and underemployment.

None of this could detract from the large inequalities in power and opportunity between us and our informants, nor should it distract attention from misunderstandings and mistakes associated with the process of fieldwork. Rather it is to recognize that the differences between us and our informants did not determine the nature of our interactions and that the differences *opened up* as well as *closed down* certain opportunities for discussion. In many situations, often through jokes or the exchange of information or ideas, we were able to 'hook up' (Clifford 1997) with young people and their parents in Nangal and Qaziwala in ways that facilitated learning and empathy.

Our position as foreign researchers not only presented difficulties in terms of our ability to develop meaningful conversations with informants but also posed questions about our commitments to the people with whom we worked and to our UK sponsors, issues which we have discussed in more detail elsewhere (Jeffery and Jeffery 1997; Jeffrey 1999). These issues were brought rapidly to the surface in October 2001, when US-led attacks on Afghanistan made some of our Muslim respondents suspicious of our motives. Many of our informants knew that our research was funded by the UK Government's Economic and Social Research Council and some believed that we sympathized with UK and US foreign policy. In addition, in October 2001 the mainly Hindu local police in Bijnor began to intimidate local Muslims under the guise of conducting anti-terrorist action, and some respondents were concerned about our possible links to state officials. We strenuously sought to allay these fears. We stressed our opposition to the practices of the UK government in Afghanistan and to the activities of the Bijnor police force. We also made repeated attempts to demonstrate our empathy with the Muslim and Dalit poor. Informants whom we met on a regular basis as well as our research assistants played a particularly important role as intermediaries and advisors during this period of the research.

Our daily practice in the field reflects a commitment to situating an account of educated un/under-employment with reference to the voices of young men and their parents. In stressing voice, we are not seeking to privilege verbal state-ments as media for the construction of agency. Nor do we imagine that young people's voices provide an unmediated 'window' into their social worlds (cf. Spivak 1988).[16] Nor indeed are we engaged in an exercise in ethnographic re-trieval, a 'display' of young men's voices for its own sake. Rather, a focus on voice, in tandem with a consideration of their broader expressive repertoire, provides a means of better understanding how young men imagine themselves as 'modern' in western UP.

In particular, we feel that accounts of voice should go beyond the *content* of verbal statements. We also need to consider what a focus on young men's *performances* of voice—the manner in which they speak, including their syntax, vocabulary, language, volume, tone and style—can tell us about their relation-ship to locally meaningful modernities (Hirschkind 2003). It is also instructive to consider voice as a *theme* of young people's practices: how young men reflect on their speech, and ideas of voice in processes of political competition.

In writing about young men, we blend extended case studies of individual young men with discussion of the broader economic livelihood strategies, so-cial relationships and cultural practices that animate and shape their practice. Again, we need to enter a series of qualifiers here. In discussing individual cases we do not intend to suggest that the individual always and inevitably provides the best vantage point from which to understand processes of social and politi-cal transformation. We do not provide a 'thick description' (Geertz 1973), if this means adhering to the notion that a single person or scene acts as a microcosm of broader economic, political and social dynamics. Nor do we wish to lend authority to the classically modern idea of the individual as a rational, and in some sense 'heroic,' social actor carving out their own world. Rather, we feel

[16]Spivak (1988) criticizes some members of the Subaltern School for assuming the existence of a homogeneous and somehow 'pure' subaltern stratum in possession of a collective consciousness expressed in its speech. We address this concern by pointing to the fractured nature of subaltern practice and discussing voice as a *cultural style*. Spivak also criticizes a tendency for academics in the global north to co-opt and misrepresent 'subaltern voices' in their own academic projects. Our response to this is pragmatic (cf. Scheper-Hughes 1995). We have tried to present the voices of educated un/under-em-ployed young men in a manner sensitive to the diversity of their views, contradictions in their narratives, and reflecting what we understood to be their meaning, style and mood.

that, to a greater extent than many other styles of writing and reflection, individual vignettes—read alongside broader qualitative and quantitative observations and data—illustrate how particular dynamics cohere to produce human outcomes, give a fuller sense of the experience of social subordination and offer telling insights into the politics of educated un/under-employment. This mode of reporting on our research will have succeeded if it allows the reader to empathize with the economic and cultural struggles of young men in western UP while also appreciating the wider structures shaping their lives.

Argument and Structure of the Book

The main argument of our book is that power and inequality mediate people's access to educational 'freedoms' and therefore that scholars should focus more centrally on how young people negotiate post-educational terrains. We advance this argument by uncovering the attempts of educated young men in rural western UP to negotiate employment markets, acquire respect and express cultural and political ideas.

Our discussion relates primarily to young men aged between 20 and 35. This definition of young people reflects how ideas of youth have been stretched in Bijnor district. As elsewhere (Parry 2005), young people's inability to move quickly from school or university into secure employment has created a generation of educated men in their twenties or early thirties who often remain unmarried, continue to be dependent on their parents financially and are widely identified as 'young' (*jawan*). This generation is different from the 'youths' of CCCS research, young people in the recent sociological literature and the teenagers studied in new anthropologies of youth. But like 'youths' discussed in other contexts, these young men define themselves separately from adult worlds, are engaged in an active search for employment and remain preoccupied with questions of culture, style and respect.

We must acknowledge three key 'silences' in our work. First, our analysis is limited to *men's* strategies. This reflects our concern with the relationship between education and access to paid employment outside the home. In the context of patriarchal norms, parents in rural north India do not usually expect young women to engage in waged work. The education of young women is nevertheless important in shaping expectations of the education that young men should possess. It is therefore relevant to note that while girls' education continues to lag behind that of boys within all the communities we studied, girls' education was rising rapidly in the two villages in which we worked. Unlike earlier generations of research on young men, we consistently seek to problematize the processes through which young men understand their masculinity and the implications of these dynamics for the reproduction of patriarchal power.

Second, our analysis focuses on *educated* men, defined as those who have passed Eighth Class; we do not discuss uneducated men's strategies at great length. The sharp rise in people's investment in boys' education makes an analysis of the strategies of educated men especially pertinent. Educated young men, while still in a minority numerically in both villages, often act as role models for other villagers and key social animators.

Another silence of this work relates to processes occurring within educational institutions. We did not conduct the type of classroom ethnography that would be required to reconstruct a detailed picture of school dynamics (cf. Srivastava 1995; Bénéï 2005), and we found it difficult to generate discussions with young men about their experiences of school. As a result, this book considers processes occurring within school rather briefly and principally as a means of understanding how young men imagine education after leaving formal education.

The remainder of the book follows a central 'story' which runs as follows. In Chapter Two we argue that the liberalization of the Indian economy has created a large stratum of educated un/under-employed young men in western UP. In rural Bijnor district this stratum included Jats belonging to a local rural elite, upwardly mobile Dalits (ex-untouchables) and a few Muslim young men from relatively prosperous households. These men had all acquired educational qualifications in local schools, spent time searching unsuccessfully for secure salaried work and identified themselves as unemployed or underemployed.

Young men had responded to educated un/under-employment in rural Bijnor district by reaffirming the value of mainstream school education and emphasizing their identity as 'modern' men. Chapter Three shows that they elaborate on this idea by pitting a vision of urbane, civilized 'educated' people against a mental picture of uncouth, savage, 'illiterates.' At the same time, the absence of employment opportunities was making it difficult for young men to sustain their 'educated' image.

Young men were differently equipped to negotiate this contradiction, a point we develop through reference to four 'analytic sets' of men, which form the central four chapters of the book (Four through Seven). In Chapter Four, we show that educated un/under-employed young men belonging to the relatively prosperous Jat caste had used their inherited wealth and social networks to enter managerial roles within agriculture or status-saving work within the private sector. These jobs allowed Jats to maintain notions of themselves as educated people. We document the emergence of new forms of Jat masculinity in which young men stressed their distance from the soil and agriculture and, by implication, from lower castes and Muslims.

A second analytic 'set' of young men is comprised of educated Dalits who had channeled their frustration at un/under-employment into becoming lobbyists and social animators for their community. Even more than the Jats, these self-styled 'new politicians' fastened onto the iconic significance of education, which they incorporated into a broader radical agenda of Dalit political mobility. The emergence of a group of educated un/under-employed Dalit young men is a key and understudied aspect of Dalit political mobility in Uttar Pradesh. But we depart from recent accounts of low caste political change in north India by identifying these new politicians' failure to transform local relations of dominance and oppression.

A third set of young men, belonging to the Muslim community, had responded to educated un/under-employment by entering craft occupations in urban areas or religious work in madrasahs or mosques. Chapter Six describes how these Muslim young men used craft or religious work to construct a vision of educated Islamic masculinity. Religious communalism nevertheless limited the capacity of Muslim young men to project Islamic identities, particularly after 9/11 2001.

A final set of young men was mainly comprised of poorer Dalits but also included some Jats and Muslims. We describe in Chapter Seven how a profound sense of melancholy distinguished these young men from their peers. Poor Dalits, in particular, were unable to acquire secure salaried work *and* were ill-equipped to cultivate sustainable and self-affirming 'fallback identities.' These young men appropriated negative representations of their behavior by caricaturing themselves as 'useless,' 'empty' or 'wandering' men. A sense of lost time figured centrally in their narratives and practices, as did education, which was sometimes castigated as a 'trap' and at other moments lauded for its transformative power. The passion with which these men expressed the tragedy of their position had compelled other young men, parents and children to reassess their attitudes to education.

The conclusion (Chapter Eight) summarizes our argument and draws out the key contributions of the book. We make three major arguments. First, we stress that educated young men's strategies impact in telling ways on processes of social change and reproduction in rural north India. The emergence of a cohort of young men eager to express their sense of education as civilization was central to the further expansion of a 'schooling revolution' in western UP and to forms of subaltern political resistance. At the same time, some educated un/under-employed young men had begun to question the value of education, and their practices were creating a new sense of irony, wariness and self-doubt among marginalized populations. Second, the book contributes to contemporary understanding of global youth and non-western modernities by documenting the sheer diversity of 'modern practices' that young people may adopt in the context of economic marginalization. We suggest that the distinctive histories of various caste, class and religious groups shape these enunciations and performances of modernity and create distinctive clusters of practice and reflection. Third, we question accounts of education as an unproblematic 'social good' within development academia. In particular, we stress the need for further research on the struggles faced by educated young people from disadvantaged backgrounds to obtain respect within post-educational terrains of social and political competition.

2

The Political Economy of Uttar Pradesh

In western UP, the context in which young men struggle to achieve their personal goals is not of their own making, and it has changed markedly over the past fifteen years. This chapter develops this point by showing how economic liberalization between 1991 and the early 2000s exacerbated problems of salaried employment creation and educational provision in the state. We examine how crises over access to education and secure work are linked to the reproduction and transformation of caste, class and religious inequalities in UP. In the second part of the chapter, our attention narrows to Bijnor district and the attempts of rural households in our study villages to navigate scarce 'markets' in education and secure employment. We show that economic liberalization has been incompatible with equitable social development in rural Bijnor district. In the 1980s and 1990s, middle caste Jats were able to reproduce their agricultural dominance in the spheres of education and salaried employment competition while relatively disadvantaged social groups—including the Chamars and Muslims—were largely excluded from education. But the agrarian social structure is not static: many educated Jat young men could not acquire secure employment, and a sizable cohort of educated un/under-employed young men had emerged among the Jats. Moreover, some Chamar and Muslim young men were obtaining secondary school education, even if they were usually unable to use this education to obtain prized jobs or other forms of economic security. This chapter therefore provides an important foundation for the rest of the book by uncovering the state-level forces and local-level parental strategies that have created a cohort of educated underemployed young men.

The Political Economy of UP

Employment and Education

Uttar Pradesh is the most populous state in India with a population in 2001 of 166 million (Registrar General & Census Commissioner of India 2002). UP is also one of the most economically 'backward' states of India. On virtually every index of human development—health, education or poverty, for example—it ranks consistently as one of the three worst performers among major Indian states (Drèze and Gazdar 1997). According to the World Bank (2002), 31 percent of UP's population lived in poverty in 2000, significantly higher than the all-India average of 26 percent.

The recent liberalization of the Indian economy has not substantially improved the lives of most rural people in UP. Between 1947 and the mid-1980s, India's approach to macroeconomic planning combined a leading role for the private sector in economic decision-making with state intervention formally aimed at accelerating growth and redistributing social opportunities (Chandrasekhar and Ghosh 2002). In the face of a growing fiscal crisis, however, and under pressure from multilateral lenders, the Indian state embarked on a series of sweeping economic reforms commonly traced to the mid-1980s but beginning formally in mid-1991 (Corbridge and Harriss 2000).

Processes of liberalization appear to have had a negative impact on rural employment generation in most parts of rural UP, at least until 2001 (Sen 1997; Chandrasekhar and Ghosh 2002). Economic reforms reduced opportunities for people to obtain government employment, historically an important source of salaried work in rural areas. In a sign that even greater efforts would be made to limit or reduce employment opportunities in the public sector, in 2001 the World Bank made an annual 2 percent cut in government employment a condition of its continuing 'Fiscal and Governance Reform' loans to UP.

Moreover, the new economic growth poles are not generating jobs in the private sector at anything like the rate needed to allow people to leave the land (Jha 2004). As Jha points out, "one of the current important anomalies in the Indian economy is that a sector [agriculture] that produces 25 percent of GDP employs 65 percent of the labour force" (Jha 2004: 2). Within the private sector, liberalization has accentuated regional inequalities within India between centers of rapid growth, mainly located in south and west India, and areas such as UP (Bhalla 1997). UP's long-established industrial base—of textile mills, especially in its second city, Kanpur—has almost completely collapsed, and UP has played almost no part in the newly emerging Information Technology, out-sourcing and other 'new industries' for which India has become renowned (Ahluwalia 2001). In addition, within UP, liberalization may have reinforced geographical differences in private salaried employment generation between the rural hinterland and the 'growth corridors' connecting major cities (Sen 1997). Simultaneously, economic reform has reduced the availability of rural credit and therefore possibilities for entrepreneurialism (Chandrashekhar and Ghosh 2002; Ramachandran and Swaminathan 2005).

Educated un/under-employment is difficult to measure. Official figures collected at employment exchanges and by the National Sample Survey (NSS) are poor guides to unemployment because few job aspirants register themselves as 'unemployed' in India (ul Haq 2003). Moreover, much un/under-employment in India is disguised by the underutilization of labor within the household, farming and informal economies. Nevertheless, ul Haq's (2003) analysis of NSS data on employment figures points to a rapid increase in unemployment at the all-India level between 1990 and 2000, particularly among educated young people. Population growth between the early 1960s and early 2000s has resulted in a sharp increase in number of young men entering the labor market. Thus in UP, according to the 2001 Census, there were nearly 50 percent more young men (21.9 million) in the age category 15–29 than there were in the age category 30–44 (14.7 million) (Registrar General & Census Commissioner of India 2004), and UP was already experiencing high levels of underemployment among young people in the 1990s (Visaria 2003). These observations help explain why the issue of unemployment featured so prominently in the successful Congress Party electoral campaigns of 2003/2004 in this State.

As new opportunities in salaried employment have dwindled in UP, recruitment to these posts has been more heavily politicized through further attempts to impose positive discrimination in recruitment. Such efforts began in the 1930s, when the British created lists of formerly Untouchable castes deemed eligible for special government assistance, the so-called 'Scheduled Castes' (SCs), also commonly termed Dalits.[1] The 1950 Indian Constitution offered the SCs

---

[1] The word 'Dalit' is sometimes used by subaltern groups to refer marginalized people in general. In the remainder of the book we use the term Dalit to refer to SCs.

legal equality and reserved for them places in public-sector employment, educational institutions and government representative bodies (Galanter 1991). Shortly after independence, Nehru established a Backward Classes Commission to investigate the condition of castes formally above the SCs in the caste hierarchy but nonetheless suffering from social and economic disadvantages. This Commission reported in 1956 with a list of 2,399 backward caste groups (*jātis*) and suggested measures to improve their position. Nehru did not implement these recommendations, but the issue of Other Backward Class (OBC) reservations resurfaced in 1978 when the Janata Party set up a civil rights commission under the chairmanship of B. P. Mandal to explore possibilities for improving the condition of OBCs. The Mandal Report (1980) was set aside for nearly a decade. But in 1989 V. P. Singh announced that he would implement its recommendations (Dirks 2003: 284–85). This move provoked vigorous protest from upper castes, who argued that reservations interfere with principles of 'merit' in job appointments, and some left-wing scholars, who maintained that positive discrimination is unlikely to address problems of poverty (e.g. Béteille 2001) and that the benefits of reservations tend to accrue to a 'creamy-layer' of richer lower castes (Pai and Singh 1997).

The scarcity of government employment and associated political conflict has been compounded by the inability of the state to provide good quality schooling. Education was central to Nehru's vision of creating a modern, secular, democratic and prosperous nation-state, and the 1950 Indian Constitution charged state governments with the task of ensuring that every individual received basic education up to the age of fourteen. Nehru believed that education would provide the 'human capital' required for development and would improve the position of groups historically marginalized by society. The partial failure of this state educational project has been the subject of numerous scholarly, donor and government-sponsored reports (e.g. The Probe Team 1999; Kingdon and Muzammil 2003; CABE 2004).

Patterns of educational achievement vary considerably across India. UP is often grouped with Bihar, Orissa, Madhya Pradesh and Rajasthan as states with a particularly poor record of educational provision and achievement (Drèze and Gazdar 1997). UP literacy rates are below national levels; in 2001, 70 percent of males and 43 percent of females over the age of seven were literate, compared to all-India figures of 76 percent and 54 percent (Registrar General & Census Commissioner of India 2002). In addition, recent research points to how the school system often entrenches social inequalities based upon caste, class, gender and religion in UP (Chopra and Jeffery 2005). Pre-colonial educational systems in UP characteristically augmented the powerful position of higher caste Hindus by systematically excluding large sections of the population from prestigious credentials (Kumar 2000). The colonial state continued to devalue the knowledge of the historically oppressed through a vigorous program of school establishment and curricular reform aimed at initiating an upper stratum of Indians in 'European civilization' and grooming Hindu higher castes and some landed Muslim elites for positions in the colonial bureaucracy (e.g. Kumar 1994; Srivastava 1998). The reproduction of social inequality through education has continued in the post-colonial period, as evident in studies of rural schooling (e.g. Drèze and Gazdar 1997) and urban education (e.g. Kingdon 1997; Faust and Nagar 2001) in UP.

The reproduction of social inequalities through schooling in the 1990s and early 2000s in UP relates closely to the liberalization of the Indian economy. Between 1947 and 1990, the government sector was becoming increasingly important within secondary schooling in the State: the Government established large numbers of secondary schools and extended financial aid to privately-managed institutions. From the early 1990s, however, there was a shift in patterns of schooling provision in many parts of UP (Mooij and Dev 2002). The fiscal crisis of the UP Government, allied to neoliberal economic reforms introduced in the early 1990s, eroded government school provision and contributed to the rapid growth of non-state educational facilities (Kingdon and Muzammil 2003). A recent report by the Central Advisory Board of Secondary Education (CABE) in India noted widespread infrastructural and curricular neglect within secondary schooling and called for an urgent review of the funding and organization of schools (CABE 2004). The privatization of secondary schooling has coincided with the politicization of education through the efforts of the Hindu nationalist Bharatiya Janata Party (BJP) to alter government school curricula to reflect the goals of militant Hinduism. By mobilizing images of India being swamped by the modernizing forces of 'the West' which threaten local and 'authentic' cultures, Hindu nationalist forces have emphasized the importance of 'value education' rooted in 'Hindu traditions' (e.g. Sundar 2004). This ideological program has been institutionalized through a program of school foundation orchestrated by the Hindu right-wing Rashtriya Swayam Sevak (RSS) (e.g. Sarkar 1996; Delhi Historians Group 2001).

Caste, Class and Religious Inequality

State neglect of employment creation and educational provision is connected to the entrenched nature of caste, class and religious inequalities in UP (Jeffrey and Lerche 2000). Three main social blocs can be identified in rural UP: upper caste Hindus; intermediate Hindu castes; and Muslims, poorer Backward Castes and Dalits.

At the top, and probably accounting for roughly 20 percent of the population of UP, are upper caste Hindus (mainly Brahmans and Rajputs, often known as Thakurs).[2] As substantial landowners, these castes have dominated lucrative salaried employment, local government bureaucracies and landownership in many parts of UP (Hasan 1998). The rise of Hindu nationalist political parties and social organizations has strengthened this section of society. The BJP held power in the UP State capital in Lucknow three times between 1990 and 2005 and governed India between 1999 and 2004. During these periods of rule, the Hindu Right bolstered the economic resources, social connections and cultural capital of upper caste Hindus through its policies and ideological drive (Hasan 1998; Jaffrelot 2003). In particular, the Hindu Right sponsored a series of high profile political campaigns in the 1990s which further marginalized and oppressed rural Muslims. These included a 'pilgrimage' (*rath yātrā*) undertaken by the BJP politician Lal Krishan Advani, in 1990, which sparked off riots and pogroms across north India, including in Bijnor (Basu 1994; Jeffery and Jeffery 1994) and the demolition of the Babri Masjid in Ayodhya in December 1992, which heightened tensions between Hindus and Muslims still further. More recently, right-wing Hindu nationalists have attempted to advance their political aims by sponsoring the testing of a nuclear device in 1998 in Rajasthan—the so-called 'Hindu bomb' (Corbridge 1999)—and, since 2001, using 9/11 as a pretext for circulating fears of a 'Muslim danger.'

[2]These figures are derived from the 1931 Census of India, the last census for which caste figures are available.

A second set of rural households belonging to Hindu 'intermediate castes' frequently control access to political and economic power in western UP (Lerche 1999). This category of household includes the Jats and upper sections of the OBCs, such as the Yadavs. The Jats are just over 2 percent of the total population of UP, but often act as local 'dominant castes' (Srinivas 1955) in western parts of the State, where, despite comprising no more than about 8 percent of the population, they monopolize landownership, non-agricultural sources of wealth, and influence within local state institutions (Jeffrey and Lerche 2000). Between the mid-1960s and late 1980s, this 'new rural elite' was powerfully represented within state and central government (Hasan 1998). Their political power allowed the prosperous peasantry to benefit from high agricultural support prices and large subsidies on agricultural inputs. Since the death of their political mentor and ex-prime minister of India, Chaudhry Charan Singh, in 1987, Jats have continued to invest profits from agriculture in attempts to colonize and co-opt the local state bureaucracy by positioning their sons in government jobs, nurturing networks linking them to the local state and establishing close connections with top district officials (Jeffrey 2001, 2002). Jats have also joined high profile farmers' movements aimed at guaranteeing access to cheap agricultural inputs and improving the terms of trade between agriculture and industry (Bentall and Corbridge 1996). In addition, during the late 1990s, Jats successfully pressured the BJP politician and Chief Minister of UP, R. K. Gupta, to include Jats in the OBC quota, in spite of their evident failure to meet the criteria for 'backwardness.' As this point suggests, since the late 1980s Jats have been prepared to cultivate links with the BJP on an opportunistic basis, and some Jats have embraced Hindu nationalist rhetoric (Jeffrey 1999).

The remainder of UP's population is mainly comprised of Muslims, poorer castes within the OBC category, often called Most Backward Castes (MBCs), and Dalits. There are elites among Muslims and Dalits in the UP countryside and a stratum of wealthy Muslims in many UP towns and cities. But rural households among Muslims, Dalits and MBCs typically possess little or no agricultural land and work in exploitative, poorly paid and insecure conditions.

Dalits in UP historically suffered from the stigma associated with being classed as 'Untouchable' (Mandelbaum 1970). Positive discrimination has failed to alter caste and class inequalities in UP in a radical way (Hasan 1998), particularly in the western areas of the state (Jeffrey and Lerche 2000). Dalits in UP continue to be concentrated amongst the poor and confined to manual wage labor, skilled artisanal work or small-scale entrepreneurship in the informal economy (Mendelsohn and Vicziany 1998; Lerche 1999).

But between 1970 and the early 1990s, most Dalits in rural UP gained slightly from the introduction of new technologies and marketing arrangements within agriculture: the so-called 'Green Revolution' (Lerche 1999). Technological change within agriculture marginally improved Dalits' real wages within agriculture, particularly in areas where they had access to off-farm employment (Sharma and Poleman 1993; Lerche 1999). Building on these small economic gains, rural Dalits in UP increasingly strove to obtain formal education and salaried employment for their sons (Nambissan and Sedwal 2002).

Moreover, Dalits have profited from the rise of the Bahujan Samaj Party (BSP) as a political force. Established in 1984, the BSP held power in UP four times between 1993 and 2003 under the leadership of a Dalit former schoolteacher, Mayawati. Drawing on the vision of upward mobility based upon education and entry into white-collar employment promoted by the Dalit hero Dr. Bhim Rao Ambedkar, the BSP encouraged Dalits to obtain education. This drive was allied to attempts to transform the symbolic landscape of UP through the creation of parks, statues, schools, hospitals and libraries dedicated to Ambedkar and other Dalit heroes (Jaoul 2007).

The BSP has attempted to place Dalits in key positions within the UP bureaucracy and improve their access to police protection and judicial redress. Mayawati also extended an Ambedkar Village Programme (AVP) by allotting Rs. 100,000 to a total of about 25,000 villages in UP that contained a high proportion of Dalits (Pai 2002: 127). These funds were principally channeled through two existing government development schemes: the Jawahar Rozgar Yojana (JRY), which offers sections of the rural poor opportunities to work on infrastructural projects and the Integrated Rural Development Programme (IRDP), charged with providing loans and raw materials to poor households (Lieten and Srivastava 1999: 223).

The efforts of the BSP to improve Dalits' access to power and resources at the local level intersected with changes in the formal system of local government in India. In 1992, the 73rd Amendment Act was enacted with the goal of increasing the power of local government in India. The Act implemented a three-tier system of local government in all states of India with populations of over 2 million people. Under this new system, *panchāyats* would play a central role in the provision of public services, the creation and maintenance of public goods and the planning and implementation of development activities, including the JRY and IRDP. The Act also provided a 33 percent reservation of *panchāyat* seats for Scheduled Castes, Scheduled Tribes and women and made provision for five-yearly *panchāyat* elections.

Rural Muslims also gained from improvements in agricultural technology and associated agrarian commercialization in rural UP in the period between 1970 and the early 1990s, particularly in the more prosperous districts of the state (Sharma and Poleman 1993). But Muslims have not usually been able to invest these modest gains in 'mainstream' education and obtain white-collar salaried work (Engineer 2001; Ara 2003). This exclusion reflects the distinctive history of rural Muslims in UP (see Jeffery et al. 2005). During the pre-colonial period there were marked divisions between a very small, upper caste Muslim elite and other Muslims castes, such as weavers, carpenters and barbers. In the colonial era, the elite established madrasahs as a means of protecting religious identities and fulfilling their religious duty to support the poor. Most notably, Muslim leaders who fled Delhi after the 'Indian rebellion' of 1857 were instrumental in establishing, in 1866, the *Daru'l `Ulūm* seminary in Deoband. *Daru'l `Ulūm* teaches a broad curriculum to residential students (cf. Metcalf 1982). By 2001, it had become the largest madrasah in India. The seminary exercises a strong influence on education in Bijnor district and adjacent areas of western UP, for example via Deoband graduates who occupy teaching posts in small madrasahs in this region. In addition to *Daru'l `Ulūm*, the influx of remittances from the Arab Middle East and geographical spread of Islamic reformist movements in post colonial UP has encouraged the growth of a range of madrasahs in the State (Jeffery et al. 2005),[3] even if many of these institutions are inadequately funded (Ara 2003).

The mass of rural Muslims remain poorly connected to educational oppor-

---

[3]Nevertheless, some Muslims in Bijnor district and other parts of western UP with a high density of Muslims migrated to Pakistan around the time of Partition in 1947. The loss of part of the elite reduced the political and social significance of Muslims in these regions.

tunities in the State; far fewer Muslims than Dalits were in formal education in UP in the early 2000s (Sachar 2006). Since Independence, the failure of the UP Government to provide cheap and accessible state education for Muslims combined with the religious communalization of formal curricula discouraged this community from investing in education within mainstream schools.

As a result of their exclusion from mainstream schools and reflecting also the absence of reservations for Muslims, few rural Muslims in UP obtain government employment, and the majority of Muslim young men are confined to work as small or medium-sized cultivators, agricultural laborers or skilled craftspeople (Sachar 2006). This also reflects Muslims' long history of working as artisans in the major cities of this state (Engineer 2001; Harriss-White 2003). In addition, Muslims lack access to the development resources that the BSP channeled toward Dalits in the 1990s, and the rise of the BJP during the 1990s exacerbated Muslims' isolation from circles of influence centered on government (Jeffery and Jeffery 1997; Ara 2003).

In sum, since the mid-1960s, a new rural elite comprised of intermediate castes, such as the Jats in western UP and Yadavs in eastern UP, has used its control over local land ownership to acquire political power and economic benefits outside the village. In these ways, intermediate castes have challenged the historical control of Brahmins and Thakurs over economic resources, social networks and political influence. But Dalits, in turn, are beginning to contest intermediate caste power by seeking new forms of political representation at the local and regional levels. These changes are occurring against a backdrop of the rapid privatization in educational services, a sluggish growth in salaried employment, and the continued economic and political exclusion of *most* Dalits and Muslims in rural UP. We now turn to exploring how these social and political changes have shaped the educational strategies of parents in rural Bijnor district.

Employment and Education in Bijnor District

Since the early twentieth century, Bijnor district's economy has been based on sugar cane, wheat and rice cultivation (Jeffery and Jeffery 1997). Between 1960 and 1990, the introduction of new agricultural technologies and high government agricultural support prices increased agricultural profits and the demand for labor. The construction in 1984 of a new road across the Ganges opened up direct links between Bijnor and Delhi and promoted commercial growth. Moreover, increases in the profitability of agriculture in the 1960s and 1970s encouraged the expansion of transport, agricultural processing, consumer goods industries and brick manufacture. But Bijnor district lacked a substantial manufacturing base and was situated outside the area of rapid industrial growth occurring in contiguous UP districts farther west.

Government employment opportunities in Bijnor district were concentrated in health, schooling, transport, agriculture and the police. The liberalization of the Indian economy reduced openings in these spheres without creating a viable source of secure private salaried employment. Partly as a consequence, the number of salaried jobs in Bijnor district declined sharply relative to the demand from high school matriculates in the 1980s and 1990s. At the same time, Bijnor district's gradual absorption into broader processes of commercialization in western UP was creating *some* opportunities for young people to enter 'service type' work, mainly in marketing, private educational institutions, telecommunication, health care or finance. Most of these jobs were poorly paid, insecure and temporary in nature. A growing shortage of secure salaried employment partly explains why upper castes in Bijnor district responded so vigorously to the extension of reservations to OBCs in the early 1990s. Upper castes organized a wave of roadblocks, civil disturbances and vandalism in urban areas of the district (Jeffery and Jeffery 1997).

Bijnor district's 2001 literacy rates were slightly higher than the state average at 71 percent of its rural males and 45 percent of its rural females. But government elementary schooling deteriorated rapidly in the district between 1991 and 2001, as elsewhere in UP. At the same time, educational entrepreneurs established a variety of non-state educational institutions in the district. This 'privatization' of schooling was most visibly evident in the changing secondary educational landscape of Bijnor town and its immediate hinterland. By 2001, there were 20 unaided secondary schools within a 3-mile radius of Bijnor. This included fourteen Hindi-medium schools, all founded since 1978 and all but one affiliated to the UP Board of Education, and six English-medium schools, established since 1987 and affiliated to the Central Board of Secondary Education (CBSE) or Indian Council of Secondary Education (ICSE). Of young people registered for Twelfth Class UP Board examinations in Bijnor, the proportion in unaided schools rose from 2 percent in 1991 to 18 percent in 2002.[4]

The prominence of English-medium institutions reflects an increased desire for English proficiency among large sections of the urban and rural population in Bijnor district. In practice, none of the avowedly English-medium schools teaches consistently and completely in English. Due to intense competition for places at English-medium schools, it was typically necessary for parents to pay large 'donations' to the school to ensure a child's admission, and parents and children were sometimes interviewed, chiefly to verify applicants' familiarity with urban middle class norms of comportment. Nine of the unaided schools in Bijnor town had an overtly Hindu orientation; they were founded, managed and run by upper-caste Hindus (Brahmins and Banias), often included Hindu gods in their name, and admitted relatively few Muslims and Dalits. But only one of these institutions was affiliated to the RSS and none admitted to sectarian Hindu goals.

The growth of madrasahs also dates from the mid 1980s (Jeffery et al. 2007). Over fifteen madrasahs were established within 3 miles of Bijnor in the late 1980s and 1990s, and existing madrasahs increased their pupil numbers. This expansion had been funded mainly by wealthy Muslims living in urban Bijnor district. A few madrasahs offered the UP Board curriculum alongside religious subjects and thus catered for Muslim students fearful of attending Hindu-dominated schools but keen to acquire 'mainstream' qualifications. Many of these madrasahs were closely linked to the *Daru'l `Ulūm* seminary in Deoband, and the vice-chancellor of *Daru'l `Ulūm* during the 1990s and early 2000s was from a prominent family in Bijnor town.

In addition to its failure to fund new schools after 1991, the government has been retreating from its commitment to pay full-time teachers within schools receiving state aid. As a result, class sizes increased rapidly in many

[4]In UP, Classes 1 to 5 are termed primary school or lower primary, Classes 6–8 upper primary, Classes 9–10 junior secondary, and Classes 11–12 senior secondary or 'inter'. The most common type of schools are primary schools enrolling children from Classes 1 to 5, 'junior high schools' catering for pupils from Classes 6–8 or sometimes 6–10, and 'inter colleges' providing Classes 6–12.

aided schools in Bijnor district during the 1990s. The private managers of aided secondary schools in Bijnor town had addressed the problem of the state's inability to fund new teaching posts by employing temporary teachers on low rates of pay. These schools passed on the costs of paying additional teachers to parents by introducing fees and by charging parents for computing, extra-curricular activities and textbooks (Jeffery et al. 2006a).

A marked feature of urban aided schools was the increased tendency of teachers to give extra-school tutorials. Low rates of pay encouraged private teachers to organize tuition, but teachers on the government payroll also provided tutorials. Some private and government teachers doubled or even tripled their salaries in this way. The tutorial system in Bijnor and many smaller towns had become a well-institutionalized form of parallel or 'shadow' schooling, with pupils attending school for five or six hours a day, and either taking tutorials in a teacher's house or attending a 'coaching center' for two or three hours in the early morning and evening.

The apparent collapse of state education in the 1990s in Bijnor district related not only to a decline in state investment in education but also to the accumulated impact of funds being channeled into teachers' salaries to the exclusion of developing educational curricula and facilities. A lack of state funds prevented critical reflection within government circles on school syllabi and there were few efforts to develop in-service training. During the 1990s, the gap between the subjects taught in school and the needs of rural students widened. Elsewhere in north India, Kumar (1998) has noted how agricultural education in state secondary schools is largely divorced from the realities of rural cultivation. In addition, the types of technical or craft-based education that might equip rural people for small-scale entrepreneurial activities were unavailable within rural schools in Bijnor district. Teachers' styles of teaching promoted rote memorization, close adherence to textbooks and cramming for examinations. With a few exceptions, teachers did not employ tutorial, case study or other methods within school that might increase students' critical judgment, promote active learning or generate understanding. Extra-curricular activities, field trips and supervised practical learning were restricted to expensive English-medium schools.

In 1986, partly out of concern at the increasing inability of the state to fund good quality education, the Indian government decided to invite external funding in elementary education (Classes 1 to 8). From 1987 onwards, international donors, particularly the World Bank, DFID and the Swedish International Development Agency introduced programs aimed at improving children's access to elementary schooling (Ramachandran 2004). In UP, the World Bank, DFID and European Union collaborated with the State Government to introduce a District Primary Education Project (DPEP) in 1993–94. The DPEP tried to increase levels of staffing in schools, establish new schools, and set up village level committees responsible for overseeing government education. A major goal was to increase the numbers of girls attending elementary schooling, by making schools more 'girl-friendly,' running motivation campaigns and establishing new schools, some of them single sex. Although DPEP may have improved aspects of girls' education in Bijnor town, as late as 2002 DPEP and its successor initiative 'Education for All' had had minimal impact on teachers' practices, class sizes and local management of schools in rural areas of Bijnor district (Jeffery et al. 2005).

The increasing importance of non-state education also marked the landscape of Nangal and Qaziwala and largely reinforced local social inequalities based upon caste, class and religion. In 2001, Nangal's population was about 5,300 of which 48 percent were Chamars, 26 percent Jats and 12 percent Muslim. The remaining population was mainly comprised of MBCs but included a small number of Brahmin households. The Jats owned 83 percent of the agricultural land in Nangal in 2001. Landownership was not the only basis for rural power in Nangal, but it remained crucial in defining a household's economic and social position. In line with local understandings of what constitutes a relatively 'rich farmer' (*amīr kisān*), rich households can be defined as those possessing over 4 acres of land. Of the 239 Jat households, 54 percent possessed more than 4 acres in 2001. Rich Jat households had reinvested agricultural surplus in small businesses. They managed a wood yard, two sugar-cane processing units, cold stores and several shops and schools.

In 2001, the Chamars possessed just 8 percent of the agricultural land in Nangal. Of the 457 Chamar households in the village, only 1 percent owned more than 4 acres and 77 percent were landless. Social inequalities in landownership were paralleled by inequalities in the material assets of Chamars and Jats:

56 percent of Chamars lived in brick built (*pakkā*) houses compared to 89 percent of Jats. Only 10 percent of Chamar households had televisions compared to 70 percent of Jats.

Up until the mid-twentieth century in Nangal, labor relations in the village were organized primarily according to caste. Under the so-called *jajmānī* system (see Raheja 1988), a range of lower castes (*kamīns*) provided specialist forms of labor to the dominant Jat caste (*jajmāns*) in return for payment in kind. During the 1950s, '60s and '70s this patron-client system slowly disintegrated as a result of the expansion of market relations within agriculture, growing political awareness among Dalits and an increase in the availability of off-farm employment. In the early 2000s, most Chamars in Nangal were employed as manual laborers within or very close to the village, often on the farms or in the small industrial units owned by Jats. Chamars were principally employed as daily wage laborers paid in cash; men earned between Rs. 25 and Rs. 50 per day in agriculture and Rs. 30 to Rs. 65 within industries such as brick kiln manufacture and sugar cane crushing. Chamar women earned between Rs. 15 and Rs. 30 as agricultural laborers and Rs. 20 and Rs. 40 within small industries.[5]

Semi-feudal labor relations continued to exist alongside capitalist forms in Nangal, however. Most notably, Jats had institutionalized a system wherein Chamars only received the leafy tops of sugar cane (*gole*) in return for the assistance in harvesting this crop (Lieten and Srivastava 1999; Lerche 1999). The existence of this system reflects the continuing importance of certain types of patron-client relation between lower castes and dominant castes within Nangal. Chamars lacked urban social contacts and frequently called on Jats for assistance in negotiations with government officials. Moreover, Chamars often depended upon Jats for fodder for their cattle and access to fields in which to defecate. These forms of continued dependence severely limited Chamars' capacity to bargain for higher wages or obtain speedy and full payment for their labor.

Nangal contained two government primary schools and local Brahmins ran three private primary schools. Jats dominated the management committee of the Nangal Junior High School, which was the larger and better-funded

[5] In 2001 one US dollar was equivalent to about 40 rupees.

of the village's two private secondary schools. The other secondary school, the Ambedkar Junior High School, catered mainly for Dalits and ran up to Eighth Class. While facilities and standards of teaching at the government primary schools and Ambedkar School were particularly poor, all the primary and secondary schools in Nangal were underfunded, were badly maintained and suffered from teacher neglect. There were inadequate amenities attached to village schools, and children often complained of having to sit outside in the hot sun during lessons. Government teachers usually arrived late for classes and were often absent from school altogether.

Within three miles of Nangal, there were two aided secondary schools offering classes up to twelfth, one co-educational and one solely for girls. These schools had suffered more than had urban aided schools as a result of the government's refusal to fund new teaching posts since the early 1990s. The private managers of aided schools located in rural areas lacked the option of employing large numbers of additional private teachers and passing on the costs to children's parents, since rural people sending their children to these schools could not afford to pay higher fees. These school managers were therefore forced to enlarge class sizes to accommodate increasing numbers of pupils. It was common for classes in rural aided secondary schools to contain over 80 pupils, and some reached 120.

Like Nangal, Qaziwala's economy was dominated by agriculture and small-scale industries, especially craft activities, small sugar cane crushing plants and transport-related enterprises. There were no sources of large-scale manufacturing employment in the immediate vicinity of Qaziwala. Muslim Sheikhs comprised 60 percent of the population of the village. The Sheikhs did not constitute a 'dominant caste' in the same manner as the Jats in Nangal, but they did monopolize access to agricultural wealth in the village: the Sheikhs owned 86 percent of the agricultural land in Qaziwala. Of the 201 Sheikh households, 51 percent had more than 1.25 acres and 16 percent possessed more than 4 acres. Some Sheikh households were fairly wealthy and had built two-storied brick houses in Qaziwala. But the majority lived in houses constructed from a mixture of earth and brick and they supplemented their meager income from agriculture by working as wage laborers or small-scale entrepreneurs in the village or Bijnor town, usually in agricultural related activities, transport, craft or construction. 'Lower caste' Qasais comprised 25 percent of the population of the village, owned 11 percent of the agricultural land and worked mainly as cattle traders and butchers. The remaining Muslim castes in Qaziwala owned negligible amounts of land. The non-Muslims in Qaziwala were almost all SCs. They comprised 2 percent of the population and were landless.

Qaziwala contained a government primary school, and there were five small private primary schools within a three mile radius of the village in 2001. The government primary school serving Qaziwala was woefully poor. The only 'teaching equipment' in the cramped and dilapidated building was a stick to beat students. The facilities in the private primary schools were little better. A government-aided secondary school, private secondary school and government junior high school, were located about two miles from the village. These were better equipped but marked nonetheless by the failure of the state to regulate post-primary schooling in the district.

In addition to these 'mainstream' schools, there were four madrasahs within or immediately adjacent to Qaziwala, three of which were co-educational. None charged students for religious instruction, but the teaching materials used for secular subjects had to be purchased. Of these institutions, the madrasah located in Begawala, just outside Qaziwala, was the most popular among Qaziwala parents. The Begawala madrasah offered classes in Urdu, Islamic doctrines and the *Qur'ān Sharīf* and enrolled over 1,200 pupils in 2001. Rich and middle peasant rural Muslims comprised most of the informal management committee and supported the madrasah financially through religious tax (*zakāt*), which was paid as a 2.5 percent share of their annual agricultural profits. Male madrasah staff also collected voluntary subscriptions (*chandā*) during tours of surrounding villages and towns, and Delhi, Surat, Mumbai and Hyderabad, during Ramzan. Begawala also received a large donation from South Africa in the early 1990s. There were close personal links between teachers at the Begawala madrasah and staff at the *Daru'l `Ulūm* seminary at Deoband.

Rural schooling in and around Nangal and Qaziwala therefore testified to the failure of the state to provide educational facilities adequate to meet the needs of the rural population, either in terms of quality or quantity. The educational intermediaries that had sprung up to fill this institutional vacuum were varied: in Nangal, they were schools catering especially for either Jat or

Chamar children; in Qaziwala they were madrasahs catering for rural Muslims. Notwithstanding these forms of infrastructural development, however, rural schools compared poorly with educational institutions in Bijnor town. The next section explores the implications of this social geography of educational provision for differently positioned rural households. We pay particular attention to Jats and Chamars in Nangal and Muslims in Qaziwala.

In Search of Distinction:
Jat Educational and Employment Strategies

When we asked Jat parents why they had sought education (*parhāī*) for their sons in the 1980s and 1990s, the most common response was that it provided opportunities for young men to obtain salaried employment (*naukrī*). In this sense, schooling was central to parental ambitions. Jat parents linked their sons' employment to their own security in old age and to the future social standing of their family. According to patriarchal norms in the village, sons were expected to enter paid employment or active work within farming or a family business by their early twenties, soon after leaving formal education. Parents typically assumed responsibility for arranging the marriage of their sons, and they imagined that marriage would occur shortly after a son obtained secure work. Jat parents also surmised that, if a son was educated up to at least Tenth Class, and particularly if he obtained a secure white-collar job, they would be able to arrange for him to marry an educated young woman from a 'good family' who would be responsible, accomplished and respectful. This was an important consideration since a daughter-in-law was normally expected to care for her husband's parents in their old age.

Jat parents spoke of boys' secondary school education as providing skills, knowledge and valuable cultural distinction. But they placed greatest emphasis on education's role in improving young men's employment prospects. In discussing men's employment opportunities, Jats made a three-way distinction between secure, well-paid and prestigious jobs within government service (*sarkārī naukrī*), unremunerative, temporary and poorly paid private service (*private naukrī*) and grueling and insecure manual labor on daily wages for an employer (*mazdūrī*), whether in industry or agriculture. Jats were concerned about the future economic security of their households in the context of the subdivision of agricultural holdings associated with the prevailing system of partible inheritance. Jats also spoke of the declining profitability of farming in light of the withdrawal of government subsidies on key agricultural inputs, especially fertilizers. Against this background, investment in boys' secondary schooling was seen as a means of diversifying economic risk. A government job, in particular, provided a regular salary, pension, over-income (*ūparī*) based on the collection of bribes (*rishwat*) and subsidized access to welfare services. By contrast, Jat parents regarded girls' education as important for creating good wives and mothers, instilling childcare skills and preparing young women for their role as civilized home makers. Parents typically withdrew young women from formal education after puberty out of a concern for young women's safety on journeys to and from school and sometimes in response to the need for assistance in the home. Some of these girls studied as non-attending students, which parents perceived to be a safe way of their acquiring higher qualifications.

During the 1980s and 1990s, Jats invested large sums of money in the pursuit of secondary school qualifications for their sons in the hope they would enter secure salaried work (Tables 1 and 2). As substantial landowners, Jats typically had a reliable source of income, could obtain loans from relatives or financial institutions and, in rare cases, they could sell land to pay for education. Landownership, or close kinship links with prosperous landowners, allowed most Jat households to manage financial crises without having to remove sons from school. These social and economic factors distinguished rich from poor Jats in access to education. Poor Jats complained much more often of the expense of formal schooling and were occasionally forced to remove sons from school in response to financial pressures, such as those arising out of the illness of a family member.

But there were similarities between the schooling strategies of rich and poor Jats that marked them out from Chamars and Muslims. Largely out of concern about the subdivision of their agricultural holdings, Jats began to use modern forms of contraception—and other means of limiting the number of their descendants—much earlier than other caste and community groups in the area and therefore had fewer children than Chamars and Muslims (Jeffery and Jef-

TABLE 1

Percentage of 13–17 year-old Jat and Chamar boys in Nangal and Muslim boys in Qaziwala in formal schooling, 1990 and 2000/2001

Education	Jats 1990	Jats 2001	Chamars 1990	Chamars 2001	Muslims 1990	Muslims 2000
Primary school	2	2	2	9	6	12
Secondary school	67	90	36	47	4	8
Higher education	0	2	0	0	0	0
Madrasah	0	0	0	0	14	21
Not in formal schooling	31	6	62	45	75	58
N	95	63	95	155	154	274

SOURCE: Village censuses conducted by authors, Sept.–Oct. 1990, Oct.–Nov. 2000 and Feb. 2001.

NOTES: This table includes children not resident in Nangal or Qaziwala but whose parents lived in the village. Percentages have been rounded. Since the numbers in some cells are very small, the percentages should be used with caution.

TABLE 2

Percentage of 18–22 year-old Jat and Chamar young men in Nangal and Muslim young men in Qaziwala in formal education, 1990 and 2000/2001

Education	Jats 1990	Jats 2001	Chamars 1990	Chamars 2001	Muslims 1990	Muslims 2000
Secondary school	15	22	16	9	3	4
Higher education	15	19	7	2	0	1
Madrasah	0	0	0	0	1	0
Not in formal education	70	59	77	89	96	95
N	79	68	135	132	105	112

SOURCE: Village censuses conducted by authors, Sept.–Oct. 1990, Oct.–Nov. 2000 and Feb. 2001.
NOTES: See notes to Table 1.

fery 1997). Thus, Jats were able to invest greater resources in each son. Jats were usually able to send their sons to the more expensive but relatively well-provisioned, private primary schools in Nangal and then to the privately-run Nangal Junior High School or secondary schools in urban areas. Many Jats improved the chances of their children's success in school by arranging private tuition in preparation for secondary school examinations with especially reputed teachers in urban areas, often paying up to Rs. 400 a month for each subject and offering their sons tuition in several school subjects simultaneously. In addition, since Jat parents were generally more educated than Chamar and Muslim parents, they were better equipped to monitor children's educational progress, liaise with teachers and instill in their sons the urbane good manners that were valued in secondary schools. Jat mothers, in particular, played a crucial role in the daily business of preparing their sons for school, supervising their homework and grooming them in appropriate forms of 'educated' comportment, forms of what Papanek (1979) has called 'status production work' (see also Donner 2006).

Jat fathers more commonly assumed responsibility for choosing schools for their sons and assisting them in making subject choices. Jat parents had relatively good access to social contacts outside the local area. These contacts could assist in their sons' schooling or provide advice about urban educational opportunities. Of Jat boys aged between 13 and 17 in 2001, 21.4 percent studied in schools outside a three mile radius of the village. Several rich Jat households had paid a substantial 'donation' or admission fee and used urban social contacts to negotiate their sons' entry into the Government Inter College (GIC) in Bijnor. Notwithstanding the general decline in state education, GIC had a reputation for particularly good examination results and discipline. Jat parents educating their children in Bijnor or farther afield sometimes sent their sons to stay with close relatives: 9.5 percent of Jat boys aged between 13 and 17 in 2001 lived with urban kin to help them get access to better schools than were available in the village. These relatives took on responsibility for supervising boys' education during term time. Adopting a different strategy, in the early 1990s parents in the three richest Jat households had sent their sons to the regional educational center of Dehra Dun for prestigious English-medium education within private boarding schools.

Jat employment strategies and outcomes also reflect the greater economic, social and cultural capital of members of this caste relative to Chamars in Nangal and Qaziwala Muslims. Parents and young men in Nangal argued that the nature of competition for government employment changed markedly in the 1980s from a system in which individual talent played a substantial role in getting good jobs, to one in which access to government employment depended much more upon the payment of a large bribe (*rishwat, ghūs*) and personal recommendation (*sifārish*). Many people believed that it was necessary to pay between Rs. 40,000 and Rs. 100,000 for even a low-ranking government job. Moreover, in the quest for government employment, young people usually had to finance extensive travel, forgo paid work for long periods and fund specialist coaching for examinations. These financial considerations placed Jats at an ad-

TABLE 3

Percentage of educated Chamar and Jat men in Nangal and educated Muslim men in Qaziwala aged between 20 and 34 by principal employment status in 1990 and 2000/2001

Education	Jats 1990	Jats 2001	Chamars 1990	Chamars 2001	Muslims 1990	Muslims 2000
Farming	50	55	4	3	23	18
Government service	11	11	4	3	9	0
Private service	8	11	4	3	9	7
Skilled craft outside Bijnor	0	2	0	0	14	29
Skilled craft local	1	0	2	5	18	16
Business	7	11	2	7	14	4
Manual labor outside Bijnor	0	0	0	3	0	2
Manual labor local	0	2	70	68	9	7
Religious services	0	0	0	0	0	4
Student	20	7	14	6	5	7
Looking/unemployed	3	3	0	2	0	7
N	76	130	50	101	22	45

SOURCE: Village censuses conducted by authors, Sept.–Oct. 1990, Oct.–Nov. 2000 and Feb. 2001.

NOTES: This table includes young men not resident in Nangal or Qaziwala but whose parents lived in the village. Percentages have been rounded. Since the numbers in some cells are very small, the percentages should be used with caution. The term 'educated young men' refers to those with at least an Eighth Class pass.

vantage over Chamars and Muslims, and also put rich Jats in a better position than poorer members of their caste in the search for government jobs (Table 3). Jats were often aware of reliable urban brokers who assisted applicants within government employment markets. Drawing on contacts in government service, Jats could also acquire the personal recommendations important in the competition for secure posts. Some Jats had used their contacts within government to occupy posts formally reserved for Dalits. In these cases, Jats claimed that there were no suitably qualified Dalits to fill the quota and they used their connections within the police and judiciary to avoid prosecution.

By the end of the 1990s, the acute shortage of secure government employment opportunities was elevating the importance of migrating in search of private-sector work. Some rich Jats were beginning to regard private sector employment as preferable to government service since it sometimes offered greater pay, prestige and independence. These households' relative wealth, access to suitable social contacts outside Bijnor district, and cultural capital allowed them to obtain comparatively secure private-sector work for their sons, often in teaching or computing. Within one of the richest Jat households in Nangal, for example, a son had been sent outside Bijnor district for specialist medical training with a view to entering private practice. Another of the richest households in the village had enrolled a son in an MBA course close to Delhi in the expectation that he would enter a multinational corporation. Outside the richest Jat households, young men unable to find government work occasionally obtained less prestigious private-sector salaried employment in the informal economy, usually within Bijnor district. Our household census surveys also showed, however, that many educated Jats aged between 20 and 34 were *not* in service employment (Table 3). Educated un/under-employment had become a pervasive problem among middle-ranking Jats, as it had among the Chamars and Muslims we discuss below.

'War Against Fate': Muslim and Chamar Strategies

Chamars and Muslims had far fewer resources to direct toward the education of their sons, and our census data showed that boys' participation in mainstream schooling was much lower within the Chamar and Muslim communities than among Jats (Tables 1 and 2). Chamar and Muslim parents spoke of the crippling expense of mainstream secondary schools and the constant financial struggle that they faced to keep their children in education, what some called a 'war against fate' (*kismat ki larāī*). Chamars were formally entitled to receive annual government scholarships for SCs of Rs. 350 per child in primary school and Rs. 480 per secondary school pupil. But Chamar parents often complained that teachers embezzled this money or that the scholarships arrived late and only in part. Lacking substantial property or the capacity to obtain cheap credit, Chamar and Muslim parents were frequently plunged into financial crises when a family member required medical treatment or when they needed to provide a dowry for a daughter's marriage. In addition, Chamars and Muslims argued that the poor standard of local education made it difficult to persuade errant and disinterested sons to remain in school. Parents said that teachers in secondary schools fail to teach or supervise students and turn a blind eye to truancy. Indeed, a common complaint among Muslim and Chamar parents was that genuine 'education' does not exist within the village and that they do not possess the money required to enroll their sons in distant schools (Jeffery et al. 2006b).

Some parents maintained that mainstream education was anyway irrelevant for their sons since they lacked the money and social contacts required to obtain salaried jobs. Instead, many Muslim parents sent their sons to local madrasahs for religious education (Table 1). Muslim parents pointed out that local madrasahs were much cheaper and better provisioned than mainstream schools and that, unlike teachers in many schools, madrasah staff did not discriminate against Muslims. Some Muslim parents also spoke of the moral deficiencies of mainstream education and the greater value of the religious and ethical training available within madrasahs. Madrasah education allowed Muslim parents to ensure that many of their children received instruction in religious practices, training in skills relevant to parenthood and acculturation in norms of good conduct (Jeffery et al. 2004).

Muslims' enthusiasm for madrasah education reflects their systematic exclusion from government and many private schools rather than a positive desire for religious instruction (cf. Sikand 2005). Indeed, Chamars *and* Muslims were keenly aware of the potential value of mainstream education for young men. Influenced by positive images of education circulated by the state, educational institutions, development organizations and the media, many Chamar and Muslim parents spoke enthusiastically of the capacity of education to improve their children's lives, stressing the role of formal school education in providing valuable skills, training and manners. Parents were also aware that a relatively high proportion of Muslim and Chamar young men who obtained a secondary school qualification in the 1960s, 1970s or 1980s went on to capture government work. Three Muslim young men from Qaziwala and eleven Nangal Chamars secured government jobs in the 1970s or 1980s. As among Jats, Muslim and Chamar parents also linked their sons' employment prospects to their future security; they believed that if their son obtained experience of high school education they would be able to acquire an educated daughter-in-law who could care for them 'properly' (*thīk-se*) in old age.

With these considerations in mind, an increasing number of Chamar and Muslim parents ensured that their sons acquired some mainstream education and remained in school up to secondary level in the 1980s and 1990s (Tables 1 and 2). Muslim and Chamar parents investing in the secondary schooling of their sons were concentrated among the richer members of their communities. But these households typically lacked the social contacts required to obtain admission to schools in Bijnor town. Nor did these households possess the very large amounts of money which the richest Jat households in Nangal could mobilize to send their children to boarding schools outside Bijnor district. Chamar children most commonly attended the Nangal government primary school or Ambedkar School and moved on to a government-aided high school near Nangal. Muslim parents in Qaziwala sending their sons to mainstream secondary schools usually enrolled them in a school two miles north of the village. Many of the Muslim young men in this school had begun their education in madrasahs and some men carried on in a madrasah and mainstream school up to Eighth Class.

Chamar and Muslim boys generally entered formal education later than their Jat peers and were more prone to repeating years. Relatively unfamiliar with mainstream schooling, Chamar and Muslim parents were less adept than the Jats at supervising their sons' education. They often said that, as illiterate people, they were unable to plan, monitor and evaluate their children's mainstream schooling effectively. The sense of being illiterate also undermined Chamar and Muslim parents' confidence and limited their ability to evaluate local school curricula critically and instill the cultural capital that confers status within educational spheres. Relatively bereft of urban contacts with knowledge of mainstream schooling, Chamars and Muslims were less capable than were Jats of seeking schooling opportunities outside the local area. Only 2.1 percent of Chamar boys aged between 13 and 17 studied in mainstream schools outside a three-mile radius of Nangal and just 1.1 percent had moved outside the village for education. No Muslims had done so, which may also reflect the greater possibility of commuting from Qaziwala into Bijnor town for schooling on a daily basis.

Continued caste and communal discrimination compounded Chamars' and Muslims' difficulties within formal education. Chamars said that open caste discrimination involving the formal segregation of lower caste students in classes and maintenance of separate eating arrangements ended within schools in the

1960s. But Chamar young men and women, as well as many Muslims, reported teachers' marking them down in examinations, preventing them from progressing through school, making demands for bribe money and singling them out for humiliating punishments on account of their caste or community background. Other young people referred to higher caste Hindu students directing intimidating language, taunts and harassment toward Chamars or Muslims. Young women were especially vulnerable to higher caste sexual harassment and the climate of fear and recrimination that this generated. Some Chamar and Muslim students said that they had partially countered the effects of casteism or communalism by: strategically mentioning or concealing their caste/community identity; publicizing acts of discrimination; seeking allegiances with sympathetic teachers; or forming close friendship networks within school.

Very few Muslim and Chamar young men who obtained secondary schooling went on to capture salaried employment (Table 3). The number of educated young men among the Muslims and Chamars searching for salaried posts rose steeply during the 1990s without a parallel increase in the number of jobs available. Chamars argued that reservations made little difference to their chances of obtaining government jobs because the competition for posts in the reserved quota was as fierce and corrupt as within the non-reserved sector. Chamars' and Muslims' less prestigious education, relative exclusion from social networks within government employment and lack of money for bribes, marginalized them in competition for government jobs relative to urban members of their caste/community and the Jats. Chamars' and Muslims' inability to develop relevant social contacts in urban areas prevented them from gaining effective access to information about the current state of markets in government employment. This reduced the confidence of these households and allowed unscrupulous brokers to extract money from Chamars and Muslims on the pretence that a government post would follow. In addition, some Chamars complained that rich Jats had been able to seize posts reserved for SCs through bribing government officials.

Conclusions

A rapidly privatizing educational market in north India and malpractice in the competition for secure salaried employment had allowed a rural elite in

Bijnor district to obtain privileged access to mainstream schooling and secure salaried employment. Most Chamars and Muslims were either excluded from secondary school education altogether or received devalued credentials. There was therefore a mutually reinforcing relationship between older forms of dominance rooted in control over land, access to urban social networks and privileged position within the Hindu caste hierarchy and social advantages based upon access to educational facilities and salaried work. The Bijnor case study therefore appears to offer an example of education's role in entrenching social inequalities.

Our case study shows that caste and religious community continue to provide a convenient shorthand for discussing rural inequality in UP. But rural people's educational and employment strategies cannot be 'read off' directly from their caste, class or religious background. Unequal access to educational facilities and salaried employment has intensified processes of class formation *within* the Jat caste, Dalit castes and Muslim community. Moreover, a growing crisis in the availability of salaried employment was increasing pressure on young men from all social classes in rural western UP, such that even large sections of the rural elite were unable to capitalize on their educational qualifications by obtaining secure white-collar jobs.

Our account of social reproduction points to three 'strata' of young men in rural Bijnor district in 2000–2002. First, there was a thin layer of educated young men, mainly Jats, who have acquired secure salaried work, principally within government. These young men enter our story at various points, but our book is not a detailed examination of their practices. Second, there was a large number of young men, principally Muslims but also many Chamars, who have not acquired any post-primary school qualifications. Again, these men will figure in our story, but chiefly with respect to how their practices shape the strategies of their educated peers. Finally, and most importantly for our analysis, we have identified a set of young men among Jats, Chamars and Muslims who have acquired at least an Eighth Class pass but who have failed to obtain their first choice of employment, which was usually work within government. These young men were becoming numerous, visible and vocal, and we now turn to analysis of their actions and reflections.

3

Masculinity on a Shoestring?
The Cultural Production of Education

This chapter explores how educated young men excluded from government work react to their predicament with particular reference to young men's discussions of what it means to 'be educated.' We seek to provide a counterpoint to scholarship based within and outside India that emphasizes the violent reactions of educated young men to exclusion from secure salaried work (e.g. Hansen 1996; Leavitt 1998) and to studies stressing young men's 'return to tradition' in the face of poor occupational outcomes (Levinson and Holland 1996; Demerath 1999). Instead, we describe a common narrative of educational value—or public culture—in which the educated un/under-employed imagine themselves as civilized and respectable *educated people*. Within these moral narratives of what it is to be educated, young men stressed their connection to symbols construed as 'modern' more than they emphasized a 'traditional' cultural style.

In making these arguments, we draw on recent scholarship exploring the cultural production of schooled subjectivities (Levinson and Holland 1996). Like Skinner and Holland (1996) and Klenk (2003), among others, we show how the notion of 'being educated' can become a vehicle for young people to communicate their sense of the modern. But more than existing studies of education's cultural meanings, we stress the links between young people's sense of themselves as 'educated' and notions of social skill. We also point to how ideas of 'being educated' are inscribed in the bodily performances of educated young men in ways that cut across caste and religion.

Ideas of school education as a form of civilization were central to the colonial projects of rule in India (Kumar 1994; Kumar 2000). The British identified a thin 'upper stratum' of the Indian population capable of acquiring education and sought to train these people—upper caste Hindu men, Muslims from the landed elites, as well as Parsis—for the rigors of modern governance. Notions of progress through formal secondary schooling were also espoused by a range of Indian political and social organizations in colonial India. In western UP, the Arya Samaj was especially influential in promoting ideas of education as social improvement, particularly among Jats but also within Dalit communities (Jones 1966; Datta 1999a). The Aligarh Muslim University was prominent in instilling similar ideas in the minds of Muslims (Lelyveld 1978).

In the post-colonial era, narratives of upward mobility through formal education have proliferated. The media have often been at the forefront of this process, depicting educated people as confident, well mannered and adept and the uneducated as the opposite. The state, educational entrepreneurs and development agencies have been no less bold in their ideological work. There is a vast array of educational institutions keen to promote notions of progress based on formal education, either for ideological, economic or 'charitable' reasons. The rise of the Bahujan Samaj Party in UP was especially important in communicating notions of progress through education to Dalits in rural Bijnor district in the 1990s and early 2000s, through pamphlets, election slogans and the periodic visits of politicians and party workers to urban and village communities. The BSP placed great emphasis on the Ambedkarite slogan 'organize, struggle, educate' in their speeches and campaigns and in their efforts to reconfigure the iconography of north Indian public space (Jaoul 2007). Notions of progress through education are not only writ large upon the landscape, however. It is also an idea that *insinuates itself* into people's everyday actions, thoughts and modes of appreciation, for example through the medium of the formal, informal and hidden curriculum within schools, and via ideas instilled from early childhood by similarly 'insinuated' parents (cf. Foucault 1980: 34).

If notions of education as progress are partly imposed 'from above,' they also reflect more localized histories. The district gazetteers for Bijnor and neighboring districts point to informal tutorial-style instruction in western UP dating back to at least the late nineteenth century (e.g. Joshi 1965). Certainly, the image of a Brahmin teacher (*gurū*) surrounded by eager pupils (*chelā*) looms large in the collective social imagination of rural people in Bijnor district. Moreover, as Sikand (2005: xxix) suggests, the recent upsurge in madrasah education in north India reflects a long Islamic tradition of rural learning organized around the notion of knowledge (*'ilm*). Thus, as far as notions of education as social improvement have taken hold in the countryside of western UP, this is likely to reflect the unfolding of successive regional projects oriented toward particular types of 'development' *and* the effervescence 'from below' of more deeply embedded ideas of education as progress.

The chapter is organized into three further sections. The next section documents educated un/under-employed young men's efforts to distinguish between the cultural styles of educated and uneducated people. We then briefly consider how far educated un/under-employed young men are 'hegemonized' by broader narratives of education as progress. Finally, we outline the relevance of this discussion for the broader themes of this book.

Imagining Education

At the cultural level, the dominant response of educated young men in Nangal and Qaziwala to their exclusion from government work in the early 2000s was to stress their superiority as 'educated' (*parhe likhe*) people. In a powerful sense, they *reinvested* in notions of education as social improvement, even in the face of their failure to find salaried work. The phrase *parhe likhe* literally means 'reading and writing' but in most contexts in rural Bijnor district it denoted someone who had attended a formal educational institution for a prolonged period of time, and educated people therefore distinguished between being 'educated' (*parhe likhe*) and 'literate' (*parh sakte, likh sakte,* literally, someone who can read and write). The term 'educated' could indicate either people who had been through mainstream education or those with prolonged experience of the madrasah system, and might refer to people with any secondary school experience or only to those with a High School (Tenth Class) pass or above. Nevertheless, and without disparaging madrasah graduates, school-educated Muslim young men tended to agree with Chamars and Jats that 'educated people' possess mainstream secondary qualifications and can read and write Hindi with fluency. Moreover, there was a measure of consensus among educated young men that someone with an Eighth Class pass was 'educated' but that a person who dropped out of school before this stage was not. Indeed, one of the most remarkable features of educational narratives was the similarity between how young men from different caste, class and community backgrounds discussed the benefits of 'being educated' and the lack of attention young men paid to gradations within the categories of the 'educated' and 'uneducated.' For example, we rarely heard young men distinguishing between those with university degrees and people with high school qualifications or discussing the differences between people with primary schooling and those who had never been to school, in spite of our asking questions about these possible differences. Emerging in part out of images of education circulated by the state, media and development agencies, a type of 'public culture' of educational distinction existed among un/under-employed young men that shaped young men's ideas about successful male adulthood.

Young men's discussions of educated difference often began with reference to speech (*bol chāl*) and voice (*awaz*) as forms of cultural distinction. Educated young men said that educated people converse in concise, grammatically sound and correctly enunciated Hindi, while illiterates speak in a village dialect (*gānv ki bolī, karī bolī*) strewn with aggression, expletives and inappropriate familiarity. An educated Chamar young man told us:

The uneducated say, "Oi! Where ya goin'?" and the educated say, "Where are you going?" The uneducated say, "Do me work!" and the educated say, "Could you please do this work?" or they say, "Please could you do this work for me?" The uneducated say, "Come 'ere an' eat," and the educated say, "Please eat." So this is the difference. There are many other differences between the way that educated and uneducated people speak.

Similarly, another educated Chamar young man claimed that:

If two uneducated men meet, and one man wants to know where a road leads, the conversation will run as follows: First man: "Where does the road go?" Second man: "It goes there." The same conversation among educated men would be. . . . First man: "Brother, could you possibly tell me where this road leads?" Second man: "Brother, this road leads over there, where are you going?"

Many educated young men referred to illiterate speech as '*dabang ke*,' a phrase that connotes blunt, rude, uncouth or 'clownish' talk. They also described the uneducated as being repetitive, guttural, monosyllabic, stuttering or 'parrot-like' in their conversations. Educated young men frequently described the ability of the educated to remain silent or talk quietly when confronting an adversary or assessing a threat. Illiterates provided the contrast: shouting loudly and in vain during everyday conversations or panicked into wild hollers by the slightest disturbance: "Like an empty bowl that rattles when you strike it."

Ideas of what it is to be educated were also elaborated with reference to clothing (cf. Tarlo 1996; Bannerjee and Miller 2004). Educated Jat and Chamar young men in both villages tended to wear collared shirts with pleated chino-style trousers, a form of young male dress popular throughout western UP, particularly in urban areas. These men also sought out opportunities to display shoes, wristwatches and dark or mirrored sunglasses understood locally as '*smart*.' By contrast, Muslim young men commonly wore clean and well-pressed *kurtā-pājāmā*[1] and a white prayer cap, a characteristic form of Muslim dress, or else changed into *kurtā-pājāmā* to pray. A small number of educated Muslim young men in and around Qaziwala had begun to wear red and white checked scarves (*keffiyeh*) which suggested membership of a community of global Muslims and, more specifically, connoted solidarity with Palestinian people.[2]

Educated young men typically argued that the educated avoid ostentation in their dress, do not tuck their shirts into their trousers and ensure that their clothes are sparklingly clean (*sāf suthrā*). By contrast, educated men said illiterates place gaudy lucky charms around their necks, tuck their shirts into their trousers and wear stained, dirty clothes. Educated young men emphasized that an educated style of dress was not so much a matter of *what* you wear—an educated person's clothes could be cheap and old—as *how* you wear it and with what level of regard for personal hygiene. Several educated Chamars emphasized this point by stating, "Our clothes may be torn but you'll never find them dirty."

[1] On the symbolic significance of this dress see Chakrabarty (2002: 51ff).

[2] We are grateful to Barbara Metcalf for drawing our attention to these scarves, which were not a feature of young male Muslim attire twenty years ago in western UP (Barbara Metcalf, personal communication, email 01/06/04).

In discussing their clothing styles, educated un/under-employed young men frequently claimed to be *smart*, *fashionable* and *modern*, using the English words.[3] In the context of discussions about clothing fashion, '*smart*' had overwhelmingly positive connotations and conveyed the ability to wear clothing in a way that impressed others. To possess '*fashion*' was to be in tune with developments in clothing characteristic of Bijnor or other urban centers in UP. A '*modern*' style referred more specifically to an affiliation with the new (*nayā*), though not necessarily 'the West,' and *modern* was a popular epithet for clothing shops, tailors, hairdressers and schools in Bijnor district. The terms *fashion* and *modern* were morally ambivalent. On certain occasions, young men criticized the impropriety of uneducated young men and young women by referring to their being overly fashionable (*zyādā fashion to hai*) or 'excessively *modern*' (*bahut hī zyādā modern*), discourses also noted by Osella and Osella (2000: 119) in Kerala.

Educated young men also spoke of the capacity of education to instill good manners (*chal chalan, adab*), refinement (*nirmalatā, tamīz-tahzīb*), moral strength (*tamīz, akhlāq*) and right conduct (*adab, nītishāstra*). Educated people perceived themselves to be civilized (*sabhyatā*), capable of displaying humanity (*insāniyat*) and therefore distinct from the illiterate man, sometimes discussed as a 'wild man' (*janglī ādmī*), 'beast' (*jānwar*) or 'stammering savage' (*barbar*). In elaborating on these ideas, educated young men described how educated people show respect in front of their elders, learn and perform religious ceremonies correctly, remain dignified in street settings and know how to behave as guests in others' houses. Illiterates provided the foil: failing to respect their parents, forgetting religious rites, displaying lustful or aggressive behavior in the street and acting as boorish and demanding guests. In expressing their views about educated and uneducated behavior, educated young men believed that illiterates not only lacked marks of distinction (*nishān*) but also acted in an immoral and irreligious manner.

An important theme of educated young men's discussions of manners was of the adaptability of the educated. They described how educated people could

[3]We did not hear young people using *ādhunik*, the Hindi word for modern, a word which Chatterjee (2004) suggests was popular in parts of north India in the nineteenth century.

shape their behavior according to the nature of social situations whereas illiterates were regularly wrong-footed. An educated Chamar young man told
us that:

When an uneducated man goes to his in-laws' home he says, "Greetings father, greetings
mother." But when he comes home he does not greet his real father and mother or even
his elder brother! The uneducated don't respect those older and younger than them.
They joke with youngsters and speak in a bad-mannered way [*badtamīzī se*] to them.
Elders should be well-mannered [*tamīz*] in the way that they speak to younger people.
The uneducated joke too much with youngsters and so the youngsters become too intimate [*khulā*] with their elders.

An educated Muslim young man teaching at the Begawala madrasah made a
similar point by recounting the story of an educated father trying to tutor his
as yet uneducated children on how to behave with guests.

[This] father told his children that when they ask whether a person is married they
should also ask about the person's children. Two young women then came to the house.
One of the man's children asked one of the women, "How many children do you have?"
The woman replied that she had three children. The child then asked her, "Are you married?" The child then asked the second young woman, "Are you married?" The second
young woman replied that she was unmarried. The child then asked her, "How many
children do you have?"

In discussing their versatility, educated Chamars, Jats and Muslims stressed
their capacity to move in an accomplished manner between practices coded as
'traditional' and those imagined as 'modern.' For example, a group of Chamar
young men celebrated the ability of educated people to switch effortlessly from
a conversation with friends in a village street to answering a call in a local
phone booth from a relative in Delhi. Similarly, a group of Muslim young men
exhibited pride at an educated person's ability to attend a computing tutorial
in Bijnor and return later in the afternoon to perform agricultural work in
Qaziwala. Educated young men imagined the educated person as an exemplary
rural cosmopolitan (cf. Gidwani and Sivaramakrishnan 2003), in the sense of
someone capable of moving between distinctive spheres, spaces or technologies with flexibility, speed and calm self-assurance. The illiterate person again
provided the counterpoint: parochial, leaden footed, inflexible and bewildered
by the 'modern' and 'traditional.'

Educated young men explained the inflexible and uncouth nature of illiterates' alleged behavior with reference to the accomplishments and capabilities (*hunar, qābilīyat, salāhīyat*) that they had failed to learn in school. Hindi is the official language of Uttar Pradesh, and of road signs, medical prescriptions, bills and legal documents. Educated men described the value of being able to read and write in Hindi and make mathematical calculations in order to act confidently in society and avoid cheats. Educated young men also regarded education as providing the knowledge (*avgat, gyān, jānkārī*) and wisdom (*'aql, hoshiyārī*) required to stand up against oppression. They stressed that education provides inner-confidence (*atm-vishvās, hauslā*) and resolve (*himmat*) and banishes feelings of fear or inferiority (*hīn bhāvnā*). Similarly, educated young men considered Hindi literacy to offer a measure of independence from others. Building on dominant motifs within television and Bollywood, educated young men said that the literate can "stand on their own two feet" while illiterates are needy and dependent, "like people leaning against a wall," "blind people" or "men stumbling in the darkness." For example, an educated Chamar young man in his early thirties told us:

Without education a man is a commonplace [*sāmānya*] thing. An educated person can read and write letters. Otherwise, one is just wandering around behind other people. An illiterate man won't know if you write down his own death and take the note to the police station. They will just wander around in a state of ignorance. If you go to a station to take a train, there the train number and time is written on a board. How will an illiterate man know when the train goes and which train to take?

Numerous stories of uneducated incompetence featured in our discussions with young men: illiterates repeatedly asking for assistance in deciphering letters, staring blankly at bus timetables, perplexed by the written instructions on the side of medicine bottles, baffled by the protocol within government offices or mistakenly signing documents harming their interests. In these examples, educated young men described the illiterate man as 'useless' (*bekār*) and lacking in development (*vikās, taraqqī*).

We observed striking similarities in the manner in which educated young men imagined and performed illiterate social practices within Nangal and Qaziwala. For example, in December 2000 on a trip to collect water chestnuts from a pond near Qaziwala, educated Muslim young men joked with Craig about how an illiterate person would react to a camera lens. Muslim young men took turns to gawp into an imaginary camera in the manner of an 'illiterate person' then collapsed in laughter in the surrounding sugar cane fields. As part of the banter that followed, several young men ran to the side of the pond to imitate an imagined 'uneducated man.' The men gazed open mouthed at each other, flapped their arms and danced on the spot. In a group conversation with educated Chamars four months later, a young man referred to seeing an uneducated woman in a local phone booth placing the mouthpiece of the phone to her ear and shouting loudly into the earpiece, "Why can't you hear me you fool!" As the laughter that followed subsided, other Chamars began imitating the uneducated. Like the Muslim young men, the Chamars allowed their mouths to loll open, bent their heads forward, half closed their eyes and beat their arms against their sides. In the autumn of the same year, a Jat young man in Nangal interrupted a conversation about village manners by rising from his rope bed to illustrate 'uneducated behavior.' Following a familiar routine, he relaxed his jaw, stuck out his tongue and waved his arms around furiously.

As these examples suggest, young men's efforts to develop and define educated and uneducated behavior were characterized by joking, horseplay and teasing. Many young men were eager to mimic uneducated speech, clothing and comportment, and the audience responded to the best performances with spirited laughter, slapping and cheers. Moreover, onlookers often interrupted performances of illiterate incompetence by shouting advice to the 'players'—"stick your tongue out," "stand pigeon-toed," "the uneducated are louder than that"—or praise particular actions or styles. On other occasions, young men made their points by engaging in what they called 'ulte' (upside down) speech: "The educated are disgusting, filthy and hopeless, and the uneducated are like gods."

A sense of the deeply ingrained quality of educated distinction ran through these narratives, jokes and performances of educated and uneducated practice. Educated young men argued that their own 'educated-ness' was not an outcome of conscious decision-making but had instead become part of their 'ūthnā baithnā': a phrase that literally means a "manner of getting up and sitting down" but more broadly connotes a structured set of dispositions—or 'habitus' (Bourdieu 1984)—inscribed in a person's reflexes, movement and tastes. Educated men expressed this idea most clearly in discussions of how they spend money, time and energy. When talking about what to eat, how to flirt with young women or what clothes to wear, educated young men sought to demonstrate the prudence, tact and discretion of the educated and the purportedly uncontrolled appetites of the uneducated for food, sex and excitement. Educat-ed young men frequently provided snapshots of the excessive consumption of illiterates: uneducated young men dribbling betel (pān) juice down their chins, gulping tea at local chāy stalls or ogling young women on the street. In these and other instances, educated young men did not imagine illiteracy as part of a traditional way of life that they had left behind, as Ciotti (2006) observed for eastern Uttar Pradesh, but as a negative form of contemporary social behavior, a type of 'bad modernity.'

This notion of 'educated' versus 'uneducated' discernment in the matter of consumption extended to conversations about hairstyles, spectacles, room decoration, drug use, alcohol, theater and books, but it came across especially clearly in young men's discussions of films. As Osella and Osella (2007: 168) have pointed out in their work on youth cultures in Kerala, and Lukose (2005) observes in her research on student cultures on university campuses in south India, cinema in India commonly furnishes important 'anchor points' in young people's efforts to craft distinctive styles in India, and the connection between cinema and 'education' was a recurrent theme of our interviews. In a typical statement, an educated Chamar young man told us:

The uneducated like films staring Amitabh Bachan, Dharmender, Sunny Deol, Sunil Shetty and Govinda. They see films with these people in. . . . And the educated like films starring Salman Khan, Shahrukh Khan and Hrithik Roshan. They see all their films. The uneducated like fighting films and the educated like popular films.

In this account, the archetypal 'uneducated films' were the 'fighting-action' films starring the actor Mithun Chakravarti popular in the late 1990s. In a group discussion with Chamars, educated young men said that they regarded the pur-ported exaggerated acting, poorly choreographed scuffles and ostentatious dé-nouement of a 'Mithun film' as emblematic of the embarrassing behavior of illiterates. The alleged failure of the uneducated to appreciate the difference be-tween films and reality—"to understand that the film is just a lie"—completed the picture of uneducated humiliation. An educated Jat young man told us:

The thing about the uneducated is that they do not understand that a film is full of ac-tors. They do not appreciate that these people do these things for show, to make a living. They see people running off with one another in films or performing dangerous stunts, and they somehow think, "I can do that, too!" And in the cinema itself they are climbing all over the screen!

Many educated young men hoped that their own educated demeanor would gradually transform the wider atmosphere (*mahaul*) of their home and neighborhood, an idea they expressed as like "a light shining out through the dark" or "sunshine streaming through a chink in the door."

In elaborating on their superiority as educated people, educated young men therefore displayed a particular vision of masculine acuity that contrasted with notions of male prowess based on physical strength (Arnold 1994), sexual prowess (Osella and Osella 2002), violence (Hansen 1996) or the display or giving of expensive consumer goods (see Osella and Osella 2000). Rather than emphasizing the limitless power of their bodies, educated young men spoke of their bodily and mental *control*. This did not equate with a vision of principled abstinence; educated young men did not say that they refrained from flirting with young women, never drank alcohol or always opposed styles of macho masculinity, for example. Instead, educated young men stressed that most of the time and certainly in the social situations that matter—in front of parents or in a public urban setting—they demonstrate good manners, discretion and educated accomplishments.

Educated young men sometimes mentioned 'slipping' into 'uneducated' forms of behavior. For example, one Chamar young man told us about an instance when he was young in which he had watched a particularly lurid action film. He recalled how he had tried to re-enact fighting scenes from the film when he arrived home. This involved balancing on top of a rope bed and throwing punches. The young man said that he fell off the rope bed and broke his leg. "That taught me not to behave in an uneducated manner. I have never seen an action film again." On other occasions, educated young men spoke of repeated lapses in their educated behavior. In a group discussion, a Jat young man admitted that he had a 'secret passion' for Mithun films even though he understood them to be 'uneducated.' A Chamar young man confided that he enjoyed taunting young women even though he knew this to be "wrong behavior for a Twelfth Class pass." In such cases, young men sometimes described themselves as temporarily 'becoming uneducated' in order to satisfy particular desires. But they stressed that their educated habitus soon reasserted itself: "like a feeling of power coming up from within" (cf. Klenk 2003).

Hegemonized Young Men?

Educated young men's moral narratives of educated difference operated as a structure of feeling (Williams 1977), a type of social consciousness that gave a distinct form to young people's cultural styles. Young men's visions of educated distinction also represented an attempt to construct an index of social respect (*izzat*) somewhat distinct from ideas of dignity based upon prestigious employment or wealth (cf. Fernandez Kelly 1994; Skinner and Holland 1996; Hyams 2000; Aitken 2001). As Hyams (2000) observed in work amongst Latinas in Los Angeles, and Klenk (2003) argued in research on women in north India, educated young people may use a sense of themselves as 'educated' to create new gendered identities that contest forms of entrenched dominance. By repeatedly stressing the cultural superiority of 'educated people,' educated young men in rural Bijnor district sought to demonstrate the value of mainstream schooling outside markets for government jobs and thereby to obtain some sort of 'pay off' for the long periods they had spent in formal education. To be educated was to be on the side of modernity, development and progress, even if one was unable to acquire economic security and prestigious work.

These narratives constituted neither purely 'hegemonic' nor 'oppositional' masculinities (Connell 2005). Educated young men's narratives echoed the discourses of dominant government, media and development organizations in many key respects, and this is particularly ironic in the case of Chamar and Muslim youth, who had historically been ridiculed for their failure to conform to upper caste Hindu norms of education, civilization and development. Moreover, educated young men's narratives were highly gendered. They usually discussed ideas of educated difference with reference to male social practices and enacted their ideas to men in settings coded locally as male, such as the village street corner or teashop (cf. Anandhi et al. 2002). By celebrating in their narratives and behavior the urbanity, confidence and pride of educated men, educated un/under-employed young men reinforced gender inequalities in access to public space. Parents and young women spoke of the dangers attached to young women traveling to and from school in the context of increasing numbers of educated, self-confident young men wandering around the villages.

Are educated un/under-employed young people therefore simply under the thrall of ideologies that serve the interests of the state and dominant classes?[4] Certainly, there is something profoundly unsettling about educated un/under-employed Chamar and Muslim young men rehearsing in moderated form notions long employed to subordinate the poor in western UP. Higher castes have used notions of their own distinctive 'civilization,' cleanliness and moral superiority to shore up their power in UP for many decades (Mandelbaum 1970), and the British used similar language in their attempts to legitimize colonial rule (e.g. Kumar 2000).

But, in as far as these young men are 'hegemonized,' they do not simply absorb ideas moving in a downward direction from above. Through their conversations, performances and debates, educated un/under-employed young men *actively and imaginatively create* positions that might look, at first blush, to be simply reiterations of dominant discourse. The creative nature of these processes of cultural production emerged in several discussions with young men. The following exchange between three educated Chamar young men provides a useful case.

Lekpal: The educated do not stare at women, but the uneducated gawp in the street.

Het Ram: No, no, the educated *do* gawp at women, but they only look at *educated* women.

Chanderpal: You are both talking nonsense. The educated and uneducated *both* stare at *all* sorts of women, but the educated do not touch women. That is the difference.

Het Ram: The educated look at educated women and the uneducated look at uneducated women.

Lekpal [slapping Het Ram on the back]: You've got it, *man*. Let's go with that!

On another occasion, three Jat young men debated the politics of tucking in one's shirt.

Yeshram: The uneducated tuck in their shirts and the educated leave them hanging out of their pants.

Indrapal: No, it's not like that. The uneducated tuck in their shirts in some places and leave other parts hanging out. The educated either leave their shirts out or tuck them in properly.

Yeshram: No, no, no. I know about these things.

[4]John Harriss asked a question in roughly these terms at a workshop on 'Ethnographies of the Political in South Asia', Southern Asia Institute, Columbia University, October, 2004. We are very grateful to him and others at this workshop for their questions and comments.

In such ways, young men debated between competing accounts of how educated people might behave before settling on a provisionally accepted version of educated behavior. This process of improvising around a central argument—that educated people are more civilized—might be usefully compared to a form of *social poetics*, in Herzfeld's (2005: 16ff) sense of the creative use of stereotypes in processes of social practice and performance,[5] or, to use a more identifiably 'regional' example, the Indian '*rāg*' (Shukla 1967): a traditional form of Hindu music consisting of a central theme on which variations are improvised within a framework of melodic formulas and rhythmic patterns. Like the '*rāg*,' young men are constantly embellishing their central theme with flights of cultural invention. At the same time, these narratives acquire their force through repetition and adherence to certain organizing schemas. This balance between repetition and structured invention is a defining feature of young men's educated cultural styles.

Equally, a sense of mischievousness and humor ran through young men's elaborations of education as civilization that marked them out from dominant notions of education as progress. Young men experimented with ideas of education as civilization in their jokes and horseplay. They interspersed intense, moral discussions of educated superiority with hints at their failure to conform to educated behavior, as in cases when young men remembered 'slipping' into 'illiterate ways,' and they repeatedly sought to outdo their peers in improvising around the central theme. None of these attributes of young men's cultural production has an easy parallel in, for example, the educational campaigns of the post-colonial state. To gloss young men's evocations of educated civility as straightforward forms of 'hegemonic masculinity' (Connell 1987) therefore risks obscuring the improvised and irreverent nature of their performances and, as we will argue in the remainder of the book, the radical ways in which the idea of education as civilization can be deployed.

[5]Herzfeld (2005: 23) explains that social poetics "is not about poetry (except as a special case), but *poetics*—not the mystically endowed semiosis of a genre, but the technical analysis of its properties as these appear in all kinds of symbolic expression, including casual talk."

Conclusions

The educated young men to whom we talked in 2000–2002 had responded to processes of economic and social restructuring in north India by celebrating the iconic significance of 'being educated.' In the narratives of educated young men, education not only provides the cultural capital that confers advantage in social situations (Bourdieu 1986), but has also come to define what it means to be civilized. Educated young men's notions of educated difference therefore offer an example of the cultural production of modern distinction. Post-structuralist writing in the social sciences has done much to challenge the use of binary concepts in social science explanation, but, at the same time, dualisms—such as 'educated' and 'uneducated' or 'modern' and 'non-modern'—course through the everyday narratives of marginalized young people in diverse global settings.

Much research on the cultural styles of educated un/under-employed young men has stressed their tendency to engage in violent, extreme and exaggerated forms of masculinity. By contrast, educated un/under-employed young men in Nangal and Qaziwala typically developed their sense of educated distinction with reference to their equanimity, patience and tact. Rather than seeking respect through self-consciously anti-modern cultural styles, educated Muslims, Chamars and Jats spoke of their versatility, and especially their capacity to grasp 'new' technologies and move between settings coded as 'traditional' and 'modern.'

These conclusions bear on debates surrounding education as a basis for empowerment. We have identified powerful local narratives that link education to social capabilities (Drèze and Sen 1995; Sen 1999). Educated young men believed in the notion that education provides a range of substantive freedoms, including a degree of political agency, better hygiene and a sense of individual self-worth. At the same time, young men's belief in education was not founded solely or even primarily on their conception of its transformative potential in the economic sphere—as a precursor to a 'good job'—but on its ability to generate embodied capacities of comportment, feeling and speech.

Following Ferguson (1999), much of the rest of our book explores how the notion of education as successful modernity set out in this chapter means different things to different people, serves a variety of political functions and is

contested by others in rural society, including many parents and the uneducated. Rather than reading off 'educated young men's identity' from an analysis
of their ideas about education, it is important to explore the diverse ways in
which Jat, Chamar and Muslim educated young men 'bend' and negotiate notions of education as civilization in the pursuit of their goals and in politicized
terrains of struggle.

More particularly, we are interested in how local political economy—and
wider regional and global dynamics—threaten young men's attempts to maintain a sense of themselves as educated people. By investing in a vision of hierarchy and placing themselves on the civilized side of this system of differences,
it was beholden on young men to live out the role they had assigned for themselves: that is, to sustain 'educated' performances. We have suggested that notions of being educated are *somewhat* distinct from ideas of progress through
the accumulation of economic wealth. But the 'somewhat' here is crucial. The
educated cultural styles discussed above depend to a significant extent on young
men having the time, freedom, money, and/or familial support required to go to
the cinema, stand around in the center of the village and wear clean shirts. What
happens when this social and economic freedom is eroded, for example when
parents call on their sons to devote more time to hard labor or when men lack
the money for a cinema ticket? Young men may improvise with ideas of what
it is to be educated to conform to their circumstances; and Osella and Osella
(2000: 120) offer an example of this possibility when they describe poor low
caste young men in Kerala using self-consciously 'fashionable' styles as a basis
for maintaining respect. But the notion of 'being educated' is not endlessly mal-
leable; it depends upon the repetition of particular 'key ideas,' such as the notion that an educated person is 'clean' in some demonstrable way. It follows that
a poverty stricken, unskilled manual laborer claiming educated airs could only
be a subject for derision. Thus, the idea of being educated 'solves' a particular
cultural problem for the educated un/under-employed—the loss of respect associated with failing to find a government job—but it potentially creates another one: the difficulty of sustaining an educated image in an uncertain economic
environment. The next four chapters explore how differently placed young men
react when a gap begins to open up between their sense of cultural modernity
and their limited capacity to realize their goals in the economic sphere.

4

From Canefield to Campus
(and Back Again):
The Social Strategies of Educated Jats

This chapter explores the social strategies of un/under-employed young men from the Jat caste. We argue that most of these relatively rich, socially well-connected and culturally confident men found avenues through which to communicate their distinction as 'educated people' in spite of their failure to find secure salaried work. Jat young men either acquired reasonably stable clerical jobs in the informal economy or moved into managerial roles within agriculture. They were often able to marry into prosperous urban households and planned to invest heavily in the education of their own future children. We show that Jat young men's strategies have been more explicitly 'modern' than 'neo-traditional' in nature and that they play a major role in the reproduction of spaces and structures of dominance in rural Bijnor district. These conclusions are central to the overall 'story' of our book but also speak directly to research on the rise of rich farmers in rural north India, a relatively neglected field of study within a wider emerging literature on the Indian middle class (Varma 1998; Fernandes 2006).

The next section of the chapter situates our research with reference to recent scholarly work on rich farmers in India and Jat cultural styles. We then use the example of Sonu, an educated un/under-employed Jat young man from Nangal, to explore Jats' response to their exclusion from prestigious government work. In particular, we discuss Jats' appropriation of notions of education as progress, entry into semi-bourgeois employment and adoption of managerial roles within farming. We then consider social differences among the Jats and relate our findings to the key themes of the book.

Rich Farmers in Post-colonial India

One of the most distinctive features of post-Independence India has been the rise of a class of rich farmers from among the ranks of a peasant cultivating class. In the mid-1960s, the Indian government shifted the direction of development planning from a model of industrial growth toward a more committed drive to improve agricultural production. C. Subramaniam's appointment as India's Food and Agriculture Minister in 1964, advice from the World Bank and changing US aid policies conspired to effect a move away from the Nehruvian policy of low food prices and institutional reform. The state focused instead on creating incentive prices for producers through the establishment of an Agricultural Prices Commission and the Food Corporation of India in January 1965. This intervention in the food-grain market was married to a drive toward agricultural production increases, principally by encouraging the application of a group of technologies developed initially in the US and the Philippines, and including high yielding varieties of grain, fertilizers, pesticides and improved irrigation.

This shift in government policy, combined with the rise of the Jat leader Charan Singh in the mid-1960s in UP, provided a platform for the consolidation and upward mobility of Jat landowners and upper sections of the OBCs across north India, but perhaps especially in western UP and adjacent areas (Duncan 1997; Hasan 1998). Between the mid-1960s and mid-1980s, Charan Singh attempted to increase the profitability of cash crop agriculture by raising subsidies on agricultural inputs and government purchasing prices for sugar cane and wheat (Brass 1985: 156; Byres 1988).

The trajectories of distinct rich peasant classes vary regionally, but it is possible to identify three central features of their reproductive strategies. First, many rich peasant households diversified out of agriculture by establishing businesses or seeking white-collar work for their sons (Rutten 1995; Jeffrey 2001; Harriss-White 2003). Second, these households raised their social standing by removing family members from direct cultivation of the soil, offering large dowries at the time of their daughters' marriages, limiting the size of their families and investing in education (e.g. Breman 1985; Upadhya 1988; Jeffery and Jeffery 1997; Gidwani 2001). Finally, rich farmers have built strong rural-urban social networks, often by co-opting the local state and cultivating an 'urban' or 'modern' style, even *within* their rural homes and villages (Jeffrey 1997, 2001). An effort to raise the collective position of the caste within the caste hierarchy—a process that the sociologist of India Srinivas (1989) dubbed 'sanskritization'—often animated these efforts at upward mobility (e.g. Breman 1985). But households emerging from the ranks of rich peasant household were often equally concerned with acquiring the accoutrements of urban *and urbane* middle class life (Upadhya 1988). As Fernandes (2006) suggests, the idea of belonging to a 'new Indian middle class' figured strongly in the individual and collective strategies of this prosperous agricultural stratum.

Recent accounts of Jat social mobility in north India fit quite well with this literature on rural elites. Jat farmers have been energetically seeking education and off-farm employment in urban areas since at least the 1900s, and possibly much earlier (Sisson 1970; Chowdhry 1994; Datta 1999a). Datta (1999a) argued that the Arya Samaj Hindu reform movement instilled in many Jats in the late nineteenth and early twentieth centuries a sense of their entitlement to compete for government salaried employment in urban areas. Through the Arya Samaj, Jats in Punjab also established a large number of educational institutions, including *gurukul* schools that prepared young men for government jobs.[1] Chowdhry (1994) pointed to the emergence of a sizable rural Jat bourgeoisie in mid-twentieth-century Punjab that had invested agricultural profits in tertiary education for their sons and in consumer goods associated with urban lifestyles.

Datta and Chowdhry argued that the social institution of caste was selectively reimagined and revived to serve the needs of a modernizing, rurally-based, elite; for example through the establishment of Jat caste associations (the Jat Mahasabha) and caste-based councils (Jat *panchāyats*) (cf. Madsen 1996; D. Gupta 1997). Research on recent agrarian political movements in western UP has placed even greater emphasis on Jat efforts to cultivate a 'neo-traditionalist' image self-consciously distinct from an 'urban' or 'modern' style. Many Jats in western UP channeled their anger at the state's alleged neglect of agriculture in the 1980s and early 1990s into political protest within the Bharatiya Kisan Union (BKU) farmers' movement. The BKU was established in 1978 but came

---

[1]For a description of *gurukul* schooling see Pandit (1974).

to prominence in 1987 in its protests against the alleged 'urban bias' of the Indian government. The BKU's demands included a rise in the prices paid by the government for key cash crops, improved agricultural marketing arrangements and greater state investment in rural infrastructure (Hasan 1998; Bentall and Corbridge 1996). Jat farmers within the BKU circulated a powerful moral discourse that contrasted honest, conscientious and impoverished farmers in rural *'Bhārat'* (the Hindi word for India) with corrupt, lazy and prosperous urban dwellers in urban *'India'* (A. Gupta 1997). BKU leaders engaged in cultural practices understood locally to connote the rural and traditional. They wore white *kurtā-pājāmā*, emphasized their primal bond with the soil and held union meetings in rural courtyards around a large smoking pipe (*huqqā*). In addition, the large urban rallies staged by the BKU in the late 1980s and early 1990s were organized around the notion of "bringing the rural into cities." They gave physical expression to this idea by establishing large urban 'camps' where they slept on their buffalo carts or beside tractor trolleys. After 1991, support for the BKU waned in the face of caste and class divisions within the movement and ideological differences regarding the union's aims and relationship with party politics (Bentall 1995; Madsen and Lindberg 2003). But images of Jat impoverishment and rural backwardness continued to be important in their political strategies. Jats employed visions of themselves as impoverished farmers to pressurize the UP State government into including them in the OBC list, and in 2004–5, Charan Singh's son, Ajit Singh, mobilized images of Jats as isolated rural agriculturalists in his movement for a separate state of Harit Pradesh to be established within UP.

We will argue that educated Jat young men in Nangal have responded to educated un/under-employment in a manner somewhat different from the political styles of Jats in the BKU movement. Rather than seeking to project visions of themselves as rural, isolated and impoverished, educated Jat young men have more commonly used notions of education as civilization to stress their connection to cultural forms imagined locally as 'urban' and 'modern.' Building on Datta (1999a) and Chowdhry's (1994) work on Jat mobility strategies in Punjab and Haryana, west of western UP, we also show how Jats tack between cultural signs coded as 'modern' and those considered 'traditional' in their individual and collective attempts to negotiate underemployment and maintain an educated image.

In developing an account of Jats' everyday strategies of dominance, our analysis bears on Mendelsohn's work on 'dominant castes' in rural Rajasthan. Drawing on ethnographic field research in Behror village, Mendelsohn (1993) maintains that the relationship between a dominant caste of Ahirs and lower castes underwent a fundamental change in the third quarter of the twentieth century. By the 1980s, the traditional system of *jajmānī* (patron-client) relations in Behror had become marginal to the overall economy of the village. Mendelsohn charts a parallel decline among higher castes in an awareness of caste as a result of the disappearance of caste councils, economic differentiation and the increasing orientation of higher castes to spaces outside the village. Mendelsohn concludes that the notions of 'dominance' and 'resistance' are no longer valuable categories in analyzing social dynamics in rural north India. Instead, he suggests that the village is comprised of increasingly atomized individuals struggling for resources located mainly outside the local area.

Our account of Jat strategies supports Mendelsohn's vision of increasing individualization but also points to contrary trends toward Jat collective organization, albeit usually outside formal institutional structures. We also show that caste remains important to the everyday strategies of educated un/underemployed Jat young men. The case of Sonu provides a useful starting point for developing these points.

Sonu

We first met Sonu when he rode up to his parents' large village home on a 250cc Kawasaki motorcycle. Clean-shaven and with carefully groomed hair, Sonu was dressed in immaculate blue denim jeans, a mauve shirt, leather boots and dark glasses. With a flourish that was typical of his style, Sonu kicked out the metal prop to support his motorcycle, strode forward to shake hands, pressed his hands together in the polite Hindu '*namaste*' to our research assistant, Chhaya, and slid open the large steel gate to his family's home. Sonu ushered us into a courtyard and soon emerged from the family home with cane chairs, tea, fresh biscuits and a bowl of salted nuts. Sonu spoke in a crisp Hindi scattered with English words like '*batch mate*' '*timepass*' and '*exam.*' He frequently leaned over to watch Chhaya taking notes. He corrected her spellings, explained the acronyms he used and checked that she had written down points correctly. Refusing a cane chair himself, Sonu perched on the edge of a cattle trough and asked us politely about the progress of our research, Craig's and Chhaya's qualifications and the cost and specifications of our jeep.

The eldest of three children, Sonu was in his mid-twenties in 2001 and had been brought up in a rich Jat family possessing 7 acres of agricultural land. His family home consisted of an eight-roomed brick house in the center of Nangal complete with flush lavatory and color television. Sonu's father, Bedpal, possessed a BEd and MA and worked in a government secondary school in Uttarkashi, Uttaranchal. His mother, Sarla, has a Tenth Class pass and came from a wealthy family in neighboring Meerut district. Sonu had attended Nangal Junior High School for classes 1–8. Keen to acquire educational opportunities outside Bijnor district, his parents enrolled him in a school in neighboring Meerut district for Ninth Class, where he lived with his maternal grandmother. Sonu left this school after a year and took classes 10–12 at the school in Uttaranchal where his father taught. After completing Twelfth Class, Sonu obtained a BSc in Mathematics from a degree college in Moradabad, a large town about 40 miles from Nangal. Sonu believed that Mathematics was preferable to Arts or Commerce subjects because it had a reputation for being '*tough*' and could create opportunities for him to work as a tutor. Bedpal and Sarla spent Rs. 20,000 a year for two years sending Sonu to Mathematics coaching classes designed to prepare him for national civil service examinations. Sonu was married in 2000 to a young woman from a large village roughly 20 miles from Nangal and who possessed an MA. In 2001, he lived with his wife in Moradabad. He returned to Nangal once a fortnight to see his mother and sister, check on the family farm and collect milk and clarified butter.

Familial support was crucial to Sonu's story. Bedpal had a keen interest in Sonu's career and advised his son on major decisions regarding education and employment. As the senior male within the household, Bedpal controlled household finances and expressed his willingness in interviews to spend on his sons' education "as far as money will allow." Bedpal had also been instrumental in withdrawing his daughter from school after Eighth Class out of a fear that she would acquire a bad name. Sarla said that Bedpal's absence from the village made it difficult for her daughter to study because of a lack of a male chaperon on her journey to school. While Bedpal's teaching employment strengthened opportunities for his sons, it had a negative impact upon his daughter, who bitterly resented her inability to attend high school.

During Sonu's educational career, Sarla was mainly responsible for ensuring that her son completed homework, arrived at school suitably dressed and groomed and was well supplied with learning aids. Sarla spoke of the difficulty of balancing her housework with caring for the schooling needs of her children, and the constant vigilance required to ensure that sons perform well in school. Sarla said that as a high school pass herself, she was in a position to assist Sonu with his homework up to Eighth Class and create a 'civilized environment' (*sabhayātā kā mahaul*) in the village. Sarla's mother, Lalita, took on these responsibilities while Sonu was studying outside Bijnor and received money from Bedpal for Sonu's board and lodging.

Sonu was eager to discuss his experiences seeking government employment. He described obtaining marks of 98 percent in the entrance examination for the Basic Teaching Certificate (BTC), which opens up the possibility of acquiring work as a government primary school teacher. He said that several young men with good social contacts (*jān-pahchān*) bribed an official to place them above him in the merit list for BTC. Sonu: "They had not even done the exam for the BTC but they still got a place ahead of me!" Sonu said that he had also received demands to pay a bribe during his efforts to negotiate a position as a sub-inspector in the UP police. Sonu: "Everywhere there is corruption (*bhrashtāchār*). What can we do?" Bedpal strove to improve his son's employment prospects by maintaining social connections within influential government bureaucracies in western UP. Bedpal frequently traveled to Bijnor or Moradabad to meet government officials and discuss the changing character of government job markets.

In line with the narratives of other young men in Nangal and Qaziwala, Sonu had responded to his failure to obtain government employment by stressing his standing as an educated person. In conversations with friends he frequently used the distinction between the 'educated' (*parhe likhe*) and the 'uneducated' (*unparh*) to label or explain people's actions within and outside the village. The picture that emerged from these conversations was of the educated as eloquent, smartly dressed, well mannered and independent, and the illiterate as foul-mouthed, disheveled, rude and needy. When Craig and Chhaya directly asked him about the benefits of education in their first meeting, Sonu looked dismissive and stated simply that "the educated are 'gold' and the uneducated 'dust.'"

Distinct from most Chamars and Muslims, however, Sonu elaborated on the benefits of education by alluding to the differences between the 'truly educated' (*sahī parhe likhe*) and the 'falsely educated' (*naqlī parhe likhe*). In this imagined opposition, the 'truly educated' possess knowledge of their accomplishments and the humility to recognize their faults while the 'falsely educated' are always '*arrogant*' and incapable of critical self-reflection. Sonu's father was equally insistent on this theme. To grunts of approval from his son, he noted:

Some young men walk around the village saying, "I have got an MA," without appreciating the proper value [*sahī qīmat*] of education. These men are qualified [*qābilīyat mil gai*] but not educated [*parhe likhe*].

Reflecting his continued enthusiasm for the benefits of education, Sonu had reacted to exclusion from government work in part by seeking further educational credentials. He was planning to take a BEd alongside an MSc in Mathematics and extend the number of coaching classes he attended. Sonu said that he enjoyed mathematics and wanted to become a *specialist* in this field. Sonu: "It is only by training and *coaching* that we learn."

Sonu had also responded to repeated frustration searching for salaried employment by seeking good 'fallback' work in the informal economy. While applying for government positions and accumulating educational credentials, Sonu also worked as a teacher in a private school in Moradabad and offered mathematics tutorials outside school. Sonu earned Rs. 1,000 as a teacher and doubled this salary by giving extra-school tutorials. Working as a teacher and tutor allowed him to monitor employment opportunities in Moradabad and the landscapes of social interaction and interest that shape young men's access to work. Sonu's teaching and tuition also made it possible for him to assist his parents financially and expand his network of urban social contacts. Moreover, the work was not too onerous and he could combine tuition, private teaching and preparation for national civil service examinations.

As a tutor, Sonu had built up a good client base among other Jat families in Moradabad, and Sarla estimated that in two years he could be earning Rs.

3,500 a month from this enterprise. Sarla: "Tuition is an excellent *side-business*, and he could continue this in his future *career*." Noting the increased demand for education in Nangal, Bedpal and Sarla were also building two rooms at the front of their village home that they envisaged Sonu could use as the basis for a private school. Bedpal and Sarla had also hired a permanent farm servant to assist with agricultural tasks to ensure that Sonu could devote his efforts to finding suitable secure employment outside farming. Sonu described teaching in a private school and tuition as acceptable short-term work:

This work is alright at the moment [*filhāl*]: for the time being, it is fine. But this is only until I can get a better job. I am someone marked out for government service.

In such ways, Sonu affirmed that he was 'in a stage of transition' toward a position more suited to his ability.

The case of Sonu points to broader aspects of Jat young men's responses to educated un/under-employment in Nangal. In particular, his case highlights three central features of the strategies of educated un/under-employed young men, which we elaborate in detail below: *reinvestment* in education, determination to find salaried employment and eagerness to remove themselves from manual toil in the fields.

Reinvesting in Education

For the type of middle-ranking government positions sought by most Jats in Nangal, young men had to attend several examinations stretched out over a year. Many young men described this process as extremely burdensome, citing the need to pay for tutorials before the tests, to memorize reams of general knowledge questions and to travel to distant examination centers. In addition, young men vented their anger at arriving at an examination to find that over a thousand people—and sometimes several tens of thousands—were competing for just a handful of posts. Young men referred to interviews as similarly harrowing. They said that they often spent the weeks before an interview petitioning friends and relatives in the hope of collecting bribe money, and negotiating with brokers (*dalāl*) who claimed to have influence (*prabhāv*) or a recommendation (*sifārish*) within government bureaucracies. Regardless of whether recruitment officials made an explicit demand for a bribe, Jats said that they often felt an internal compulsion to offer money. Indeed, stories of bribery had taken such deep root, that some young men gave bribes even *after* having received a formal offer for a post in the belief that the post would not be confirmed until money had been paid.

In response to these frustrations, the majority of educated un/under-employed Jat young men in Nangal had internalized a sense of themselves as urbane educated people. Like Sonu, they often placed particular emphasis on the capacity of education to inculcate key skills relevant to work outside Nangal. Such narratives accorded closely with the 'public culture' of educational value we described in Chapter Three. But, like Sonu, a few Jat young men had begun to make distinctions between their own 'true education' and 'falsely educated' peers. They occasionally laughed about how people with 'just Eighth Class pass' from a village school believed themselves to be 'educated' and parodied other educated un/under-employed young men wandering around the village, "who think they are educated but behave like illiterates." These narratives were colored by caste prejudice. But educated un/under-employed Jat young men also criticized members of their own caste whom they felt had not fulfilled their parental expectations or 'educated' potential.

A substantial number of educated Jat young men reacted to failure to obtain a government job by seeking further educational credentials. Like Sonu, some of these men believed that by acquiring additional qualifications they could improve their prospects in the search for government work. Other Jat young men said that they continued to study simply as a means of countering boredom and appeasing their parents. They told us that their university degrees provided a sense of progression, allowed them to meet occasionally to talk with friends, offered experience of urban life and conferred an identity—student (*vidyārthī*)—that bestowed a measure of social distinction or at least social acceptability. The cost of studying for a degree in local government and private colleges was low—usually between Rs. 1,000 and Rs. 3,000 a year—compared to the capital and income of most Jat households. The personal cost to young men of enrolling for a degree was also minimal. Lecturers rarely turned up to teach in local colleges, students typically visited their degree college just once or twice a week, and there was no assessed coursework for most degree programs; students had to do little more than appear for examinations to obtain their qualification. In addition, many students prepared for examinations by purchasing 'cheat books' that contained model answers to a range of questions likely to appear on an exam paper. Few young men said that they were interested in their degree courses or imagined that their education would provide skills or information useful for their careers. Many admitted to possessing little or no knowledge of the discipline which they were studying. Struggling in poorly funded colleges, with few teachers willing to provide instruction, and disillusioned by the limited relevance of their syllabi, students frequently imagined their colleges as '*degree shops*,' the sole utility of which was to provide a paper certificate.

Reflecting on their educational trajectories, Jat young men said that they planned to send their own children to English-medium schools, preferably outside Bijnor district in Meerut, Dehra Dun or Delhi. Educated un/under-employed Jat young men criticized teachers in local schools for failing to provide a practical (*vyāvasāyik*) and moral (*nīti*) education. They said that local teachers fail to appreciate the distinction between reading (*parhnā*), by itself, and evaluating or digesting what has been read (*gunnā*). Teachers, they say, spend their days worrying about their own affairs rather than attending to the learning needs of students. In discussing the future education of their children, educated Jat young men also emphasized the importance of their children receiving refinement (*sanskār*)[2] in the home and of finding schools that re-created parents' loving care (cf. Bénéï 2005).

In discussing the possible educational prospects of their own future children, educated Jat young men often discussed the important role not only of parents, but also of a wider kinship network, in providing a secure educational environment. Like Sonu, many of these men had spent part of their educational careers being supported by relatives in urban 'satellite households,' in which maternal grandparents often played an especially prominent role: caring for children during term time and offering some financial support for their education. Educated young men frequently argued that these arrangements offer

---

[2]Our research assistants argued that '*sanskār*' in rural Bijnor district usually refers either to the influence of a past life on a person's nature—their 'instinct' or 'intrinsic nature'—or, as in the sense here, the influence of parents on a person's character.

the benefits of being among one's family alongside the advantages of pursuing urban-based education undisrupted by the "dirt and soil" of the village.

These considerations encouraged educated young men and their parents to seek an urban young woman for a bride. Jat young men were unanimous on this point: that their future wife should be educated, content with working inside the home and committed to creating a civilized atmosphere for their children's education. This came across especially in the words that Jat young men used to describe a 'perfect wife': *homely*, modest (*sharmindā*), loving (*pyārī*) and good mannered (*adab*).

Many Jat young men therefore interpreted their educated standing not only as a marker of distinction (*nishāna*), but also as a sign of the movement of their family out of village 'uselessness' (*bekārī*) toward urban success (*saphaltā*) and development (*vikās*). Rather than reinventing overtly 'traditional masculinities' in the manner of some BKU activists, disappointment in the search for government jobs had encouraged the majority of rich Jats to 'scale up' their educational and familial ambitions, acquiring further degrees themselves and planning prestigious schooling careers for their children. We will point to more radical reactions to underemployment among a handful of Jats in Chapter Seven, but the weight of evidence suggested that rich Jat young men's belief in the value of education intensified during the experience of struggling in vain for secure white-collar work.

The 'scaling up' of Jat educational ambitions in response to un/under-employment was geographical as well as social: educated Jat young men imagined the process of personal and familial development as one of moving out from the village to acquire connections, property and reputations in successively larger urban settlements and, if possible, abroad. For example, some of the richest Jat young men in Nangal spoke of Bijnor town as an unsuitable environment for the education of their children. Drawing upon invective usually directed at village life, these men described Bijnor as 'rustic and unruly' and said that their offspring would study in the more sanitized and civilized environment of Meerut, Dehra Dun or Delhi. Our conversations with Jat young men around their children's education suggested not only that they wanted to 'place' their children in major urban centers but also that they were committed to constructing the expansive social and political webs of relationships that would nourish their children's careers.

'Semi-bourgeois' Work

Like Sonu, Jat young men argued that as 'educated people' (*parhe-likhe log*) and as Jats they should not engage in manual labor (*hāth kā kām*) but seek instead 'pen work' (*pen chalāne kā kām*) in urban areas. Similar research on Jat caste mobility in Punjab has shown that the attempts of Jats to claim a higher position within the caste hierarchy and their desire to cement their middle class standing has been bound up with an effort to disengage from manual labor, which was increasingly imagined as 'unclean' and 'demeaning' (Chowdhry 1994; Datta 1999a). In some cases, this move out of manual labor began with Jat men's efforts to ensure that their wives did not work in the fields (Chowdhry 1994). In other instances, Jats' disengagement from physical toil occurred through men seeking off-farm employment within the army or local bureaucracies (Stokes 1986; Datta 1999a). By the 1960s in western UP, caste- and class-based aversion to manual labor had become common within the wealthiest Jat households (Pradhan 1966), and the vast majority of educated Jat young men from all economic backgrounds argued that manual labor is useless, dirty and 'lower caste.'

In talking of their desire for 'pen work' Jat young men were not referring solely to desk-based employment but to any occupation that did not involve manual labor and that implied some measure of professionalism and acquired skill. For example, Jats defined work as a bus conductor, private tutor or car dealer as forms of 'pen work,' but employment as a tailor, mason or electrician as *hāth kā kām*. Jats commonly identified a hierarchy of private clerical occupations: 'excellent' private service (*bariyā naukrī*), such as engineering or medicine, 'good' service (*achchhī naukrī*), for example work as a salesperson for a private company, and 'modest' service (*chhotī-motī naukrī*), such as work as a shopkeeper, driver or teacher in a private school (cf. D. Gupta 1997). Eighteen percent of educated Jat young men aged between 20 and 34 were engaged in private service employment or a related form of business in 2001. Of these 23 men, 5 were in 'excellent' work, 6 were engaged in 'good' employment and 12 young men were in occupations categorized locally as 'modest.'

In contrast to many rich Jat farmers in neighboring Meerut district (Jeffrey 1999), Jat young men in Bijnor lacked the social contacts and knowledge required to migrate abroad in pursuit of employment. Despite their occasional claims to be interested in working in foreign countries or India's metropolitan centers, their horizons were usually limited to entering service occupations within Bijnor or neighboring districts. They particularly favored work within relatively new employment sectors, such as positions as teachers in private coaching institutes, contractors on government development projects, 'team leaders' in pyramid sales organizations and marketing agents for pharmaceutical firms. These 'semi-bourgeois' jobs (Bourdieu 1984) were insecure and poorly paid and offered few opportunities for in-service training and promotion: they were usually 'modest' salaried jobs (*chhotī-motī naukrī*). But the relatively undemanding and flexible nature of this work allowed young men to continue their studies alongside paid employment, offered opportunities to spend time with friends and enabled young men to make daily commutes from their rural homes. Moreover, these posts made it possible for Jat young men to advertise their involvement in lucrative, clean and self-consciously 'modern' employment. Employers assisted young men in this task by offering them the accoutrements of secure salaried work, such as a computer, briefcase, impressive job titles and headed paper.

Importantly, these short-term occupations offered Jat young men an opportunity to locate themselves on a 'pathway to development' (*vikās kā rāstā*), whereby they would graduate from temporary clerical work to more lucrative and secure careers. That the region of western UP as a whole was imagined to be undergoing 'development' (*vikās*) was significant in opening up space for Jat young men to promote their transitional status. Many Jat young men emphasized the temporary nature of clerical jobs or small-scale business concerns by referring to their employment as '*timepass*' rather than '*serious*' work. One Jat informant working as a clerk in a private factory told us, "All I do all day is *timepass*, you could even say that *timepass* is my job!" But Jats were sometimes ambivalent on this point. In constructing their work as '*timepass*,' these men risked drawing attention to the insecure, poorly paid and 'menial' nature of much of this activity. At other moments, Jats referred to their work as responsible, serious and stimulating, and some Jats vigorously denied that they conducted their work only as *timepass*.

Consideration of Satpal, a Jat young man in his mid-twenties from Nangal offers a richer sense of the types of 'semi-bourgeois' work conducted by educated Jat young men and their attitudes to such employment. Satpal had a BA from the government degree college in Bijnor town and belonged to a rich Jat family in Nangal. Unable to secure government employment, he had entered business with a Brahmin young man called Pramod whose family also came from Nangal. Satpal and Pramod had used money from their parents to establish 'Cosmos Internet Café' in Awas Vikas, close to where we lived. Satpal made the rather implausible claim that his work was a form of 'social service' (*samāj sevā*) and that he hoped to attract poor villagers from around Nangal to the internet café. Satpal was also keen to promote a pyramid selling scheme he had entered and which was sponsored by a large Indian company based in Delhi. The scheme offered those who could recruit another 360 people into the pyramid a week's holiday in a five-star hotel in Mumbai. It also provided people with a name badge, cloth briefcase, three imitation leather files and pens labeled with the company's name. Satpal and Pramod were confident about the future. Pramod told Craig:

We live in an age of information [*info kā zamānā hai*]. India is very good on IT internationally. We chose Cosmos because I wanted to target the poor; we are not *pure businessmen*. In Canada, Indians run 70 percent of the Information Technology industry. You see there is a dual benefit with Cosmos: *earning while you are learning*.

When we left Bijnor in April 2002, however, Satpal's internet business had attracted little trade and he had recruited just 18 people to the pyramid selling scheme.

As in the cases of Sonu and Satpal, educated Jat young men had commonly used money provided by their parents to establish small businesses, often shops, fertilizer agencies or phone booths. These enterprises typically provided meager financial returns, but, like clerical jobs in the informal economy, they brought Jat young men into contact with urban areas and allowed them to construct images of themselves as people 'in transition.' In other cases, educated Jat young men had used funding provided by their parents to establish more substantial businesses. Among the very rich, three Jat households had invested in extensive transport enterprises for their sons to run. These businesses provided considerable prestige and allowed their owners to project an image of physical and social mobility. In addition, young men running transport businesses could make large illegal side incomes by carrying stolen goods.

A small number of educated un/under-employed Jat young men had entered more explicitly criminal activity. Three Jat young men who had failed to obtain government employment admitted to having been involved in *gundāgardī* (criminal work) in Bijnor. One of these men had extorted money from fellow students in his degree college using intimidation and muscle power, one had engaged in petty theft and one was involved in the sale of black market goods. These men saw no contradiction between being educated and engaging in criminal work. Rather, they claimed that as educated people they are well equipped to improvise around rules, an idea they expressed through use of the term *jugār*. Jats were able to practice criminal activity by maintaining close relationships with the mainly upper or middle caste Hindu police force. Jats in Nangal had been entering the police force since the 1960s. Although government rules prevented police recruits from being posted in their home district, friends or relatives within the police could provide Jats in Nangal with advice about how to avoid prosecution and guarantee police complicity. As in neighboring Meerut district (Jeffrey 2000), Jats frequently claimed to be able to influence the police force.

Jat young men also sought to utilize the cultural capital residing in their caste status to enter private clerical employment. Jats said that during interviews for jobs in private service they would tactically reveal their caste identity by using the honorific, 'Chaudhry' in front of their name, a term specifically applied to the Jats. There was a consensus among Jats that they are morally obliged to assist other members of their caste and that they also *feel* that they should help. A Jat young man responsible for informally hiring temporary assistants in a government office in Bijnor said that on meeting a Jat he feels "a strange feeling of happiness welling up from inside." Similarly, Satpal claimed that people would not obtain clerical work in the informal economy if they behaved in a '*Chamārī-sī*' manner. *Chamārī-sī* literally means 'like a Chamar' but among Jats it usually connoted clumsy, embarrassing or overly 'showy' behavior. The casual use of '*Chamārī-sī*' as an index of awkwardness was indicative of an array of practices and judgments that marked out Chamars as unworthy of relatively lucrative jobs in the informal economy and thereby bolstered the position of the Jats.

Jat parents were often willing to allow their sons to prolong their educational careers and move between insecure employment during their twenties and early thirties, and they supplemented their son's incomes from semi-bourgeois work or business. In line with broader gendered assumptions in western UP and India, Jat parents expected young men to spend a period of their early adulthood 'wandering about' and experimenting with different forms of work (de Haan 2003). Many of the fathers of educated un/under-employed Jat young men in the early 2000s had themselves spent long periods searching in vain for salaried employment in the 1970s or 1980s. For example, Sonu's father, Bedpal, spent eight years seeking a good job before he secured employment as a government teacher. These older Jat men tended to sympathize with their sons' position and protected them from the comments of other villagers. Bedpal frequently referred indignantly to the mixture of bad luck and corrupt practice that prevented Sonu from succeeding in the search for government work. Bedpal labeled Sonu an "Indian Administrative Services hopeful"—someone with all the hallmarks of becoming a high-ranking public servant—and cited the failure of local recruitment officials to grant Sonu a place as indicative of their bovine stupidity and venality. In such ways, Bedpal attempted to boost Sonu's confidence and protect him from criticism while also maintaining the social standing of his household in the village.

The earlier entry of a substantial number of educated Jats into secure government employment had also shored up the economic position of many households and allowed them to bear the cost if one son spent a long period in status-saving but low paid work. There were many Jat households in which one son was in secure government work while another spent time experimenting with different forms of private service. In this situation, the government-employed Jat man often provided his brother with loans, acted as a source of moral support and defended his sibling from accusations of laziness or failure.

Jat parents had self-interested motives for seeking to prolong the period over which young men claimed to be 'searching for government work' while engaged in semi-bourgeois jobs. By allowing young men to work in often poorly-paid service-type employment, parents could advertise their sons as people on the brink of obtaining secure salaried work (*naukrī milnewālā ādmī*), 'men in a state of becoming' (*honewāle ādmī*) or 'youthful men' (*jawānī ādmī*). This improved parents' chances of marrying their sons into wealthy, urban, well-connected families, obtaining a high dowry and acquiring a daughter-in-law (*bahū*) who would raise their social standing.[3] Sonu's wife came from a well-connected rural Jat family and, as an MA graduate with an 'urban' (*shehrī*) style, her presence in the home contributed to the impression of Bedpal's household as upwardly mobile. Like other Jats, Sarla knew that her daughter-in-law would be likely to nurse her in old age and she cherished the prospect of being cared for by a young woman with a good education, taste and a polite demeanor. In addition, Sonu's wife's family gave him a large dowry by the standards of a seven-acre Jat farmer. The dowry included a Samsung color television, double bed, two steel chests, gold jewelry, sofa, fridge, expensive clothing and Rs. 40,000 in cash. Bedpal and Sarla said that the bride's family offered the dowry of their own free will (*apnī marzī se*). But Sonu's parents marketed their son as someone in line for prestigious salaried work and this would have created the expectation that a large dowry was appropriate. Our wider observations suggested that young men who could claim to be in some type of service job were able to command larger dowries than equally educated young men who could not make such a claim.

Jat parents actively assisted their sons in the search for good fallback employment within state bureaucracies or the private sector. In addition to Sonu's story, we heard of a rich Jat in Nangal who used his friendship with an influential local landlord living close to Bijnor to ensure that his two sons obtained clerical posts in a private Delhi shoe factory run by the landlord's son. Similarly, a retired Jat police inspector in Nangal capitalized on his influence within upper echelons of the police to ensure that his son and nephew obtained temporary posts in the local constabulary. In these and several other examples, Jats were able to trade on their middle caste status and historical associations with local government to forge effective social links. Moreover, where rich Jats did not possess close connections in relevant sections of government or the private economy, they were often able to hire reliable urban brokers (*dalāl*), who acted

[3]Senior members of a family controlled most aspects of a marriage, and the father of the potential bride tended to initiate negotiations. Marriages were broadly isogamous: parents generally sought to marry within a family of equal wealth and standing. Jats were averse to marrying within descendants of the same couple three or more generations back or within the same village. They tended to obtain information on suitable marriage partners through friends, relatives and acquaintances, one of whom would act as an intermediary (*bīchauliyā*) in negotiations between two families.

as paid representatives for candidates during negotiations with recruitment officials. In these ways, Jat parents, especially fathers, found ways to improvise (*jugār*), even in the absence of secure government work.

Dust, Soil and Shifting Jat Masculinities

Jat parents often pressured young men to assist with farming and abandon poorly-paid clerical or business work after their marriages. Parents were concerned about their household developing a bad reputation if a son spent too long engaged in overtly 'temporary' employment. Moreover, many Jats required help managing their farms. Of the 130 educated Jat young men aged between 20 and 34 in Nangal in 2001, 55 percent had become farmers.

Young Jat farmers often stressed the importance of education for post-Green Revolution agriculture. They claimed that only 'educated people' are capable of making the fine calculations required in sowing, harvesting and marketing their crops. Educated Jats emphasized the need to pay close attention to the activities of the Cane Society responsible for buying sugar cane from farmers and the importance of being able to read the receipts that the Society sent farmers. These young Jats also said that as educated people they are able to practice a 'scientific agriculture,' and they spoke of learning about new farming practices from agricultural manuals issued by local Cane Societies. In addition, educated Jats said that they possess the manners, confidence and charm required to negotiate with government agricultural extension officers, Cane Society officials and other representatives of the state. This is especially important in the context of widespread malpractice within the marketing of sugar cane, management of land records and government regulation of agriculture more broadly. A person often has to make repeated visits to crowded offices, negotiate with numerous officials and negotiate a complicated terrain of influence and malfeasance to obtain timely and full payment for sugar cane or record a land purchase, for example (Jeffrey 2002). Educated Jat young men said that—as educated people—they possess the knowledge to chart their way through these political fields, the charisma required to charm officials and the equanimity necessary to wait patiently for a task to be accomplished.

At the same time, however, many educated Jats entered agriculture reluctantly and stressed their distance from most aspects of manual agricultural work. This was not new: a few educated men who had entered agriculture in the 1970s and 1980s spoke of their initial dissatisfaction with such work. But there was a consensus that educated Jat young men had become increasingly reluctant to enter agriculture and lacked interest (*shauq*) in the manual labor associated with farming. These Jat young men emphasized their desire to remove themselves from the daily grind of preparing ground, irrigating their land and harvesting crops. Reflecting this idea, an educated Jat young man told us, "The word 'JAT' used to mean 'Justice, Action and Truth,' but it now stands for Justice, *Administrator*, Truth.'" Observing the attitudes of his sons to agriculture, a Jat father noted:

We used to have a saying: highest is farming, middle is business, below this service and bottom is begging [*Uttam khetī, madhyam ban, nīch naukrī, bhikh nidān*]. In previous times, agriculture was the most excellent, and people thought of salaried employment as being below farming and business. . . . Now things have been turned upside down. Service is now seen as best and agriculture now occupies third spot. Business and begging remain in the same positions.

Assisted by their parents, Jat young men had found ways of managing the contradictory imperatives of becoming farmers while maintaining an urbane and civilized demeanor. As in Sonu's case, and paralleling trends among rich farmers in Gujarat (Rutten 1995; Gidwani 2001), wealthier Jat households often protected their sons from physical work on the land by employing a farm servant on a relatively long-term (six- to ten-month) contract. The farm servant was often a local Chamar, though Jats were increasingly looking outside Bijnor district for lower caste servants, who were cheaper to employ and were perceived to be less inclined to remonstrate with their employers. Farm servants undertook tasks such as preparing the soil for cultivation, irrigating crops and attending to buffaloes, and received between Rs. 800 and Rs. 1,200 a month as well as food and a place to sleep.

The Cane Society responsible for marketing farmers' sugar cane issues requests to farmers to deliver a certain quantity of their crops on a particular day. If farmers miss this deadline they suffer financial penalties or may lose their right to deliver cane to the sugar factory. It is therefore important to Jat farmers that their cane is harvested and delivered rapidly. In this context, all but the poorest Jat households employed small work teams to cut sugar cane (see Srivastava 1995). These teams were paid on piece rate contracts, which had the significant benefit for Jats of ensuring that their crops were harvested in a timely manner and reducing their need to supervise laborers. Jats tried to discipline local Chamar laborers employed in piece rate teams by refusing to grant them payment for work they perceived to be 'poorly performed' or by issuing verbal threats if Chamar laborers refused to assist in an urgent agricultural task.

Through these strategies of hiring labor, Jat young men were free to adopt a relatively 'hands off' approach to agriculture. They typically expressed a purely aesthetic attachment to their fields and land and claimed to dislike touching the soil. They toured fields on their motorcycles to check on laborers, spent long periods talking to friends in the Cane Society offices or concentrated their attention on farm accounts (cf. Gidwani 2001). Describing the typical activities of her husband, in his late thirties in 2001, a Jat woman told us, "He does not have any interest in agriculture (*khetī kā shauq nahīn hai*)." She continued:

The agricultural work is done by a farm servant. He [her husband] just goes once or twice by scooter and does a round [of the farm]. Sometimes the sugar cane has to be weighed, so he remains there watching or there is some other essential task and he goes to oversee it. Otherwise, he is only interested in business or salaried work.

In neighboring Meerut district, many Jat farmers had responded to their desire to escape agricultural work by planting mango orchards, which require less supervision than sugar cane.[4] But mango growing had not emerged on a large scale in Bijnor district, where Jat farmers typically lacked the funds to forgo income while mango trees are growing and where pollutants from the brick kiln industry harm tree growth.

Aside from renegotiating the tasks in which they engage as farmers, educated Jat young men who had entered agriculture tried to portray themselves as '*modern* men.' They did so in part through acts of conspicuous consumption. Many parents provided their sons with the money required to develop urban consumer identities. By riding a motorcycle, wearing an expensive designer watch and donning pleated chino-style trousers, for example, Jat young men projected

---

[4]In one case, a Jat farmer in Meerut district has mounted a tannoy system, with speakers attached to mango trees. This allows him to instruct laborers from the comfort of a hut on the edge of the orchard.

their detachment from the daily business of rural cultivation and sense of being marked out for 'better work.' This involved Jat young men in occupying village space in a particular way. Groups of Jat young men congregated outside shops in the center of Nangal with the explicit goal of demonstrating their civilized comportment and ownership of consumer goods. The consumption strategies of these men acted as an important conduit for the entry of urban cultural styles into Nangal. By the early 2000s, many Jat households possessed televisions, refrigerators and motorcycles. The richest households owned washing machines, cars and three-storied rural homes. These rich Jats sometimes referred to their quest to "construct an urban home in the village." There was a gathering sense in the early 2000s that Nangal—with its three banks, six primary schools and population of nearly 5,000—was becoming a small town (*chhotā shehr*) rather than village (*gānv*) and a managerial class of young Jat farmers was at the forefront of this shift. In this instance, as in the case of semi-bourgeois work, Jats used the terms '*modern*' and 'urban' (*shehrī*) as synonyms.

Another means by which Jat young men sought to convey their educated accomplishment while working as farmers was by boasting of their familiarity with urban India and the cultural styles associated with what Fernandes (2006) terms 'the new Indian middle class.' Jats signaled their familiarity with urban cultures by inserting English words and phrases into Hindi sentences, discussing popular films and directing attention toward their schooling in Bijnor or elsewhere. Jat young men referred in particular to their knowledge of town-based corruption (*shehrī bhrashtāchār*) as a basis for signaling their urban credentials. We witnessed numerous conversations in which Jat young men appeared keen to demonstrate their awareness of the complex series of payments, negotiations and deceptions that allegedly characterize corrupt transactions in government employment markets. Running through these descriptions was a sense of excitement at the complexity of malpractice, and of corruption as a game (*khel*) with players (*khilārī*), rules (*niyam*) and winners (*jītwāle*) and losers (*harnewāle*). Jats occasionally likened trickery (*dhokebāzī*) within the competition for salaried employment to other types of *bāzī*, a word that may be translated either as 'game,' 'play' or 'enthusiasm.' The following exchange between Sonu and Amit, another educated Jat young man, provides a sense of Jat young men's tendency to admire particularly effective 'moves' or 'masterstrokes' within the 'game' of seeking salaried work. We were discussing a tendency for candidates for police posts to cheat in the medical tests that are performed as part of the recruitment process. Sonu and Amit seemed eager to discuss the topic and they reveled in the following story, which Amit told amid bursts of laughter:

Bribery in medical tests happens like this. A candidate, for example one with weak eyesight, bribes the examiner to send a copy of the eye test in advance of the examination. The candidate memorizes the letters on the eye test board. You know, the board has a big letter at the top and smaller letters beneath. . . . During the eye test, the candidate and the examiner are the only people who know that the candidate is cheating. The other people sitting there don't realize the trick!

Jats did not condone malpractice within government employment markets, and many were furious that they had lost out in this sphere. But, as the case of Sonu and Amit suggests, their frustration at 'corruption' was tempered by an eagerness to demonstrate that they were 'players' in this arena and that they knew what was happening in the interview rooms and recruitment centers in and beyond Bijnor. In this and other cases, Jat young men referred proudly to members of their caste who had bent the rules in novel or daring ways, particularly where the result was to marginalize lower castes. Rather than depicting themselves as rural innocents tricked out of government employment by rapacious government servants as Gupta (1995) records in work elsewhere in western UP, educated Jat young men in rural Bijnor district spoke of their familiarity with cultures of corruption, worldly knowledge and guile. It followed that, although some Jat young men felt disheartened at having to rely on social networks to find work, the majority accepted that personal considerations would be important in their attempts to enter reasonably secure private or government employment, and even sometimes boasted of their network of social contacts. We frequently heard educated Jat young men claim cheerfully to possess a '*setting*,' by which they meant a durable network of social contacts to whom they could apply for assistance in the search for positions in service.

These observations signal a broader point. Men like Sonu were distinguished from many Chamars and Muslims not only by their greater wealth, social networks and effective cultural capital, but also by what Bourdieu called a '*sens de placement*': a capacity to accumulate and store knowledge of their position within the different 'games' in which they were engaged. Here 'position' referred to their place within local social hierarchies and their shifting position within dense social networks that were oriented around the pursuit of credentials, jobs and political influence. Possessing a *sens de placement* implied mastery of a particular form of cosmopolitan skill: a social and spatial capacity to combine the 'modern' and 'traditional' and navigate political terrains. Cognizant of this aspect of their power, Jat young men accused educated Chamar young men of lacking knowledge of their position, of being 'above themselves' or of "wandering about the village uselessly."

Young Jat farmers' attempts to broadcast their civilized standing and *sens de placement* were underpinned by relationships of trust, reciprocity and friendship they had established with Jats and upper castes outside the village. These friendships had often been formed in the private schools that Jat young men had attended and were founded on similarities in the opinions, speech and comportment of upper and middle caste young men. We did not detect among upper caste young men a sense of regarding Jats as 'rustic' 'backward' or members of a 'new rich' who should therefore be treated with disdain. Rather, middle castes were fairly successful at generating a sense of shared caste-based solidarity with higher castes (cf. Srinivas 1955).

Few educated Jat young men used their *sens de placement* to enter politics. Jats lacked a strong regional political party representing their interests in the early 2000s. The politics of middle caste educated un/under-employment in rural Bijnor district appeared divorced from the formal pronouncements of political parties and lacked a leader—such as Mahendra Singh Tikait—around whom young male dissatisfaction could take shape. There were notable similarities between the views of some educated Jat young men and the rhetoric of Hindu right wing political organizations, and ten educated young men from Nangal were involved in RSS-led demonstrations in Bijnor in the early 1990s. Several educated young men participated in protests against VP Singh's decision to implement the recommendations of the Mandal Commission in 1991 (Jeffery and Jeffery 1997). But the political tactics of educated Jat young men excluded from government work in 2000–2002 were generally more subtle, fragmented and narrowly aesthetic in nature than action undertaken during the BKU protests of the late 1980s or anti-Mandal agitations and Ayodhya temple movement of the early 1990s.

Social Difference among the Jats

Most Jats possessed over four acres of land or some form of relatively lucrative off-farm employment. For many purposes, the Jat caste in Nangal could
be treated as an economic 'set.' But there were considerable internal divisions
within the Jats based upon wealth, and intra-caste social differentiation became
more marked and visible in the 1990s. In particular, by 2001 there was a small
collection of poor Jat households who possessed less than four acres of land
and lacked access to a secure off-farm income. A consideration of this group
provides a clearer picture of how educated un/under-employed Jat young men
were responding to their exclusion from prestigious government employment.

Bedhu and his wife, Seema, were poor Jats owning about two acres of agricultural
land and living in a small two-roomed house in Nangal in 2001. They had two sons
and a daughter. Bedhu, who was an Eighth Class pass, had secured a job as a clerk
in a local government sugar mill in the early 1980s. Seema had never been to school.
Bedhu and Seema sent their eldest son, Intu, to Nangal Junior High School up to
Eighth Class and arranged private tuition for him in English and Sanskrit. Bedhu
and Seema were aware of emerging educational opportunities in Bijnor town but
lacked the resources or social contacts to negotiate entry to a Bijnor secondary school.
After Eighth Class, they therefore sent Intu to a government-aided inter college three
miles from Nangal in the administrative center of Haldaur. Intu excelled at sports in
Haldaur, and the family was impressed with the standard of education relative to the
village, but Intu's examination results were poor and mid-way through Tenth Class
he dropped out of school.

Intu lacked the qualifications required to compete in national civil service
examinations and his parents could not afford the type of coaching that Sonu
had obtained. Instead, Bedhu used social contacts in Bijnor to arrange a low-
ranking temporary government job for Intu in the Home Guard. He did not
take to this employment, however, and returned to Nangal after a few months
to work on the family farm. Intu married in 2000 and his first child was born
early in 2001. Aware that their small farm would not be able to support a family,
Bedhu's mother petitioned Bedhu's younger sister's husband to arrange a low-
ranking government post for Intu in a government sugar mill. This job offered
a salary of only Rs. 900 a month, but it was secure. Dismissive of the low salary,

Intu turned down this opportunity. In desperation, Bedhu and Seema encouraged him to establish a shop in Nangal. In 2001, they had raised Rs. 20,000 in starting capital. Intu seemed upbeat about the enterprise. He said that he enjoyed traveling to and from Bijnor collecting stock and ideas of what to sell. At the same time, Seema had contacted a relative from her natal home who had promised to find Intu a clerical job in a government sugar mill.

Intu said that he regretted not concentrating more on his school work and he planned to invest heavily in the education of his own children. He claimed that education provides knowledge of the world, the confidence to start businesses and the capacity to speak, move and comport oneself with distinction. Intu boasted that as an educated person he was able to make informed decisions about how to establish his business, behave respectably in urban settings and keep accounts. But he was concerned at the possibility that his shop might not be successful and he eagerly awaited news of the job at the government mill. In addition, Intu could not afford the fashionable clothes worn by most Jat young men in Nangal.

These themes, of the poor Jat young men's struggle to acquire secondary school credentials and of the subsequent difficulties they encountered seeking secure salaried work, were repeated in many other interviews with poor Jat young men. Rich as well as poor Jats in Nangal identified an upper stratum of Jats, who they said are entitled to label themselves 'Chaudhrys'—on the grounds that they possess government jobs, good private service or large farms—and other members of their caste "who are just Jats." Among poor Jat young men we heard frequent complaints about the deteriorating standard of village schools and the relative merits of urban institutions, from which they were excluded on economic grounds. The mismatch between their ambitions and economic realities had created considerable resentment; young men frequently complained about the expense of contemporary formal education, corruption in government employment markets and the state's failure to offer scholarships to the middle caste poor.

In the context of this sense of resentment, poor Jats commonly described Chamars as being in a privileged position in relation to the acquisition of educational credentials and salaried employment. They argued that Chamars had been '*pampered*' by the Government through the system of scholarships and

reservations. They also spoke bitterly of the ostentatious consumption practices of Chamar young men. Poor Jats offered fanciful descriptions of Chamars
"wandering around the village listening to walkmans," "building three-storied
houses" or "holding feasts that last through the night." Tugging at his *kurtā-
pājāmā*, one educated underemployed young man from a landless Jat family
asked, "How can I afford the pants and shirts of those rich Chamar bastards?
Everything is now upside down." Jats, and poorer members of the caste in particular, sometimes made similar comments about Muslims. They claimed that
the state was constantly preoccupied with assisting Muslims, who also had
'their own' schools, charitable institutions and rich businesses. More commonly, however, educated Jat young men from poorer backgrounds distinguished
between the injustice of their poverty and 'inherently backward' (*pīche*) Muslims. Adopting a tone of moral condemnation and disdain, Jats claimed that
Muslims have little interest in education and prefer to have large numbers of
children, whom they install in small craft workshops from an early age. Indeed,
many Jats used the terms 'illiterate' (*unparh*) and Muslim interchangeably. At
this everyday level, Jats were appropriating aspects of the political ideologies of
right-wing Hindu nationalist organizations.

We should not exaggerate the disadvantages of poor Jats. Even when they
came from poor backgrounds, almost all Jat young men possessed a type of
'latent' cultural capital—embodied in their speech, clothing and comportment and condensed in their identity as Jats—that conferred privileges within
most government bureaucracies and sections of the private economy outside
Nangal. Moreover, like Intu, poor Jat young men were usually able to draw on
social contacts in influential positions, often connections established through
marriage, to acquire employment in the urban informal economy or temporary government jobs in Bijnor district. The idea of being in possession of
'*jān-pahchān*'—'known and recognized figures'—neatly expresses Jats' social
advantages. Young men from this caste had a sense of being favorably located
in politicized networks of shared recognition even if they lacked material resources. Indeed, one Jat young man from a poorer family told us, "Being Jat in
Bijnor [district] is like having an invisible license." In addition, within Nangal,
many poor Jat young men were able to press richer kin into assisting them

in establishing small businesses. If all other options were exhausted, poor Jat young men could work as tractor drivers on the farms of their richer peers.

In explaining why they offered financial or other assistance to poorer members of their caste or kinship group, rich Jats said that they felt a sense of duty (*farz*) to poorer kin and members of their caste. But prosperous members of the caste were equally concerned at the social implications of a member of their kin or caste group having to resort to manual wage labor in the village. Several Jats told us that "Jats do not work on the fields of others" and linked this 'social fact' to Jats' alleged 'independence.' The existence of a suite of 'fallback options' and caste-based networks of support meant that only two educated Jat young men aged between 20 and 34 were engaged in manual daily wage labor in Nangal in 2001—an extraordinary statistic in the context of the scale and intensity of the employment crisis in the region.

Conclusions

Educated Jat young men unable to obtain prestigious government work had mobilized economic, social and cultural capital to acquire jobs within private service, business or agriculture that were consistent with their educated standing. These Jat young men were so confident of their continued future success that they imagined deepening and extending their educational investment for their own children in spite of their own experiences of struggling to obtain employment.

Jat fallback strategies were a collective achievement, a point that Mendelsohn (1993) tends to downplay in his account of a formerly dominant caste in rural Rajasthan. Jat young men's families played a central role in supporting their efforts to acquire education and negotiate educated un/under-employment. Jat young men's parents were usually educated up to at least Eighth Class, and some of their fathers had experience of negotiating educated un/under-employment in an earlier period. Members of a wider kinship group were similarly important in assisting Jat young men. In addition, everyday caste sentiments and social networking remain central to Jat efforts to find a way to manage educated un/under-employment even while social differentiation among the Jats renders open to question the value of caste as a category for analyzing their strategies.

This chapter therefore adds further weight to the argument rehearsed in Chapter Two that Jats have, on the whole, been relatively well equipped to meet the challenges presented by economic liberalization. Just as many Jats avoided becoming educated un/under-employed by marshalling inherited economic, social and cultural capital to obtain government work (Chapter Two), those who had found themselves without government employment used the same resources to prevent downward mobility and sustain the educated cultural styles we described in Chapter Three. In the rapidly changing context of western UP, maintaining one's economic standing and sense of cultural superiority was a significant and hard-won achievement. These trends—toward either upward mobility or maintenance of social position—cannot be summarized as forms of 'sanskritization,' where a caste collectively adopts the practices and linguistic traits of a 'higher' status group (Srinivas 1989). Rather, they reflect the attempts of individual households to improve or defend their standing in society.

At first reading, the strategies of young Jat men from landowning families contrast starkly with the picture of Jats that emerged from discussions of the BKU movement in the late 1980s and 1990s (cf. Bentall 1995; A. Gupta 1997). Instead of cultivating an overtly 'traditional,' agricultural, village-based identity or developing an oppositional politics targeted against city cultures, Jat young men excluded from salaried employment typically stressed their affiliation with urban and modern masculinities and distanced themselves from 'sons-of-the-soil' cultures. Indeed, Jats increasingly voiced ideas of development (*vikās*) in opposition to the image of the 'dirt and soil' of the village.

But we must not draw too stark a contrast between our material and earlier work on Jats and the BKU. First, Jat men had largely removed their wives from agricultural work in the 1970s and 1980s because this activity demeaned their households. The efforts of educated un/under-employed Jat young men to distance themselves from the soil are therefore part of a longer history of agricultural disengagement rather than a radical historical break. Second, many observers of the BKU movement noted tensions within the organization over members' allegiance to rural cultural styles. Tikait frequently criticized BKU activists who wore shirts and trousers coded locally as 'Western' (A. Gupta 1997) or who dropped English words into their sentences (Madsen 1996). Such cultural differences were important in the disintegration of the BKU movement in the mid-1990s (Madsen 1998). Third, as Osella and Osella (2002) point out, the cultural practices of Indian youth typically involve them in moving back and forth between styles coded as 'modern' and 'traditional,' and the Jats are no different in this respect. Jat young men continued to place emphasis on the importance of intra-caste arranged marriages with young women who possessed knowledge of rural 'tradition.' Moreover, educated Jat young men were ambivalent when discussing their rural homes. Many of these men spoke of the village as a place of peace, clean air, good water and abundant wildlife and contrasted the countryside with the polluted, crowded and unfriendly nature of urban areas.[5]

Jat young men also explicitly acknowledged their willingness to make political capital out of their image as 'backward' (*pīche*), 'simple farmers' (*kisān*) if and when the opportunity arose. For example, many Jat young men referred to their successful attempt to obtain OBC status in UP in 2000 as a highly strategic political tactic. In contrast to the argument made by some scholars (e.g. Datta 1999b) that Jats were 'trading in' their caste status in return for the benefits of OBC status, Jats saw no contradiction between proclaiming their warrior caste (*kshatriya*) standing while striving for OBC privileges. Indeed, they said that their acquisition of OBC status signaled their political maturity as agents in networks of political maneuvering that extended well outside Bijnor district and UP.

In most respects, the strategies of educated Jat young men we have described accord with the image of rich farmers' strategies in other parts of India and provide support for Fernandes' (2006) recent emphasis on the iconic power of the image of a 'new Indian middle class.' Like the farmers discussed by Upadhya (1988) and Rutten (1995), Jat young men have retreated from the daily business of agricultural cultivation, used extra-village social contacts to acquire useful

---

[5]This was especially evident in a long discussion we held with two Jat young men about the wild animals that surrounded Nangal. These men enthusiastically described their frequent forays into the fields to search for jackals, foxes, and leopards.

fallback employment and 'counter-resisted' the attempts of those lower in the caste hierarchy to emulate their success. Rather more than Upadhya (1988), Rutten (1995) or Fernandes (2006), however, we have pointed to the role of ideas about education in shaping the diversification and identity strategies of young rich farmers. The compulsion to appear and act in an educated manner animates Jat practices, drawing them toward particular occupations and shaping local practice in numerous other ways.

Consideration of the strategies of rich Jat young men largely supports Sen's emphasis on education as a basis for creating substantive freedoms. Even in the face of a shortage of secure salaried jobs, most Jats were able to use education to acquire social goods, including reasonably well-paid work, social confidence and respect. Moreover, Jats themselves voiced their enthusiasm for education, linking the possession of school qualifications to local ideas of skill (*hunar*), knowledge (*jānkārī*), good manners (*tamīz*) and refinement (*sanskār*). At the same time, our material suggests that it was Jats' accumulated wealth, social networking opportunities and other forms of inherited cultural capital rather than education alone that had acted as the springboard for their success. Power and culture mediate people's access to education and to the 'entitlements' commonly associated with being successful at school.

The next chapter develops this argument by considering the practices of a small group of educated Chamar young men who constructed themselves as 'new politicians.' Distinct from the Jats, these Chamars linked notions of 'being educated' to formal political processes and action. While the Jats used education to reinforce caste difference and to support individual strategies of upward mobility, a few Chamars believed that education provided a basis for challenging caste as a measure of worth and for advancing the interests of their caste as a whole.

5

Dalit Revolution?
New Politicians in Uttar Pradesh

Our focus shifts in this chapter from dominant Jats to a small group of relatively wealthy Chamars in Nangal. A few Chamar young men had responded to their exclusion from secure salaried work by cultivating identities as political actors. Indeed, one of the most important consequences of rising educated un/under-employment in western UP has been the emergence of a set of 'new politicians' (*naye netās*) among comparatively prosperous Chamar young men. This chapter explores the strategies and reflections of this Dalit elite. Prolonged formal education had provided new politicians with crucial skills, cultural capital and confidence. But the activities of these *naye netās* have failed to change established relationships of dominance in rural Bijnor district to any substantial extent.

In making these arguments, the chapter engages with recent research on Dalit social mobility in UP. Jaffrelot (2003) has argued that a 'silent revolution' is occurring in rural north India wherein lower castes are challenging the power of established elites. Jaffrelot draws on archival evidence, secondary sources and interview material to describe how lower castes have asserted themselves in electoral politics. Jaffrelot charts the emergence of OBCs as a formidable political force in the 1960s and the subsequent rise of Dalit political parties in the 1980s and 1990s. These parties offered lower castes a new voice in processes of state policy formation and governance such that "power has been transferred, on the whole peacefully, from upper castes to various subaltern groups" (Jaffrelot 2003: 494).

Jaffrelot does much to improve our understanding of the democratization of north Indian political competition since 1947. But he is less useful as a guide to the everyday politics of dominance and resistance in north India. Jaffrelot stresses a process of empowerment among Dalits in rural UP that is not supported by most village-level research. For example, several studies document Dalits' lack of local political power in the 1990s (Lerche 1999; Jeffrey and Lerche 2000). Others have referred to Dalits' continued oppression within agricultural labor relations (Srivastava 1995; Lerche 1999). Dalits are also still relatively excluded from education and employment markets (Nambissan and Sedwal 2002).

Jaffrelot does caution against exaggerating lower caste empowerment: he identifies both the partial nature of their political achievements and the counter-resistance of the higher castes. But he nevertheless argues that a 'transfer of power' is significantly advanced. He also makes the still bolder claim that, insofar as a revolution has not occurred, it will work itself out in 'several decades' (2003: 494). Teleological notions of inevitable political progress through time—of a gradual and unstoppable 'unfolding' of democracy—therefore haunt his account of a 'silent revolution.' While Jaffrelot evaluates an impressive array of evidence to support his claim that lower castes have colonized *formal* political arenas, he is less exhaustive in his account of ground-level change.

The research of Pai (2000, 2002) largely supports Jaffrelot's assertions, and he uses her work in his book. Building on survey research conducted in three villages on the outskirts of Meerut, western UP, Pai (2000) describes a new generation of educated, securely employed, Chamar young men who have overturned established relationships of dominance in rural UP. These men represent Dalit interests within local government councils (*panchāyats*), act as intermediaries between their community and the state and organize social mobilization (cf. Jeffery et al. 2001). Gupta (1998) makes a similar argument based upon more ethnographic fieldwork in a small village he calls 'Alipur' in Bulandshahr District, western UP. Gupta argues there has been a shift in the relationship between rich and poor in Alipur as a result of a rise in non-farm employment, the decline of the traditional '*jajmānī*' system of labor relations and the strengthening of *panchāyats*. Gupta charts a move from a relationship of bondage, whereby low caste agricultural laborers were tied to particular forms of work on the farms of richer cultivators, to a relationship of brokerage, wherein rich farmers depend upon the votes of the poor to be elected onto the village council. Whilst stopping short of arguing for a wholesale change in social relations, as does Pai (2000), the implication of Gupta's analysis is that poorer low castes greatly improved their position in rural society in the 1970s and early 1980s.

This chapter provides a counterpoint to such optimistic accounts of Dalits' social mobility and to Jaffrelot's broader idea of 'silent revolution' by reaffirming the importance of notions of 'dominance' and 'resistance' in understanding rural struggle. We argue that the 'silent' capture of political power by Dalits in UP has not translated into revolutionary shifts in economic and social structures or in everyday power relations. Party political change is unlikely to improve the prospects of Dalit mobility without a redistribution of economic and social resources on the ground. We make these arguments through reference to precisely the cohort of energetic intellectuals that Jaffrelot (2003) and Pai (2000) regard as crucial to processes of social transformation: *naye netās* among Dalit educated young men. The chapter describes *netās'* political work, their role as social animators and the reactions of other Chamars in Nangal to the rise of these men.

New Politicians as Political Intermediaries

Inspired in large part by the ascendance of the BSP, a few educated Chamars in Nangal had channeled their frustration at educated un/under-employment into work as local political brokers. This reaction to exclusion from government employment was exhibited by only *some* Chamars, and we discuss the strategies of the majority of Chamar young men in Chapter Seven. But these *naye netās* were highly influential in Nangal. People sometimes used the epithet 'new politician' semi-humorously to mock the aspirations of ambitious young men, but they often employed the term more seriously to indicate men who circulated political rhetoric in the village and assumed organizational roles within local institutions. Rural people referred to these men as 'new' politicians because they belonged to a section of rural society—the Chamars—that had formerly been excluded from local representative and participatory politics. Villagers also used the term 'new politicians' to distinguish local young men with political aspirations from the more established Dalit politicians who regularly contested national or State-level elections and had developed a regional power base. Finally, the term 'new' suggested the connection between these ambitious young men and notions of progress (*prāgatī*), development (*vikās*) and the *modern*.

Six of the 38 educated un/under-employed Chamar young men aged between twenty and thirty-four in Nangal exhibited the traits of new politicians. Like the educated political entrepreneurs studied by Lynch (1969), Khare (1984) and most recently Jaoul (2007) in urban areas of UP, these men generated support for low caste political organizations, assisted in social awareness campaigns and acted as 'cultural brokers' in the transmission of new ideas (Wolf 1956). In a study of 69 villages in Rajasthan and Madhya Pradesh, Krishna (2002) has written of the rise of *naye netās* in *rural* India who work as political intermediaries at the local level. Drawing on earlier accounts from urban north India and on Krishna's work, this chapter shows that an increase in formal education, combined with widespread un/under-employment, has encouraged the emergence of a new stratum of low caste leaders working as lobbyists and gatekeepers to the local state.

Brijpal came closest to conforming to the ideal type of a Chamar *netā*. Brijpal usually wore a clean white *kurtā-pājāmā* with smart leather sandals. He brushed his hair carefully across his head and sometimes carried a small leather briefcase. His Hindi contained many Sanskrit words and he was careful to speak politely and avoid expletives. In these respects, Brijpal typified the cultural style of Chamar new politicians: confident, composed and scrupulously attentive to matters of self-presentation.

Brijpal lived in a small two-roomed brick house near the center of Nangal. He was 34 in 2001. Brijpal had studied up to Eighth Class at the Ambedkar Junior High School (AJHS) in Nangal, went to a government aided inter-college in Haldaur for classes 9 and 10 and then attended another aided inter-college in Bijnor for his senior secondary school education. After leaving school, Brijpal obtained an MCom from the government degree college in Bijnor. At the same time, he studied for a polytechnic diploma in commercial practice from a private technical institute close to Bijnor. Brijpal completed his formal education at Nainital where he obtained an MA at a government degree college. Brijpal was married in the late 1990s and had one son and one daughter, both aged under five during our fieldwork.

Brijpal grew up in a household possessing 0.8 acres of agricultural land. His parents worked as manual wage laborers in the village and were uneducated. Brijpal's father-in-law had a job in a legal office in Nainital, and Brijpal's younger brother ran a courier agency in Bijnor. Lacking close relatives in influential positions within government service or large amounts of money to bribe state officials, however, Brijpal had been unable to obtain a government job. In the mid-1990s, Brijpal worked on a voluntary basis as a clerk in a government *tahsīl* (sub-district) office, partly as a means of looking for permanent work. By 2001, Brijpal had resigned himself to having failed in the quest for a secure government post.

As an 'educated person,' Brijpal said that he should not engage in manual labor, nor did he appear to have contemplated migrating in search of employment. Instead, Brijpal had sought opportunities for small-scale entrepreneurship and white-collar work in the local informal economy. Brijpal had set up a moderately successful agency selling cigarettes in the village, using social contacts he had established in Bijnor and the knowledge he had acquired through his commerce qualification. This job involved maintaining good relationships with higher caste suppliers in Bijnor and selling cigarettes to local retail outlets and on the street. In addition, Brijpal mobilized urban social connections to obtain short-term contracts to supply labor for government construction projects in the village. Brijpal's wife, Meena, drew a salary of about Rs. 1,500 a month as a government *anganwādī* (nursery) worker in Nangal. Brijpal and Meena were therefore slightly better off financially than many of his peers working as manual wage laborers, but much less wealthy than the majority of Jats.

Brijpal's case offers insights into the social location of new politicians. *Netās* were all male. Young women were discouraged from engaging in the types of public oratory and local political maneuver that form the staple of a new politician's work. Most *naye netās* came from relatively wealthy backgrounds, by Chamar standards, and possessed a comparatively extensive range of social links in urban areas. Of the six *netās,* four had university degrees, one had a Tenth Class pass and one an Eighth Class pass. Three of the *netās* managed moderately successful small businesses in Nangal, two worked as contractors on construction projects funded by the state's Public Works Department and one had a temporary job in a government bank.

All the new politicians were married, in three cases to young women from urban areas and four *netās* had at least one child. The parents of young women had usually married their daughters to *netās* in the expectation that their sons-in-law would obtain government service outside Nangal. But parents-in-law had not put *netās* under pressure after they had failed to obtain secure government work. The capacity of new politicians to make money in the informal economy or through temporary government employment, allied to the good reputation they had developed in Nangal, diffused possibilities of marital conflict and typically seemed to prevent the *netās'* in-laws from intervening in their lives.

Brijpal pursued his political activity on several fronts simultaneously. In 1987, he enrolled in the Dalit Shoshit Samaj Sangarsh Samiti (DS-4), a political organization founded by the Dalit politician Kanshi Ram that aimed to improve Dalit society and increase their representation in politics (see Jaffrelot 2003: 393 ff.). In 1984, the BSP replaced the DS-4 within party politics, but the DS-4 survived as the BSP's youth wing and Brijpal joined the BSP in 1993.

At the village level, Brijpal formerly sat on the Ambedkar Junior High School (AJHS) management committee in Nangal. This was an unelected and unpaid position but it provided influence over the appointment of teachers and management of school funds. Brijpal had also served as a committee member within the government *panchāyat*, had contested one *panchāyat* election unsuccessfully and hoped to stand for *pradhān* (village council chair) again in the near future.

Brijpal played an important role as lobbyist for other Chamars in their dealings with the state. His experience working in a government *tahsīl* office provided a range of local social contacts and offered him valuable inside knowledge of state bureaucracies. Brijpal also possessed personal qualities, such as confidence, charisma and tact, required to manage relations with local state officials. Chamars often called upon Brijpal to assist with routine work that entailed interacting with government officers, such as obtaining loans through the State Bank, filling in forms for pensions and petitioning the *pradhān* to improve Chamar sections of the village. Brijpal had acquired a reputation as someone who 'gets work done' (*kām karnewālā*). Chamars also approached Brijpal and other new politicians after particular 'atrocities' (*atyāchār*)—such as an attack on a Chamar laborer—to assist in negotiating with lawyers, the police and senior district-level officials.

Brijpal's skill as a mediator came to the fore in March 2001. During annual celebrations associated with the Holi festival, a fight erupted between Jat and Chamar young men in Nangal. Chamars claimed that Jats had been pelting them with stones, while Jats argued that Chamars had set light to a portion of their sugar cane fields. Jats called the police and insisted that they arrest several Chamars. Chamar young men then approached Brijpal to negotiate with the primarily upper caste Hindu police force, a task Brijpal performed with alacrity and skill: no charges were brought against Chamars, and the incident was soon set aside. Brijpal said that he often had to pay bribes as part of efforts to convince officials to intercede on his clients' behalf. But he claimed that he did not gain financially from his political work. Brijpal described himself as an intermediary (*bīchwālā*) rather than broker (*dalāl*).

Brijpal's case illustrates wider themes. Like Brijpal, other *naye netās* in Nangal did not hold formal political offices outside the village, but three others claimed to have 'good relationships' (*achchhe jān pahchān*) with BSP politicians, and politicians frequently sought *naye netās*' help in garnering support before an election, raising political funds and communicating political ideas. The Chamar *netās* often sat on the management committees of local schools, held positions within the *panchāyat* and assisted in the introduction of new government programs. Influenced by the rise of the BSP in UP, *netās* worked within local non-governmental organizations representing Chamar interests, which included a youth group, rotating credit scheme and adult literacy program. In addition, *netās* commonly assumed the position of mediator within clientelistic networks that linked rural Chamars to local state officials. Like organic intellectuals in other contexts (Gramsci 1971), these men acted as political fixers in the efforts of friends and relatives to accomplish tasks through state officials. These forms of political brokerage were reversing relationships between age and authority among Chamars in the village. Educated *naye netās*, with knowledge and experience outside Nangal, were better able to exercise power than were older caste members, who were increasingly dependent on younger men.

Three of the six *naye netās* with whom we spoke said that they specialized as lobbyists. Brijpal was particularly skilled in negotiating with the police, land revenue officials and the judiciary. Another *netā*, Tejpal, felt more comfortable mediating between rural people and the State Bank, where he was employed as a peon, or with the Block Development Office. A new politician called Amit concentrated his political efforts on mobilizing government support and funds for a Dalit hostel that would house visiting wedding parties and provide space for readings from Ambedkar's work.

It is important to distinguish between the social and political work of Chamar *netās* and the efforts of government-employed Chamars to assist members of their caste. Chamar *netās* frequently argued that they are better positioned to help rural Chamars in their dealings with the state than educated Chamar young men who had entered government service. Some *netās* claimed that Chamars in government, who usually lived with their families in urban areas, had forgotten the plight of Nangal's Chamars. More commonly, they argued that Chamars who had obtained government positions did not have the time, influence or confidence required to assist their peers in the village. *Netās* stressed that Chamars in government generally occupied low-ranking posts and remained fearful of offending upper caste superiors. One *netā* described a Chamar in service as a man "with his tongue caught between his teeth": someone unable to 'speak up' in the face of exploitation and malpractice. Moreover, government employees are forbidden to engage in political activity.

Against the grain of *netās*' statements, however, we spoke to two educated Chamar men within government service who had played major roles in assisting Chamars in Nangal. Birendra, a Twelfth Class pass, had obtained a reserved job as an office assistant in the Survey of India in 1971 and was posted in Delhi in 2001, where he lived with his family. In 1978, Birendra established the AJHS in Nangal. Despite living outside the village, he continued to play an advisory role in the development of the school and planned to improve the institution further when he retires and moves back to Nangal. Birendra had also established an Ambedkar Youth Organization (AYO) in the late 1970s. The AYO attempted to spread knowledge of Ambedkar's teachings by organizing debates and dramas around the theme of Ambedkar's life. The AYO had also raised funds for the AJHS and was building a function-room for Chamars in Nangal in 2001. In his early thirties in 2001, Jaibir had been similarly influential. In 1997, Jaibir obtained a post cleaning and repairing shoes in the Bijnor police force. In this position, he came into daily contact with senior figures in the police. On the basis of the social relationship he had developed with the Superintendent of Police, Jaibir was able to mediate between Chamars in the village and the police force. He assisted in resolving disputes involving Nangal Chamars and police officers, and helped individual Chamars who he felt had a legitimate basis for complaining about police maltreatment. This evidence counters an argument made by some observers of India that the entry of large numbers of Dalits into government employment may deprive the community of political leaders (see Parry 1999), and, though he did not directly say so, we suspect that Jaibir imagined himself as a type of *naye netā*.

Notwithstanding this evidence, however, Chamars in government jobs stressed that the pressures of their work, relative remove from rural affairs and limited influence prevented them from responding quickly and effectively to the demands placed on them by rural members of their caste. The Chamars in government service therefore supported the view of *netās*, that educated young men excluded from government work were better able to assist other Chamars in the village in their negotiations with state officials.

Changes in local government had provided new opportunities for *naye netās* in the field of village politics. One of the richest Jats in Nangal, Balbir Singh, held the post of *pradhān* of the village *panchāyat* between 1960 and 1988, and another rich Jat assumed this position between 1988 and 1995. Until the early 1990s, Chamars in Nangal did not radically question the right of the Jats to 'lead' the village within the *panchāyat*, and only once put forward a Chamar candidate for the position of *pradhān*. During this period, rich Jats periodically sought re-election by distributing largesse within the poorest parts of the village and intimidating voters on the eve of elections (see also Lieten 1996; Lieten and Srivastava 1999).

But the 73rd Amendment Act of 1992, in reserving *panchayat* seats for SCs, offered a new path along which Dalits could seek power. In 1995, Jogender captured the post of *pradhān*. Jogender's wife, Guria, had formally won the post, since it was reserved for a SC woman. But Jogender assumed effective control of the *panchāyat*. Jogender told us, "I just gave her the pen to sign the paper. I went to all the meetings and did all the work." Jogender's wife expressed little interest in the work of the *panchayat* and disliked village politics (cf. Pai 1998). As *pradhān*, Jogender raised Chamars' awareness of their entitlement to state assistance and their confidence in complaining in the face of government inaction and corruption. He also improved the economic fortunes of some poor households by increasing the proportion of development resources reaching Chamars. Jogender ensured that 38 households received Rs. 20,000 loans through the Integrated Rural Development Program and he said that he had favored Chamars, widows and the very poor in dispensing these loans. We were unable to verify these claims but our research in the Block Development Office suggested that Jogender's period of office coincided with an improvement in Chamars' access to Jawahar Rozgar Yojana (JRY) funds. For example, in 1999–2000, Rs. 139,500 came through the JRY, which provided about 2,700 days of labor per year for Dalits, equivalent to roughly five days of work each for landless households in Nangal and much more than Chamars had received when Jats had controlled the *panchāyat*. Jogender had also bolstered Chamar access to scholarship money; according to Block Development Office records, Rs. 149,500 was allocated to Nangal children for scholarships in 2000/2001, only slightly below the figure we would expect on the basis of our household survey and over double the amount that Chamars received before Jogender became *pradhān*. Rural people frequently complained about scholarship money arriving late or of small sums being appropriated by the *pradhān* or schoolteachers, but most Nangal villagers said that they received at least three-quarters of the money to which they were formally entitled when Jogender was in post.

Jogender and other *netās* said that their work as intermediaries depended on their knowledge of local government, current affairs and social and political dynamics outside the village. *Netās* read widely and listened to radio news programs. They also spent long periods in specific areas of the village, such as the bus stop and *panchāyat* office, where they could catch up on local gossip, make themselves available to local people and signal their capacity to play mediating roles. Like Jats, they alluded to the importance of a *sens de placement* in their everyday social practice (Bourdieu 1984). *Netās* also said that developing

a strong political profile depended upon reflecting critically on one's performance within government offices and other political spaces. They claimed that
convincing government officials to assist with particular tasks required making
polite appeals for help, absorbing setbacks graciously and cultivating an atmosphere of mutual respect. *Netās* tended to distance themselves from confronta-
tional styles, which they regarded as undignified and counter-productive.

Netās' attempts to improve Chamars' access to state officials and generate
Dalit associational life moderated rather than transformed processes of local
class and caste domination, however. Upper and middle caste Hindus, particularly the Jats, continued to control local government bureaucracies in Bijnor
district, as they did in most other parts of western UP. Reflecting this dominance, the police usually sided with Jats in struggles over land, labor or other
resources. For example, in 1998, the police and a local land revenue officer assisted Jats in illegally transferring a large portion of land in the center of Nangal
from Chamar to Jat ownership. In 1999, the police intimidated Chamars, who
had unfurled a BSP flag in Nangal, and confiscated the flagpole. In 2001, the
police and judiciary turned a blind eye when many Jats withheld payment for
agricultural labor and harassed Chamar women working in the fields. In some
high profile cases involving transparent state malfeasance, *netās* tended to be on
hand. But in smaller and everyday state/society interactions *netās* had to ration
their time and energy according to personal considerations. Each new politician had a limited stock of 'influence' (*source*),[1] and there were simply too few
netās to serve the large number of poor Chamars in Nangal in their negotiations with the state and dominant Jats.

Moreover, *netās* lacked a coordinated approach to changing rural society.
This point became glaringly evident in 1997 when, after a series of factional
disputes between different *netās* in Nangal, a delegation of new politicians went
to petition the BSP-led state government in Lucknow to obtain financial assistance for the AJHS. Ironically, this poorly planned and delayed expedition
arrived in the state capital on the day that the BSP fell from power. The *netās*

---

[1]*Netās* sometimes traded on their *potential* to draw on social contacts. In these cases,
for example threatening a local policeman by referring to one's link with a politician,
their stock of '*source*' is not depleted. But *netās* often have to contact senior officials for
favors, and in this sense '*source*' is finite.

returned empty handed, and the Jat-run private secondary school in Nangal remained much better funded than the AJHS. Problems of coordination emerged
again in 2002, when, in spite of constituting over half of the village population,
Chamar new politicians were unable to win the *pradhān* elections in Nangal
due to internal divisions within their caste. Broader consideration of Dalit associational activity in Nangal points in a similar direction: only 24 Chamar
households had become involved in the Dalit rotating credit scheme and few
Chamar young people attended the AYO. A *netā*-led adult education scheme
ceased altogether due to a lack of interest and Jats had blocked the efforts of
Chamars to build a hostel.

Dalit initiatives also failed because *netās* sometimes prioritized their own
interests over those of their caste. Despite trying to help many Chamar families,
Jogender defined himself as a profit-seeking broker. He admitted that he had
made a substantial amount of money working as *pradhān* and had done little
to reduce poverty. In other cases, *netās* failed to help other Chamars in spite
of their best intentions. Jats were well equipped to counter-resist lower caste
political assertion at the local level by entering government employment or
private service and deepening their investment in education. In government offices around Nangal many *netās* encountered higher castes who ridiculed their
posturing, were better qualified, more knowledgeable and confidently sought
to reassert their dominance. An understanding of the dialectics of dominance
and resistance in contemporary Nangal requires attention to the capacity of
naye netās to mediate between 'society' and 'the state'—which is a 'new' form of
political activity in rural western UP—*and* consideration of older structures of
dominance that prevent them from effecting a more radical shift in power.

What emerged quite powerfully over the two years of our visiting Nangal,
was not just the frequency with which higher caste dominance reasserted itself
in the practices of the police, politicians and other state representatives but
also the strength of Chamars' *feeling* of their poverty and social isolation. The
prevailing political mood was one of despondency, cynicism and thinly veiled
anger. Rather than being part of what some *netās* called the '*chain*' linking particular rural people to higher officials, local people said that they felt themselves
'isolated' (*akelā, nāektā hai*), 'powerless' (*bekār*) or 'wandering' (*ghūm rahe*). A

belief that others lacked the capacity to empathize with the poor was woven through this sense of exclusion. In the type of statement that we heard repeated numerous times, a Chamar male laborer lamented:

Who will cry about our sadness? Who will listen to us? . . . How can we complain to lo-cal state officials? The people to whom we would complain are the same people about whom we would be complaining. So in this situation, we can do nothing. The Jats, in their big houses, are drinking our blood.

That this laborer used plural pronouns in describing his isolation is significant. There was a sense of collective possibility among Chamars in the early 2000s that was not apparent in the early 1990s in Nangal (Jeffery and Jeffery 1997) or in neighboring Meerut district in the mid-1990s (Jeffrey 2001). But this sense of possibility had not led to a substantial transformation in the relationship between caste and power.

Our account of *naye netās'* political practices presents an interesting con-trast to Krishna's (2002) discussion of political entrepreneurs in Rajasthan and Gujarat, where similarly self-styled 'new politicians' are allegedly capable of building "inclusive institutional structures" at the local level. Krishna also credits *naye netās* with a capacity to escape caste as an ordering principle in society. He writes, "By looking to caste as a possible source of influence for themselves, they [*naye netās*] know they would be playing into the hands of the old leadership" (Krishna 2002: 78). By contrast, we have suggested that Chamar *naye netās* work mainly for Chamars, and their efforts have been piecemeal and contradictory even in this respect. The divergence between our conclu-sions and those of Krishna (2002) largely reflects differences between the social geography of Rajasthan/Gujarat and of western UP, where inequalities were more marked. But the differences in our accounts also relate to theoretical and methodological issues. In employing Putnam's (1993) work on social capital, Krishna detracts attention from the roles played by class, caste and gender in-equalities in his research area. Moreover, Krishna's large-scale survey-based re-search, while possessing obvious strengths, leaves him rather poorly equipped to discuss how other villagers perceive *naye netās'* practices or measure their successes. To cite just one example, Krishna records that 53 percent of rural people responded to a questionnaire by indicating that they approach *naye netās* in their negotiations with the police. But this tells us rather little about either how far marginalized agents are capable of convincing *naye netās* to act on their behalf or about durable inequalities in the negotiating positions of differently placed rural people. Adopting a more ethnographic approach, we have suggested that new politicians only marginally improve the access of the rural poor to resources in western UP and that *naye netās* are thoroughly embroiled in processes of caste, class and gender reproduction.

Urbane Geographies: New Politicians as Social Animators

Netās' role as social animators was more important than their function as political intermediaries. Chamars have long circulated ideas critical of dominant castes in the village, and their resistance to upper castes in western UP was recorded in the district gazetteers as early as the 1890s (Nevill 1922). A few Chamar men in their seventies and eighties were able to recall songs they had learnt in their childhood that expressed anger at caste oppression. Het Ram, a Chamar laborer in his early eighties, was among the keenest exponents of these songs, which frequently took the form of two or three line sung poems called *ālhās*. Het Ram often sang in small gatherings at his house, and several *naye netās* referred to him as an inspiration. On one occasion, Het Ram had been speaking about caste discrimination during his childhood in Nangal. He remembered higher castes refusing to let Dalits drink from taps in Nangal and of having to scoop water from irrigation channels, "like a beast." Het Ram then launched into the following *ālhās*:

> Through ascetism you can rule and bring together separated families.
> Those whose time has come will die, others won't.
> Why die like a jackal? Grab your reins and dagger.
>
> *Tap karne se rāj mile hai, bichāre mile kutumb parivār*
> *Jis ki āyi wohi māregā, aur koi māregā nāhīm*
> *Kyom maut maro gīdar ki, apne sūt laho krpān*
>
> If someone insults you, don't speak. If they insult you again, don't use your sword.
> If they insult you a third time, plunge a dagger into their face.
>
> *Ek gālī par nā bolu, dūsrī par nā karu talwār*
> *Tīsrī gālī par, mumh mein thūms du tarwār*

As in these cases, Het Ram's songs lacked direct reference to caste, but they emerged out of intense feelings of discrimination and were geared toward provoking anger, determination and courage in their Chamar audience through general references to heroic action.

Nangal's new politicians were more explicit in their denunciations of caste and their speeches engaged more tangibly with questions of political and social change in Nangal. Building on Khare (1984), we identify four key 'moments' in the cultural production of *naye netās* in relation to caste, politics and social transformation. First, they identified a set of ideas imposed upon them by others that they imagined as oppressive, illegitimate and repugnant. Second, they established the capacity of the marginalized to resist stigma and subordination. Third, they located and sought to remove their disadvantages with reference to a new cultural ideology based upon formal education. Finally, they pointed to the role of the state in supporting their efforts to eliminate accumulated deprivations. The remainder of this chapter discusses these four 'moments.' We refer particularly to the two most active social animators among new politicians in Nangal: Brijpal and Yashvir. Yashvir was married with two young sons and came from a family owning one acre of land and living in a village close to Nangal. Having failed to find salaried employment, Yashvir worked on a temporary basis at a private school. Across rural Bijnor district, we met several educated un/under-employed Dalit young men who had become private teachers, and some of these men labeled themselves 'new politicians.'

Identifying Oppression

Naye netās sought to provoke anger and moral indignation among other Chamars by referring to continued caste discrimination in the village. They circulated these ideas during functions at the AYO or in public gatherings in Nangal. But they also discussed the evils of casteism (*jatiwād*) during everyday conversations around the village. Many of these statements focused on routine forms of caste discrimination perpetrated by the Jats. For example, in a discussion with other Dalits in a public (mixed caste) area of the village, Brijpal told us:

Look at the atrocities committed by Hindus! They dump their liquor bottles close to Dalit houses. They have made liquor so cheap so that Dalits can buy it. Hindus do not accept that god is for everyone. No-one can buy god. We won't stay silent. We will raise our voices against these atrocities [atyāchār]. We will tell other people that we are not below anyone. We want to have equal rights [haq] in the eyes of society.

In this and other cases new politicians used observations regarding everyday casteist practice to make broader points about the continuing social and spatial isolation of Dalits.

Our conversations with these men did not support the recent argument made by Deliège (2002) that ideas of untouchability are 'disappearing' in India. Indeed, we observed several instances in which Dalit new politicians spoke explicitly about the continued practice of untouchability (see also Lerche 1999; Frøystad 2005; Ciotti 2006). For example, during a group discussion among Dalits, Brijpal remembered that:

One woman here lifts her sari right up to her knees in case some Chamar child somewhere might touch it! If some Chamar had touched her handpump, then she will wash it 10 times, will perform a religious ceremony and only then consider it clean [sāf-pāk]. If any Chamar sits on her bed, then she will wash the entire bed, so that once it is clean again she can sit on it. Here in the Hindu religion there is a great deal of discrimination [bhed bhāv].

New politicians claimed that the introduction of regular village-level elections occasionally offered opportunities for Dalits to obtain favors from Jat candidates, in line with the research of Gupta (1998) in Bulandshahr district. But netās typically offset these observations with references to the long-term marginalization of the Dalits and their vulnerability to caste discrimination and aggression. Yashvir argued loudly that:

These Hindus remember us because of votes or when they have to rape one of our sisters or wives, then, in order to escape the court, they call us their own. And when there is no need for our vote, then they dishonor us. It is only to escape punishment that we become their 'brothers.' And when there is any atrocity perpetrated against us, then they break the connection with us.

As this assertion also suggests, physical and sexual violence perpetrated by Jats against Dalits, especially Dalit women, was a recurrent theme of netās' discourses which repeatedly returned to the subject of caste-based 'atrocities.'

Chamar netās also referred to caste discrimination within schools. They remembered being mocked and unfairly punished by teachers and pupils, marked down in examinations and made to perform humiliating punishments. Brijpal spoke bitterly of his efforts to avoid being stigmatized among his peers:

I didn't keep it [my caste identity] quiet. If I had stayed quiet then the upper castes would have openly insulted me by making jokes about Dalits. After I had said that I'm a Dalit, at least I knew that they wouldn't insult me to my face. Of course they carried on behind my back, but who looks at what's happening behind one's back?

Other *netās* said that they tried to avoid open caste discrimination within educational institutions by obscuring their caste background or choosing schools with high proportions of Chamar students.

Establishing Dalits' Capacity to Resist

The discussion of caste discrimination was often a preface to new politicians' descriptions of Dalit political agency. *Netās* argued for Chamars' capacity to resist oppression by referring to a small number of Dalit 'great men' who had triumphed in the face of higher caste injustices. *Netās* derived these stories from the speeches of Dalit political leaders and they sometimes aped the gestures and rhetorical devices of leading politicians. Brijpal spoke passionately in his clipped Sanskritized Hindi:

Jagjivan Ram[2] visited a Hindu temple and afterwards they washed the whole temple with milk! They thought that the whole temple had been defiled by Jagjivan Ram's visit. So you see the huge differences that people construct in their minds? We should oppose any religion in which people believe temples are ruined by Dalits' feet. Jotirao Phule[3] was invited to a Thakur [upper caste] wedding. A Hindu priest was reading from a sacred text. When the priest saw Jotirao Phule he said: "Who invited him to the wedding? This has made the whole wedding pointless! The marriage has been ruined! Who invited him?" When people heard the priest's words, the Thakurs said, "*Pandit ji* what can we do?" The priest replied, "Something can still be achieved by beating the Chamar over the head with some shoes and driving him back home." On hearing this, the upper castes did what the priest had said. They beat Phule and sent him home. Phule was badly insulted by this. He decided that he should commit suicide. He saw no point in living when he wasn't going to be given any respect. While traveling along a road, Jotirao met

---

[2]Jagjivan Ram (1908–86) was a Chamar from Bihar who became a leading figure in the Congress movement from the 1930s onwards.

[3]Jotirao Phule (1827–90) was a member of the 'untouchable' Mali (market gardener) caste who became a prominent low caste activist in south India.

another Chamar who asked him, "Jotirao, where are you going?" Jotirao replied that he was going to kill himself. The Chamar said that dying is not a solution to the problem of disrespect. "You must fight for your rights [*haq*]," he said.

At this point our Muslim research assistant, Shaila, asked Brijpal about the identity of Jotirao Phule. Brijpal's answer was instructive:

Jotirao Phule got the first BA. It was in his name that the name of the Rohilkhand University was changed. So he was a Chamar, a very intelligent person.

Brijpal's identification of Phule (a member of the Mali *jāti*) as a Chamar suggested his eagerness to link the battles of *naye netās* in Nangal to a much broader *Dalit* struggle against injustice. But the broader point we take from Brijpal's speech is his determination to place educated Dalit men and masculinities at the center of an account of effective resistance to higher caste oppression. In this and other cases Brijpal built a narrative of Dalit progress through struggle around the figure of the educated Dalit man equipped with the stoicism, intelligence and resolve required to counter entrenched injustice. The audience's appreciation of these narratives did not seem to reside in the presentation of something strikingly new but in the accomplished and stirring performance of a known story and in the emotional power of references to shame, suffering and resistance.

New politicians said that Dr. Ambedkar's emphasis on the ability of Dalit elites to mobilize the low caste poor was a constant source of inspiration, and Ambedkar figured prominently in Dalit motivational speeches. In a small courtyard surrounded by Dalit households, Yashvir told Craig, Shaila and an audience of roughly fifteen Chamars and Jats:

There was once a Round Table Conference.[4] India's biggest leaders went to it. Gandhi, Nehru and Ambedkar all went there. While people were talking at the conference, Ambedkar put a chair on his head. So the English asked, "Ambedkar *jī* what is the problem?" Ambedkar then said that Dalits in India have no place. "High castes discriminate against them. They won't sit with them. They won't eat or drink with them. Dalits sit at their feet. They keep the Dalits in slavery." Ambedkar then said: "Tell me one thing: should the first train into a station be the first one to leave or should a later train leave

---

[4]This speech refers to the Second Round Table Conference held in London in 1931 when Ambedkar opposed Gandhi's claim to represent all Hindus including 'untouchables'.

first? You people are discussing India's freedom. But even before Britain enslaved India, Dalits were enslaved by high castes. So first you should set us free, only after that should you give India freedom." The English then asked Nehru and Gandhi whether that is how they behave with Dalits. Gandhi and Nehru then denied that this is the situation in India. They said that they do not differentiate between castes and that Ambedkar was telling lies. Ambedkar then said to the English, "You go yourselves and see the situation."

An inquiry was then sent to India to find out about this [the condition of untouchables]. So Nehru and Gandhi went in the middle of the night and distributed *dhotīs*, *kurtās* and *topīs* [loin-cloths, shirts and hats] among the Dalits. The clothes were a brilliant white [*safed-jhak*] with a touch of indigo added. When the Dalits put on the *dhotī-kurtī* they were happy and Gandhi and Nehru embraced them [*gale lagānā*]. Gandhi and Nehru said: "We're all brothers. There's no difference between us." They then said that if anyone comes and asks, they should say that Gandhi and Nehru are like brothers. The next day the inquiry came to the Dalits. The Dalits said that Ambedkar is telling lies: "Gandhi and Nehru are like brothers to us. We eat with them and we sit next to them." Ambedkar cried a lot when he found out that *dhotīs* and *topīs* had been given as an incentive. He said, "Two men have cheated 140 million people."

But Ambedkar was very well educated. He was a jurisprudent [*vidhi-vettā*] and had great knowledge of the law. He alone wrote the Constitution. No-one else had as much knowledge. He was very qualified [*qābil*]. Even then, he was one of us. He wrote the Constitution [of India]. Otherwise, the high castes would have written it for themselves. He wrote sections [*dhārāye*], paragraphs [*anu-chchhed*] and notes [*tippanīya*] in an excellent way. He wrote the constitution, but even then he thought about Dalits and gave them reservations.

Brijpal also spoke in reverent tones of Ambedkar's resolve, particularly with reference to Ambedkar's decision to convert to Buddhism in protest against caste discrimination.[5] Brijpal said that in the early 1990s he decided to follow Ambedkar's example and convert from Hinduism to Buddhism. Brijpal:

Why should we believe in a religion in which there is no respect [*sammān*] for us? These Hindus do not look at us with good gazes, they do not give us respect. So why should we believe in this religion?

Of the six *netās* in Nangal, three had converted to Buddhism. Brijpal spoke

[5]Ambedkar vowed in 1936 to seek a religion that offered 'liberty, equality, and fraternity' and that did not lend ideological support to economic oppression. In 1956, Ambedkar publicly converted to Buddhism in Nagpur, central India, together with roughly 500,000 other ex-untouchables (see Omvedt 1994; Jaffrelot 2005). Fewer than twenty Chamars in Nangal had converted to Buddhism.

of Buddhism as India's authentic and original religion. He imagined Buddhists as internationalists, whose faith provided a means of looking across borders and assisting marginalized groups. Brijpal cited the international outcry at the Taliban's destruction of Buddhist statues at Bamiyan as evidence of Buddhism's global reach, and he maintained that Buddhists in China, Africa, Sri Lanka and Japan would intervene on behalf of India's Dalits.

The efforts of new politicians such as Brijpal and Yashvir to inspire and mobilize Dalits through reference to a selection of Dalit 'great men' parallel the political strategies of local Dalit political leaders in urban UP (Jaoul 2007). Jaoul has recently written of a vibrant symbolic politics among Dalits in the UP city of Kanpur that makes similar use of stories of Dalit humiliation and enjoins ex-untouchables to resist upper caste oppression through reference to Ambedkar's example. As in the Nangal case, the Kanpur *netās* described by Jaoul do not typically have close links with political parties or positions in government employment but trade instead on their charisma and rhetorical skill.

Promoting a New Cultural Ideology

To a greater extent perhaps than Jaoul (2007), however, we want to emphasize the importance of education as a new cultural ideology undergirding new politicians' struggles (see also Ciotti 2006). In spite of their exclusion from salaried work, Chamar *netās* were among the most energetic advocates of the idea that education provides valuable skills, knowledge and civilization. Brijpal's zeal in describing the 'benefits of education' (*parhāī kā fāydā*) typified the attitudes and demeanor of Chamar *netās*. Brijpal stressed the importance of being able to read and write Hindi and make basic mathematical calculations in order to challenge entrenched caste power. He said that education offers knowledge of local politics, legal matters and social and political dynamics occurring outside the village. Brijpal also believed that formal education provides a basis for Dalit intelligence (*hoshiyārī*) and ensures that they are self-aware (*jāgarūk*), individually and collectively. In this vein, Brijpal explained that his education was crucial to his ability to act as a gatekeeper to the local state. He argued that as an educated man he is able to store information about the peccadilloes of numerous government officials and cultivate the requisite balance of confidence and humility required to "get work done."

Like other young men, new politicians elaborated on ideas of formal education as a basis of social worth with reference to the alleged differences between
'educated' and 'uneducated' people. *Netās* tended to agree that someone with
an Eighth Class pass was 'educated' and a person who dropped out of school
before this stage was not. More than other educated un/under-employed young
men, however, *netās* emphasized the importance of education in instilling civilization and self-belief. Reflecting the views of other *netās*, Brijpal told us:

The greatest benefit of education is the appearance of civilization that it provides. Men
become civilized. They develop good manners. Others see the benefits: they know that
we are well-mannered. . . . Educated people fearlessly demand their rights. Education
provides so much confidence that the educated aren't afraid of any [government] official. And people don't try any nonsense with the educated because they know that the
educated possess knowledge and understanding of the law.

Netās discussed confidence with reference to the terms *himmat* or *hauslā*, which
commonly connoted courage in the face of adversity. But they were equally eager to stress the importance of *self-confidence* encapsulated in the Hindi phrase
atm-vishvās. Reflecting a commonly-held view, one *netā* asked, "How can I expect others to respect me, if I do not respect myself?"

Netās used ideas of the iconic importance of education to critique caste as
a measure of social worth. They argued that a person's ability to acquire and
display an educated demeanor offers a more appropriate basis for assessing
their standing in society than caste (*jāti*). *Netās* used a strongly moral discourse
with reference to those aspects of Chamars' 'habitus' formerly associated with
their caste subordination. They praised the meticulous hygiene and careful
self-presentation characteristic of educated Dalits, "whose homes are so clean
that the flies slip off the surfaces." *Netās* contrasted images of educated Chamar
cleanliness and order with those of higher caste young men who drink alcohol,
refuse to wash and greedily hoard money in their houses. This critique was
directed not only at local Jats but at a much broader regional history of neglect
and discrimination. In insisting upon education rather than caste as a measure
of respect, Chamar *naye netās* criticized and sought to replace the abstract categories employed by the state to label them, such as 'Scheduled Caste' or 'Below
the Poverty Line (BPL),' and stress their entitlement to participate in modern
politics as knowing, moral, erudite agents.

As in the case of Jats, Chamars' sense of themselves as *educated people* involved them in renegotiating their relationship to the local environment. These new environmental subjectivities entailed stressing their remove from the "dust and soil" of the village and determination to improve Chamar neighborhoods of Nangal. In discussing the idea of a new Chamar hostel in Nangal, several *netās* repeatedly emphasized that it should be neat and clean (*sāf suthrā*). New politicians regularly expressed their enthusiasm for local spaces imagined as 'ordered' and 'hygienic': parks, English-medium schools and middle class suburbs in Bijnor.

But in espousing education as an alternative measure of respect, *netās* offered a limited critique of the caste system. They did not seek to eradicate social hierarchies or associated forms of subordination, but argued instead that these stigmatizing labels should not be attached to them as 'educated people' (cf. Lynch 1969; Khare 1984; Gooptu 1993). Brijpal maintained that higher castes who behaved in the manner of illiterates deserved disrespect. Indeed, his ultimate goal was to invert the caste system so that Chamars stood "right at the top." This point emerged with startling clarity during a conversation with Brijpal regarding the challenges facing Chamar politicians. As we were talking, Brijpal drew an expensive roller ball pen out of his top pocket. Brijpal: "You have to imagine that society today is like this." He placed the pen with its nib pointing toward the sky. "The Brahmins are the nib of the pen, the *kshatriyas* are its upper portion, the *vaishyas* are the lower portion, the *shudras* are still further down, and we—the Dalits—are at the base." Brijpal paused to check that we had understood. "We are trying to make society like this." He moved the pen to a horizontal position. Slowly a smile began to play across his face. "But my dream is for society to be like this." Brijpal moved the pen through another ninety degrees so that the nib was pointing toward the floor. "The Dalits would be at the top!" He continued:

But we lack the power to put us at the top [*ūpar*] and the high castes at the bottom [*nīche*]. We simply do not have the power for such a massive change. How could we achieve so much?

Brijpal moved the pen back through ninety degrees so that it was horizontal. "For this reason, we are striving for equality." In this way, Brijpal explained that *naye netās'* quest for equality and mutual respect was pragmatic rather than ideological; while Dalit supremacy is the ultimate aim, equality is a more achievable goal.

Similarly, Chamar *netās* were ambivalent about the possibility of including Muslims in their quest for power. On certain occasions, Brijpal and his peers stressed that they were 'raising their voice' on behalf of all oppressed communities, in line with the idea of a '*bahujan samāj*' ('majority of society'). But we met many Muslims who disagreed with this assessment, saying that the BSP did not reliably represent their interests. Indeed, Chamar *netās* also sometimes emphasized their own progress through reference to the relative 'backwardness' (*pīche*) of rural Muslims, who they depicted as having too many children, possessing little interest in education and being somehow more intimately connected to the "dust and soil" of the village.

These contradictions in the cultural ideologies of new politicians opened up space for Jats to contest *naye netās'* visions of education as a basis for Chamar respect. Several educated un/under-employed Jat young men argued that new politicians lacked 'proper' (*thīk*) schooling credentials or were only *shaksha* (qualified) not *shikshit* (educated). They also said that *naye netās* retain certain distinctive markers that single them out as uncouth, such as nasalizing their vowel sounds, engaging in inappropriately showy acts of consumption or failing to appreciate the 'true value' of education.

The contradictions of new politicians' discourses of education as civilization also created tensions between *netās* and their parents. Among the Jats discussed in Chapter Four, the schooling experiences of educated young men and their parents were relatively similar, and the fathers of almost all Jat educated young men possessed high school qualifications. By contrast, none of the fathers of Dalit new politicians had spent more than five years in formal education and only one of their mothers had any school experience. New politicians insisted that honoring one's senior kin is an important attribute of the educated person, but they nevertheless sometimes referred to their parents as backward, dull (*sust*) or lacking in intelligence (*hoshiyārī*), and many parents felt embarrassed and angry at being labeled in this manner. Parents stressed the time, money and energy they had invested in educating their sons as indicative of their knowledge and good sense.

Appealing for Government Assistance

In contrast to the new politicians studied by Jaoul (2007), who frequently stressed their opposition to political interference, *netās* argued that effective Dalit political mobilization could only occur through the capture of state power and that the BSP leader, Mayawati, was capable of radically improving Chamars' political prospects. In the view of Nangal's *naye netās*, Mayawati had already reformed the UP bureaucracy and improved Dalits' access to a variety of government programs. Brijpal proudly showed off a book on Mayawati's life entitled *The Iron Lady* while speaking of her determination to ensure that government officials assist disadvantaged groups. That Mayawati was a former schoolteacher was significant: she was seen as embodying an ideology of progress through formal schooling. Brijpal claimed that, during Mayawati's tenure as Chief Minister, teachers had arrived at local schools promptly and government bureaucrats had been compelled to curb corruption and discriminatory practices. Building on these observations, Brijpal argued that the BSP is capable of creating an environment conducive to the expression of a new Dalit educated courage (*himmat*) and unity (*ektā*).

Brijpal was convinced that Mayawati's return to government would trigger wide-ranging reform of the police, judiciary and other arms of the local state. This faith was founded in part on a vision of the BSP building links across social divides to establish a common program of action among the 'majority of society' in UP. Brijpal emphasized Mayawati's equal treatment of Dalits, Muslims and OBCs. Also underlying their belief in the BSP was a sense that the government might effectively address problems of Dalit poverty and social isolation through policies aimed at improving Dalit representation within educational institutions and government. *Netās* energetically advanced the view that, while inadequate as a basis for wholesale Dalit empowerment, SC reservations are an important tool for social mobility and a symbol of Ambedkar's political labor.

The Popular Receptions of *Netās'* Ideas

In circulating discourses critical of upper caste discrimination, identifying a new cultural ideology distinct from caste and stressing the capacity for the state to assist in processes of Chamar empowerment, *netās* played a crucial role in politicizing the local population. New politicians' narratives had enhanced public awareness of caste discrimination, or at least provided opportunities for rural Chamars to voice an awareness of discrimination. *Netās* had also encouraged discussion of party and regional politics in the village, generated support for Mayawati and the BSP and contributed in numerous less tangible ways to raising the political awareness of rural people. Chamars frequently said that they had learnt about their rights by listening to men like Brijpal and young Chamars in Nangal remembered particularly inspiring Dalit teachers in their schools from whom they absorbed political ideas. Moreover, *naye netās'* narratives of education had been important in persuading parents of the value of sustained mainstream schooling. The following statement from an uneducated Chamar laborer in his late fifties—the neighbor and friend of a *nayā netā*—was typical of ideas we heard repeatedly in our interviews with Chamar parents in Nangal:

Educated children learn a lot about good behavior: about the benefits and damage of different things and about cleanliness and health. . . . The thing that I want is for education to change the aura [*māhaul*] of our home. For example, I am illiterate and I would shout loudly, "Bring me tea," but the educated person remains silent before tea is brought. The educated bring a tray with a kettle and teacups to a table, but we would just serve tea in an iron pot. So this is the difference between the educated and the illiterate.

But *naye netās* had been only partially effective in convincing other Chamars of their vision of progress. Chamars frequently challenged *netās'* vision of Dalits' collective strength. Chamars commonly argued that they lacked the unity (*ektā*) required to engage in movement-based politics or launch a strong bid for state power. A Chamar woman told us:

All the people in our brotherhood [Dalits] are fighting one another. They don't have unity. One lot go east while another lot go west: they can't go along together. And actually our people [Dalits] are all poor. No-one listens to the poor. Everything is a result of poverty.

Many Chamars said that the poor are socially isolated, and that even close relatives avoid associating with impoverished households. Chamars frequently recounted a popular local saying: "Even the dogs don't approach the empty handed."

Furthermore, some parents complained that education offered only an 'empty promise.' They talked instead of the dignity of labor, value of learning outside school and educational importance of life experience (*anu-bhav*). In a discussion with several Chamar laborers in Nangal, for example, one parent said that his nephew's education occurred "in the brick-kilns and fields: through labor." Some Chamars cited the examples of Nangal's *netās* as indicative of the failures of school education. They mocked the pretensions of *naye netās* and characterized their speeches and story-telling as overblown and even ridiculous.

Most Chamars were also skeptical about the potential for Mayawati to transform people's lives. Chamars said that they vote for the BSP and that Mayawati's tenure as Chief Minister had been of 'some benefit,' for example in ensuring that government officials arrived at work on time. But many Chamars argued that their problems were too acute, varied and entrenched to be solved by the BSP. Similarly, they said that SC reservations in Government employment amounted to a sop thrown to Dalits to prevent widespread unrest. These Chamars often went on to argue that a government truly committed to raising Dalits' position in society would improve laborers' rights, living conditions and wages and their access to basic education, health care and infrastructural facilities.

This political skepticism strongly reflects the continued subordination of Chamars within economic hierarchies in Nangal and the daily realities of poverty. Despite piecemeal state attempts to redistribute land under Indira Gandhi's government in the 1970s, the Chamars possess less than 8 percent of the total agricultural land in the village and their plots are concentrated in the least fertile areas. Our village census also pointed to a lack of economic progress among Chamar households between 1990 and 2001, measured in terms of consumer good ownership and the ability to extend or strengthen their houses. During our survey of Nangal in February-March 2001 and interviews over the following year we heard twelve accounts of Chamars failing to obtain timely and complete payment of their wages from Jat employers and sixteen stories of Jats' attempts to coerce Chamars to work in the fields. Many of these stories were told by women who often suffered the worst consequences of marginalization and Jat social dominance, including violent attack, sexual harassment and rape. In 2001 there were floods in Nangal that further exposed the vulnerability of Chamar livelihood strategies and instilled a new urgency in their discussions of their quest for a living wage, decent living conditions, protection from higher caste harassment and basic medical and educational goods.

Disillusioned by *netās*' narratives of progress, and their associated ideas of acquiring power through education and state-led development, Chamars, especially women, occasionally stressed the need for more radical and violent political resistance. They talked of their desire to "tear down Jat houses" or "set Jat fields alight" in order to improve Dalits' prospects and protest against the perpetuation of semi-feudal social relations within agriculture. We heard versions of the following statement, made by an uneducated Chamar woman, many times during our field research:

Someone should set fire to the Jats' fields since they do not give laboring work and they only give us leafy sugar cane tops [as payment for cutting cane]. In my heart, I want to go into the Jat fields and set fire to them. We [Chamars] go to do laboring work in the Jat fields and these bastards swear at us and we come home dejectedly. May they be cursed, may they become ill, may their children not be able to walk. In their hearts, the Jats do not want the Chamars to be able to have stoves burning in their homes, that Chamar children should die hungry. They will be doomed. I get very angry about the Jats. They make us work like animals the whole day in their fields, and when the afternoon comes, they give us leafy sugar cane tops in place of money. God alone will make justice for us. We have to endure their tyranny.

Another Chamar woman who worked as a laborer for the Jats told us:

There is no daily wage labor here, people are forced to go outside to earn money and they come back here to defecate. And Jats even benefit when we defecate in their fields, because some time later it turns into fertilizer! Poor people can eat and drink nothing. Grain is Rs 30 for 2.5 kg and that is cooked daily, so they do not even get enough food.

Rather than imagining progress to occur through the empowerment of their own community, Chamars in Nangal more commonly argued that their own social improvement depended upon the destruction of higher caste power: a leveling *down* rather than leveling *up*. One uneducated Chamar laborer told us:

We're fed up with our poverty [*garībī se tang āgaye haim*]. It feels like there should be an earthquake here like the one in Maharashtra [referring to the Gujarat earthquake of February 2001]. Everything would be finished, neither the patient [the poor] nor the illness [poverty] would remain.

Pointing at three-storied brick-built Jat houses in Nangal, a Chamar man who worked as an agricultural laborer told us:

Now you look over there at those high houses. Now look back in our direction. Here no-one has a good house, no-one has any land. We don't have enough grain to eat and look at them! They have grain standing inside their big houses. So when this difference is eliminated, only then will we build a *bahujan samāj* [movement for the majority of society].

Many Chamars therefore perceived development (*vikās*) as a process that must be creative *and* destructive, one centrally concerned with removing power from dominant groups.

Conclusions

Educated un/under-employment has provided fertile ground for the growth of a small cohort of 'new politicians' who were trying to raise the standing and confidence of their community and express subaltern voice. The political support accorded to Dalits had meant that they emerged in particular within the Chamar caste in rural Bijnor district. Chamar *naye netās* were changing how the rural poor relate to the state. This cultural project is part of regional processes of identity formation and mobilization. But, as in the case of Jat social mobility, the rise of *netās* does not represent a broad-based collective effort at raising the position of the whole caste in a process akin to sanskritization (see Srinivas 1989; Charsley 1998). Rather, and in line with Mendelsohn (1993), the rise of *netās* reflects a more fragmented process of social uplift whereby a small number of educated men seek to improve the social standing of their households and community outside the parameters of the Hindu caste system.

The oppositional political mobilization we have described fails to accord with images of the educated un/under-employed as hostile, destabilizing and anomic. Nor did Chamar *naye netās* inhabit an authentic space of subaltern resistance somehow inevitably opposed to the political vocabulary and ideological goals of the post-colonial state, rural capitalist expansion or patriarchal power. We have described instead *naye netās'* accommodation, negotiation and lobbying, forms of political endeavor oriented around a moral narrative of education, financed in part by people's engagement in capitalist production and centrally concerned with co-opting the local state.

Our description of *naye netās*' practices provides some support for Pai's (2000) and Jaffrelot's (2003) accounts of Dalit political mobility and Sen's much broader vision of education as freedom. Prolonged schooling has provided some Chamar young men with the skills, knowledge and confidence to act as representatives for their wider community and circulate new political ideas. Moreover, *naye netās* vigorously sought to convince others of the benefits of education. But new politicians' visions of transformation ran far ahead of local social and economic realities. Most Chamars in Nangal were poorly connected to patronage networks centered on government and were pessimistic about the future. Seeds of doubt about formal education's value in delivering substantive freedoms had taken root alongside the flourishing of discourses celebrating schooling's transformative power.

The disjuncture between our study and those of Pai (2000) and Jaffrelot (2003) reflects methodological differences. Jaffrelot's history of lower caste political change lacks close reflection on the links between national level policy changes and everyday social praxis. Pai (2000) is more attentive to these connections, but, like Krishna (2002), she moves too readily from the accounts of a small group of Dalit 'intellectuals' to draw broad conclusions about social upheaval. Pai also studied highly unusual villages: semi-urbanized settlements with a plentiful supply of off-farm employment in a prosperous part of western UP. Gupta's (1998) more ethnographic analysis of changing rural politics reflects to a greater extent on the diversity of Dalits' political sensibilities. But he worked in a village where almost all Dalits owned land and which lacked a strong class of rich farmers; unusually for villages in western UP at that time, only one of the rich farmers in Alipur owned a tractor in the early 1980s. Pai and Gupta might respond by arguing that Nangal itself is in some way 'unusual.' But in as far as Nangal is atypical, it is in ways that would make it *more* not *less* likely that social transformation would be occurring: Nangal possesses a relatively high proportion of Chamars and is located in a district historically associated with the rise of Mayawati.

We have therefore provided an alternative account to optimistic readings of

Dalit empowerment. Our appeal is for a closer engagement in studies of north Indian political change with what Li (2005) calls 'metis,' which she defines as contextualized forms of knowledge and practice that lie outside the purview of state planners, and which tend to be ignored in much political science research. We return to this point in Chapter Eight. First, however, we consider the practices of educated un/under-employed Muslim young men (Chapter Six) and discuss the strategies of educated un/under-employed Dalit young men who are from poorer backgrounds than those of the *netās* (Chapter Seven).

6

Muslims' Strategies in an Age of Insecurity

Zamir

Craig first met Zamir in November 2000 cycling along the road between Qaziwala and Bijnor. Craig was returning from Qaziwala after a morning of interviews in the village and Zamir was going to Bijnor for a tutorial. Twenty-four at the time, Zamir came from a moderately well-off Muslim Sheikh family. He was unmarried and had five brothers and three sisters. On this first meeting, Zamir spoke enthusiastically about his involvement in a karate school in Bijnor, his skill as a farmer and his membership of "Heavenly Gym," a new fitness center on the edge of Bijnor. "I want to become like the very best heroes, with a strong mind, powerful body and pure spirit." Over the following year, Zamir became a friend and eager informant.

Zamir's 'typical day' gives a sense of his dynamism. He rose each day at 5 AM, ran five miles and returned to milk the family's buffaloes. Between 7 AM and 10 AM, Zamir worked on the land. His father, Iqbal, suffered from a long-term illness and it had fallen to Zamir, as eldest son, to take on farming responsibilities. Zamir prepared, sowed, irrigated and fertilized the land, collected buffalo dung, drove and maintained the tractor, supervised laborers on the farm, checked on marketing arrangements and kept accounts. When Craig cycled into Qaziwala village each morning, he often saw Zamir driving his tractor along the main village street: "I'll teach you to drive this thing one day. It's good fun!" At 10 AM, Zamir cycled three miles to Bijnor for a computer class. At noon, he cycled back to the village to continue farming work. At 3 PM, Zamir returned to Bijnor for karate practice followed by either an English or Advanced Accountancy tutorial. He then cycled back to Qaziwala again at 5:30 PM. Zamir said that the rest of his day entailed studying for his BCom. When we repeated his 'typical day' to check that we had the schedule right, Zamir grinned and said: "You have forgotten one thing—I never forget to pray five times a day."

Zamir's parents, Iqbal and Feroza, spoke earnestly of the transformative potential of education. They said that children require religious education (*dīnī tālīm*) *and* worldly education (*duniyā ki parhāī*) to lead full and successful lives. The family believed that Hindi education was important for obtaining salaried employment and for reading documents, road signs and the instructions on medicine bottles. But they perceived religious education to be a source of knowledge about morality, manners and religious good practice. Iqbal and Feroza had enrolled Zamir at the Qaziwala government primary school at the same time as encouraging him to attend the Begawala madrasah. While studying in Begawala, Zamir learnt to read and write Urdu and recite the *Qu'rān Sharīf* from memory (*Hāfiz Qu'rān*). In spite of this success, however, he saw his future in mainstream education. At the age of about 12, Zamir left both the government primary school and the Begawala madrasah to enter secondary school at Bijnor Inter College (BIC), a Hindi-medium private school that was run by a Muslim committee, appointed its own teachers, and enrolled a large number of Muslim students. Iqbal and Feroza lacked the money required to send Zamir to one of the English-medium schools used by Jats. After passing his Tenth Class examinations from BIC, Zamir moved to the Government Inter College in Bijnor and then to a government degree college in Bijnor, where, by 2001, he was studying for a BCom. Zamir also received tutorials in English and Accounting, which cost him Rs. 350 a month each, and he attended computer classes outside school.

Yet Zamir had been unable to obtain government work. During a physical test for the army, the doctor told him that his heart rate was too fast. His father said that Zamir should have given the doctor a bribe (*rishwat*). Zamir stated that something like a 'price list' exists for different government jobs. At the bottom of the scale, he said, people pay about Rs. 40,000 or Rs. 50,000 to become a police officer, while at the top of the price list, people might spend Rs. 400,000 to secure the post of District Magistrate. Zamir: "Three things are necessary to get a salaried job: of most importance is money, then social contacts, then knowledge."

Zamir had used a portion of the profits from his land to finance his enrollment at a private computing course in Bijnor. He claimed that candidates for computer-related jobs were less likely to have to pay bribes. According to Zamir, people without computing skills who use bribes to secure government employment that entailed computing found it impossible to maintain their position. He said that people in a government office ask a new appointee, "You've got the job, but what can you do on the computer?" As a result, Zamir perceived computing as a means of obtaining government employment without having to pay a bribe. He said that if he failed to obtain a government post he would either work on his family farm or enter business. Zamir told us: "One of my dreams is to leave the village, start a profitable business and then come back to help Qaziwala. I would build a high school for the poor, improve all facilities, banish poverty." By the end of 2001, however, Zamir had started to visit Delhi to explore opportunities to enter embroidery or tailoring work in the capital either as an apprentice or small-scale entrepreneur.

Valuing Education

There are specific aspects of Zamir's case that make him unusual in Qaziwala. Owing to his father's illness, he had greater say over his future than most other Muslim young men. Moreover, Zamir's family was wealthier than many Muslims in Qaziwala and belonged to the relatively advantaged Sheikh caste. Notwithstanding these points, Zamir's case provides insights into the position and practices of educated young men in Qaziwala more broadly. This section of the chapter discusses these insights with reference to the mood of educated Muslims' and their perceptions of education. In the next section, we discuss Muslims' attempts to find what they regard as 'good work' outside the sphere of government employment. Finally, we consider two sets of threats to these strategies: from uneducated Muslim young men with alternative visions of education and from growing religious communalism in the region.

The discussion in this chapter relates primarily to the 45 Muslim young men in Qaziwala aged between twenty and thirty-four in 2000 who had obtained an Eighth Class pass, whom we term 'school-educated' in the remainder of the chapter to distinguish them from a second set of seven 'madrasah-educated' Muslims in Qaziwala, who had not obtained an Eighth Class pass but had extensive experience of madrasah education. Forty of the 45 school-educated men are Sheikhs, and 32 of this set were from households possessing more than 2.5 acres of land. The five non-Sheikh school-educated Muslims were from landless households or families possessing very small plots. Five of the seven madrasah-educated Muslims were Sheikhs and they came from households possessing more than 2.5 acres of land. The other two madrasah-educated young men came from landless households. The terms 'school-educated' and 'madrasah-educated' should not obscure the diverse character of Muslim young men's educational experiences: many of the 'school-educated' had studied in madrasahs for long periods and all the 'madrasah-educated' had at least Fifth Class Hindi.

Like Zamir, most Muslim young men had entered school in the hope of obtaining a government job. In many cases, young men said that this was a 'distant hope' (ummīd) rather than expectation. Of the 45 school-educated Muslim young men aged between 20 and 34 in 2000, roughly a third had applied for government employment. None of them had succeeded. As we noted in Chapter Two, Muslim young men tended to lack the economic, social and cultural capital required to impress government officials in competitive markets for government jobs.

Paralleling this exclusion, Muslim young men were generally unable to obtain the types of 'semi-bourgeois' employment acquired by some Jats. Only three of the 45 school-educated Muslim young men in Qaziwala in 2000 had captured a private service position. Muslims tended to lack the social connections and confidence required to enter private service work, such as jobs as salespeople within pharmaceutical companies and tutors in urban coaching institutes. Some Muslim young men communicated this exclusion by referring to their lack of the 'style' and influence necessary to enter good private service. They also mentioned encountering religious discrimination in the competition for these occupations; higher caste Hindus in Bijnor commonly labeled school-educated Muslims as 'Osama types' or 'terrorists.' Although not all Muslim young men were excluded from jobs considered 'excellent' or 'good' within private service—the presence of a sizable Muslim middle class in Bijnor created some openings for enterprising rural Muslims with good educational qualifica-tions—these opportunities were scarce relative to those open to Jats. Muslims were also poorly placed when compared to new politicians from prosperous Chamar backgrounds. Whilst possessing more land than the families of *naye netās*, even the richest Muslim Sheikhs usually lacked the social connections in local government bureaucracies required to obtain work as contractors on development projects or clerks in state offices, and they also lacked reservations in government employment.

Faced with exclusion both from government work and the modern sectors of the private service economy, one school-educated Muslim young man in Qaziwala, Rauf, spoke of intense feelings of resentment, and we discuss his case in the next chapter. Generally, however, the mood among school-educated un/under-employed Muslim young men was pragmatic and forward-looking. In a group discussion with Muslim young men, Zamir made the following state-ment, which was greeted with many expressions of agreement:

If we don't get a salaried job, we just think that it is a matter of fate [*nasīb*], fate [*taqdīr*] [repeated loudly]! If, after so much study and so much trying, we still fail to get salaried work, we become sad and angry. When we sit together, we become frustrated about this sometimes; but this frustration only lasts ten or fifteen days. We soon get over these types of problems.

Young men's broadly positive responses to the experience of failing to obtain salaried work partly reflect their continued enthusiasm for a vision of prog-ress through education. In spite of poor occupational outcomes, these men be-lieved they had benefited from spending a substantial period studying Hindi and mainstream school subjects.

School-educated Muslim young men sometimes expressed their enthusi-asm for mainstream schooling by decrying the Urdu-based, religious educa-tion taught within madrasahs. For example, a school-educated Muslim young man told us:

I have seen the education that occurs in an Urdu madrasah. I've seen big *maulwīs* who can't read where a bus is going. In a way they are very educated. But they can't tell where a bus is going; they must ask someone else. So religious schooling [*dīnī tālīm*] is one thing and being educated [*shikshit*] is something else. If you want to earn a living some-how or do some work, being educated is necessary, and it is also needed for service.

Conversely, young men educated principally within madrasahs sometimes spoke of the sole value of religious education and denigrated mainstream schooling. This point emerged powerfully in a conversation that Craig held with Feroz, a teacher at a madrasah close to Qaziwala. Sitting in the central courtyard of the madrasah drinking tea, Feroz emphasized the capacity of Islamic education to instill equanimity, tolerance and respect. He bemoaned the failure of school education to inculcate the same qualities. Feroz said:

You tell me one thing: when people block the roads, who does this? It is college students. You've never heard of madrasah students who have blocked the roads. So tell me: in whose learning is there good sense and discernment? It is a good thing not to cause people worries. If they are going on some necessary work—like someone is taking an ill person to see a doctor—and the college students block the roads, what sense is there in this? . . . In our religion it has been said that you must never ignore what a mother, father and teacher say, because these are the people who give us knowledge about religion and the world. With them we must never be disrespectful. What kind of learning do you have if you are disrespectful to your elders and betters and don't listen to what they have to say?

Feroz claimed that Urdu-based learning, unlike mainstream schools, provides knowledge of how to conduct religious practices correctly, lead moral (*aqlāqī*) lives and comport oneself in a civilized manner (*adab*). Feroz collapsed the distinction made by many other Muslims between worldly education (*duniyā ki parhāī*), taught in schools, and religious education (*dīnī tālīm*), offered in madrasahs, by identifying the *Qu'rān Sharīf* as the locus of both religious and worldly knowledge (cf. Sikand 2005).

Madrasah-educated young men elaborated on the immorality of school education with reference to the linked themes of consumption and time. Feroz and another madrasah-educated young man, Mohsin, claimed that school-educated young men had become indoctrinated into a 'false view' of time and modernity. In their view, educated men had become embroiled in the immediate pursuit of consumer goods to the neglect of spiritual reflection on the after life. In a conversation with Craig, Feroz said:

You run your life according to this world's calculations—"now I don't have this," "now I don't have that." While you carry on thinking in this way, your life will pass. But *we* live according to our religion. We don't want money in the Bank or lots of good things in our house. We just think that we should be able to eat well and feed our children well.

We think about today. We don't think about tomorrow. Allah is the master of tomorrow. We don't live only in this world; we also go to another world. We worry more about *that* world than about this world, [we worry about] where we will go after we die.

Mohsin was similarly opposed to rural consumerism and cultures of monetary wealth. He told Roger:

I earn less than you but nonetheless I am happy because I am living the Muslim way. You are not living the Muslim way and therefore your expenses are more and ours are less. We think that divine worship is very good and you think Hindi and English and Hindu things are good, that's why you have a shortage of money and we don't. If we do have a shortage, we give thanks to Allah. We say to Allah, "We give you hundreds of thousands of rupees of thanks that you have given us so much." In all conditions we thank Allah because he is the giver. People have no capacity. Everything comes from Allah's hand. He is the one who rears everything. Not even a leaf can go hither and thither except by his will.

Madrasah-educated young men were not arguing that Muslims should adhere to a former way of life, but that they should revitalize religious practices and systems of thought in order to distinguish themselves from the 'illiterates' (*an-parh*) of the village and the badly-behaved school-educated men alike.

At stake in these discussions was the very notion of what constitutes a *human* way of life. Madrasah-educated young men said that the idea of pursuing worldly wealth inculcated within mainstream schools deprives people of the moral qualities that define what it is to be human (*insān*). Feroz:

Knowledge of religion is our aim [*maqsad*] and earning a living in the world is our necessity [*zarurat*]. We must not make our necessity into our desire. Necessity is alright up to the limit of necessity. If we go beyond this, human beings cannot stay as human beings, they become animals.

Such ideas provided a contrast to the narratives of school-educated Muslim and Chamar young men, who typically referred to poverty and illiteracy as the forces confining many people to 'sub-human' or 'animal' lives.

We should not exaggerate the prevalence of the views expressed by Feroz and Mohsin, however. The other five madrasah-educated Muslim young men in Qaziwala distanced themselves from the notion that madrasah education is inevitably superior to that available within schools. For example, Irshad, a teacher in Begawala madrasah, told Craig:

Look, I'm not the type of man who thinks that children should all do religious education and become *hāfiz* or clerics. I believe that children should follow their hearts and become what they want to become, because religious education is such that, if you don't have a desire to learn, it is useless.

Irshad's statement suggests a wider point. Madrasah-educated and school-educated Muslim young men typically acknowledged the value of *both* Hindi- and Urdu-based education. This was reflected in a tendency among young men to refer to the benefits of education in general without thinking it necessary to specify a particular type of knowledge or educational regime. Like the Jats and Chamar new politicians, educated Muslim young men believed that education in this rather abstract and ideal sense changes how people converse, move, eat, think and make choices in their lives. And like other young men, Muslims used the terms 'educated' (*parhe likhe*), 'modern' and 'in possession of development' (*vikās, taraqqī*) synonymously.

Within this broader public culture of education, school- and madrasah-educated young men tended to emphasize two points in particular. First, they stressed a type of rural cosmopolitan ease founded on their capacity to negotiate between rural and urban areas and their movement between spaces and styles coded as 'religious' and 'worldly.' For example, Zamir made repeated reference to his ability to practice for computer classes while supervising sugar cane laborers in his fields, and he stressed that he never set out for English tutorials without his prayer mat tucked under his arm. Second, more than Jats and Chamars, educated Muslim young men emphasized the discipline of those who had spent long periods in mainstream schools or madrasahs, often with reference to their bodies and strength. Zamir was a case in point: he said that as an educated person he had the good judgment and equanimity required to practice karate in a responsible manner. He also claimed that as an educated person he is capable of controlling his emotions during fights: "I don't become too bothered, but I often win." Similarly, Zamir's brother, Afroz, who was training to be a *maulwī*, emphasized that he follows the strict daily madrasah regime of prayer, study, rest and refreshment. By cultivating an image of cosmopolitanism and self-control, educated Muslim young men challenged depictions of educated Muslims as violent ideologues or 'terrorists.'

As with Chamars, Muslim young men's attempts to stress the value of education acted as a limited critique of the Hindu caste system. Educated Muslim young men did not contest the idea that rural society is organized into distinct strata separated according to their accomplishments, discipline and intelligence. Rather, they stressed that education was the most important marker of difference. At the same time, and paralleling Jat discourses, we occasionally heard Muslim Sheikhs referring to lower caste Muslim Qasais as innately 'uneducated.' In these cases, Sheikhs used education to reinforce notions of caste, even whilst they challenged the religious communalism of upper caste Hindus.

While valorizing education as an ideal, school-educated Muslim young men in Qaziwala were downbeat in their discussions of local schools. The majority of these men had acquired primary education at Qaziwala Government Primary school, which they usually combined with religious education at Begawala madrasah. They then moved to government-aided inter-colleges in Bijnor or near Qaziwala. Paralleling Chamar experiences, Muslim young men usually remembered their time in school as a struggle to pass examinations, avoid harsh physical beatings and move from one class to the next. They spoke bitterly of a lack of teaching aids, physical amenities and conscientious or inspirational teaching. In particular, school-educated Muslim young men referred to the dilapidated state of the Qaziwala Government Primary School and they criticized the teachers for their absenteeism and tendency, when they did turn up, to abuse pupils and send them on errands. These men said that teachers at the aided inter-colleges they attended pressured them into taking tutorials by threatening to mark them down in examinations if they did not pay for expensive private classes outside school. Several school-educated Muslims said that the teachers in schools discriminated against Muslim pupils by delaying their progress through school and singling them out for humiliating punishments.

School-educated as well as madrasah-educated Muslim young men frequently compared the deteriorating situation in mainstream schools to the relatively high quality of education available within madrasahs. Mirroring the views of parents, educated men claimed that madrasah teachers pay closer attention to instruction, are less discriminatory and maintain better discipline—often with less physical violence—than mainstream schoolteachers. Educated men said that local madrasahs, like local mainstream schools, tend to lack facilities, but they spoke enthusiastically of the resources available within madrasahs else-where. For example, Zamir's brother, Afroz, praised the standard of education available within the madrasah he attended in Delhi: the strict daily program of activities, teachers' close attention to their progress and the grand architecture of the buildings. Reflecting this general enthusiasm for madrasah education in the context of a lack of mainstream school opportunities, educated un/under-employed Muslim young men said that, when they became parents, they would try to send their own children to a combination of schools and madrasahs.

Alternative Routes: Manual Labor and Islamic Masculinities

Farming and Artisanal Work

School-educated Muslims typically identified a range of ways in which they could maintain an educated cultural style aside from entering white-collar em-ployment. For example, one man told us:

Whether or not people find [white-collar] work, education is still necessary for every-thing. The population of India is 1000 million or more. So not everyone can get jobs in government service and not everyone can do that type of work. For this reason, edu-cation and employment are completely different things. Education is not a means of earning money. Education opens people's minds and provides knowledge of good and bad behavior. There are so many benefits associated with education that are not linked to getting a service job.

Other school-educated Muslim young men explicitly argued that people like them should not feel ashamed of entering 'hand work' (*hāth kā kām*). One told us:

If we all became the same then who would do the work? Once, poor people prayed to Allah to make them rich. Allah then made everyone equal in wealth. Allah then thought that he should give everyone a test. He made some people's houses fall down. There was then no-one to rebuild the houses. Who was there to build houses? Who could do the little work when all were the same?

While school-educated Muslim young men did not feel bound—as 'edu-cated people'—to enter 'pen work,' they said that it would be inappropriate for an educated person to become a daily wage laborer (*mazdūr*). As educated people they had no aversion to contact with the soil or machinery but they felt that they should not suffer the humiliation of working under the regular supervision of a labor contractor and being paid a daily wage. Such sentiments reflect the difficulties that daily wage laborers faced in receiving payment for the work as well as the ubiquity of verbal and physical harassment perpetrated by rural employers. Only three of the 45 school-educated Muslim young men from Qaziwala aged between 20 and 34 in 2000 had entered daily wage labor in the local area.

The majority of school-educated Muslim young men came from fairly prosperous farming households. Eight of the 45 school-educated Muslim young men in Qaziwala in 2000 had become farmers. The wealthiest Muslims could ensure that their educated sons did not perform the most grueling agricultural tasks, however. For example, within the richest Muslim household in Qaziwala, the eldest son, Dilshad, had developed a style of young 'gentlemanly farming' that mirrored Jat practices in important respects. We vividly remember Dilshad gingerly picking his way along field boundaries to avoid damaging his expensive Delhi-bought shoes while prodding the ground to check on soil quality and peering through dark glasses at the progress of laborers. Dilshad apart, though, most school-educated Muslim young men participated in manual labor on their farms. Unlike Jat young men, whose education often entailed their spending long periods under teachers', parents' or tutors' supervision, school-educated Muslims typically maintained a close connection with farming from a young age, before or after the school day, and in vacations. Moreover, few of these men would agree with those from the upper caste Hindu urban bourgeoisie who imagined agricultural labor as 'dirty' and backward.

Skilled artisanal work was an even more popular occupation than farming for school-educated Muslim young men in Qaziwala. In 2000, 20 of the 45 school-educated young men in the village worked in skilled manual employment, which they had usually obtained by using kinship and friendship connections. Of these 20, five were employed in Delhi, four in Bijnor town, four in Kashmir, three in Qaziwala and four elsewhere. Tailoring, machine embroidery and metalwork accounted for 14 of the 20 men. Nine of the 20 worked under bosses in small workshops and the other eleven were self-employed. Young men entering artisanal work under a workshop boss typically underwent an unpaid

apprenticeship of between six months and two years and then earned between
Rs. 2,000 and Rs. 6,000 a month. The earnings of self-employed skilled manual
workers varied considerably. Those who had recently set up artisanal businesses close to Qaziwala or Bijnor earned as little as Rs. 1,500 a month, roughly the
same as a manual wage laborer in the village. By contrast, some self-employed
carpenters in Bijnor earned Rs. 5,000, and young businessmen belonging to the
Nai caste running hairdressing salons or beauty parlors in Kashmir earned up
to Rs. 8,000 a month.

We interviewed 12 school-educated Muslim young men who worked as artisans, and the example of Sarfraz highlights key aspects of their experiences.
Sarfraz was twenty in 2001 and grew up in a landless Muslim household belonging to the Sukkhe caste. He was unmarried. His father, Imtiaz, was a cloth
trader in Qaziwala and earned about Rs. 2,000 a month. His mother, Rehma,
looked after Sarfraz and his four younger brothers and three younger sisters at
home. Imtiaz said that he had decided to educate his children after observing
educated Muslim young men in Qaziwala obtaining government employment.
Sarfraz took classes 1–5 at a primary school close to Qaziwala whilst also studying Urdu and *Qu'rān Sharīf* at Begawala madrasah. He then enrolled at an aided
inter-college in Bijnor for classes 6–10. Sarfraz had tried to obtain low-ranking government employment in various offices in Bijnor. He explained that,
without close social connections in the right department or the money to pay
bribes, his efforts were in vain.

In response to his failure to obtain government employment, Sarfraz joined
a Muslim-run workshop on the edge of Bijnor, where he removed dents from
cars and painted over the repaired bodywork. He said that a school friend in
Bijnor had introduced him to this job. Sarfraz was employed on a one-year,
unpaid apprenticeship. He enjoyed the work and expected to earn Rs. 3,000
a month after his apprenticeship. Sarfraz said that his job was better paid and
required greater skill than his father's work selling cloth in the villages, and
he derived satisfaction from learning about the vehicles he repaired. Sarfraz
hoped to establish his own 'painting and denting' workshop in the future. He
had investigated shop rents in Bijnor and decided upon the best position to site
a business. Imtiaz had saved Rs. 50,000 to assist Sarfraz with the Rs. 200,000
required to establish a substantial workshop in Bijnor. Although both Imtiaz

and Sarfraz expressed their opposition to the practice of demanding a dowry, Imtiaz appeared to hope that a portion of the remaining Rs. 150,000 would be obtained from Sarfraz's future wife's family as either a dowry or a loan at the time of marriage. Sarfraz also hoped that his painting and denting work might deliver up opportunities to migrate to Delhi or Saudi Arabia. Sarfraz claimed that his education enabled him to perform his work better than his uneducated peers. He said that education allows him to keep accounts, work diligently and comport himself politely with customers.

Rehma and Imtiaz believed that investing money in Sarfraz's education had not only improved his capacity to obtain and perform relatively well-paid work, but had also enhanced his marriage prospects. According to Imtiaz, education had improved Sarfraz's temperament, comportment and knowledge, such that he would be an attractive match for the parents of educated young women. Rehma and Imtiaz were hopeful that Sarfraz's future wife would assist in the education and proper upbringing of their future grandchildren. Marriages within their caste, said Rehma and Imtiaz, always take place with people who are relatives (*rishtedār*) rather than outsiders (*gair log*). Imtiaz explained their reasoning:

The advantage of this type of marriage is that we know our relatives and they know us. There is no trickery. The boy's side and the girl's side know the plus and minus points of the match.

Imtiaz added that arranging a marriage within one's 'family circle' (*khandān*) also reduces the possibility of a girl's parents complaining should her new husband not obtain 'good work.' Sarfraz was similarly positive in discussing his future marriage. He said that he wanted his wife to be at least Eighth Class pass, but he trusted his parents to make all the necessary decisions. He could not envisage his employment prospects adversely affecting the marriage negotiations or his future relationships with his wife, parents and in-laws.

As the case of Sarfraz suggests, educated Muslim young men saw no contradiction between being educated and engaging in skilled manual employment. Rather, they associated artisanal work with a type of genteel Islamic masculinity. Educated young men spoke of the dexterity, concentration and patience required to conduct such work, which they typically considered less arduous and cleaner than other forms of manual employment. Some also argued that artisanal work entailed devoting their whole bodies to acts of labor and thereby inculcated forms of embodied discipline and 'virtuous toil' (nekī mehnat). In addition, many educated Muslim young men believed that by moving to urban centers to conduct skilled artisanal work they could reinforce their status as educated people engaged in development (taraqqī). Educated Muslim young men engaged in skilled craftsmanship frequently returned from Delhi with stories of the excitement of urban life. Some educated Muslim young men also boasted that their machine embroidery work was of 'export quality' and destined for foreign markets or that working on embroidery machines was like, "driving a car very fast." The frequency of stepwise migration, whereby young men would move from working in Bijnor to Delhi or from Delhi to Ludhiana, Surat, Mumbai or Kashmir, also contributed to young men's sense of artisanal work as part of a 'route' (rāstā) to the 'modern,' and they used the English word modern to refer to their lifestyle. At the same time, most young men said that they viewed their migration as a temporary measure. They claimed that they would return to Bijnor district to establish their own businesses once they had built up sufficient wealth and experience. Our household censuses suggest that at least a third of the previous generation of educated young men who were recorded as conducting artisanal work outside Bijnor district in 1990 were back living in Qaziwala in 2000.

As in Sarfraz's case, a few educated Muslim young men believed that their craft occupations might uncover opportunities to migrate abroad. Two educated Muslim young men, both from wealthy households in Qaziwala, had migrated to the Arab Middle East to work in embroidery outlets. But Qaziwala Muslims said that it is typically necessary to pay about Rs. 200,000 to negotiate entry into artisanal work in the Middle East, and that even after paying this money many brokers trick young men. As a result, most of the educated Muslim young men chose to channel their energies into obtaining work in Bijnor, Delhi or Kashmir, where Qaziwala Muslims had been migrating since the 1970s and where they could draw on the social and financial support of friends and kin.

The case of Sarfraz also points to the connection that many educated Muslim young men made between 'being educated' and marrying well. Muslim men usually said that as educated people they would not only be able to marry a beautiful and accomplished young woman but also be able to demonstrate the empathy and equanimity required of a good husband. These men rarely worried about their in-laws becoming frustrated at their failure to find government work, often because they had married (or expected to marry) within an extended kinship group. These educated Muslim young men also claimed that few Muslim parents expected young men to enter government work. As one man commented, "Our in-laws realize that it is just a distant hope."

Religious Employment

In response to their exclusion from white-collar employment, a few madrasah-educated or school-educated Muslim young men who had obtained parallel madrasah training sought work as an Islamic cleric (*maulwī*) or teacher in a madrasah. In 2000, one school-educated and two madrasah-educated men aged between 20 and 34 had entered religious employment as teachers in madrasahs and one school-educated man taught Urdu on a temporary contract in a government-funded school. They were all Sheikhs and came from relatively rich households.

Three of these men had attended the *Daru'l `Ulūm* seminary in Deoband. *Maulwīs* at Begawala had social links to the Deoband institution and were experienced in grooming students for the *Daru'l `Ulūm* entrance examinations. The early educational career of Zamir's younger brother, Afroz, provides insights into the trajectories of young men trained in madrasahs outside the local area. Afroz was 20 in 2001 and unmarried. Between the ages of five and thirteen, he received Hindi education up to Eighth Class and Urdu-based education at Jhandapur madrasah close to Bijnor. The Jhandapur madrasah was opened in 1989 with remittance money from the Arab Middle East. In 2003, this co educational institution had roughly twenty teachers and 400 students. In addition to studying *Qu'rān Sharīf*, Urdu, Farsi and Arabic, Jhandapur pupils could follow the standard UP School Board curriculum, including Hindi and English, at a primary and lower secondary school established next to the madrasah and run by the same management. After showing more aptitude for religious education, Afroz moved first to Begawala madrasah and then to a boarding madrasah in Bihari Colony, Delhi, with his younger brother. They did not have to pay fees for the Delhi madrasah, which imposed on its male students a strict program of study, prayer and exercise. In 2001, Zamir was assisting Afroz in preparing for the examinations for *Daru'l `Ulūm*, where Afroz intended to train as a cleric. Zamir explained that out of about two hundred candidates appearing for the examination annually, the top one hundred would pass and the top fifty would receive scholarships. Afroz said that as an Islamic cleric he would not earn as much as someone in government or private service. He also told us that some school-educated Muslim young men teased peers who had left mainstream school to train as clerics by stroking long imaginary beards and calling out, "Mullah! Mullah!" But Afroz saw nothing shameful about having collected mainstream qualifications yet still wanting to do religious work. He perceived employment as a cleric as a means of becoming reasonably prosperous, pursuing opportunities to live and travel outside Bijnor district and obtaining peace of mind (*sukūn*).

Not all those in religious work agreed with Afroz's evaluation of the benefits of this employment. Educated young men working as teachers in madrasahs typically earned salaries of between Rs. 1,500 and Rs. 2,500 a month, slightly above that of local manual wage laborers, but well below the money earned by government employees or by successful artisans in urban areas. For example, Irshad began his own schooling determined to enter government employment. But his father wanted him to enter madrasah education, and Irshad eventually gave way. Now established as a teacher at Begawala madrasah, Irshad told us:

I will speak from my heart. With respect to worldly matters, I am not happy. I am poor. I don't have money because in this line there isn't much money. Now I have just one job: to please Allah. If there is nothing for me here, then I pray to Allah that I will receive my reward [*ajr*] up there.

At other moments, however, Irshad was more positive about his work: he stressed the respect accorded to madrasah teachers in the local area and the sense of moral purpose that his job provides. Indeed, most madrasah-educated young men agreed with Afroz that religious work is preferable to secular white-collar employment. They contrasted the 'straight' system through which people obtain positions as clerics with the corruption, religious discrimination and atmosphere of mistrust they encounter in the search for government work. Madrasah-educated young men also said that people employed by the state are compelled to engage in bribery, illegal favoritism and demeaning forms of flattery. Like Afroz, madrasah-educated young men emphasized the security, independence and peace of mind offered by religious work. For example, Feroz told us:

We earn about Rs. 2,000 and the people in government offices earn about Rs. 10,000. But we are still better off than the government worker because we have peace of mind [sukūn]. In this world there is a shop for everything, but there is no shop for peace of mind.

Many young men said that religious work provides religious merit (sawāb) and honor (nekī) and 'clears our path to god' (upār kā rastā hamārā sāf ho gyā). Most madrasah-educated young men perceived their religious work not as a 'fallback' form of employment that they had been forced to accept in the absence of secular white-collar work, but a prize obtained through conscientious labor and the blessings of Allah.

The Counter-narratives of 'Uneducated' Men

The attempts of educated Muslim young men to develop appropriate 'fall-back strategies' in response to educated unemployment must be read alongside the efforts of the uneducated to question the value of education and the apparent 'success' (sa-phalatā) of educated Muslims. Of the 292 young men aged between 20 and 34 in Qaziwala in 2000, 240 (83 percent) had neither obtained an Eighth Class pass nor extended madrasah qualifications. Among these 'uneducated' young men, 47 percent worked as manual wage laborers in 2000, 30 percent were skilled artisans and 21 percent were in other forms of business, mainly the cattle trade and butchery. Thirty-two percent of these 'uneducated' men had some experience of formal education. Among this set of men, a minority claimed that they made a positive decision to leave formal education, for example after becoming aware of the difficulty of obtaining white-collar employment or because they were repeatedly beaten by teachers. But the overwhelming majority of young men said that their households had lacked the money for them to remain in education or that their parents had curtailed their studies when they failed to achieve good results or demonstrated a lack of enthusiasm for their studies.

Very few of these uneducated men could read or write Hindi and they had internalized a vision of themselves as 'illiterate' (*an-parh, ku-parh*). They typically echoed their educated peers by arguing that education provides key skills, knowledge and civilization. Influenced by wider narratives celebrating the benefits of education, and citing the difficulties they faced in negotiating urban settings without school skills, many uneducated young men said they regretted their inability to remain in school. The example of Afzal is illuminating. A twenty-three year old carpenter, Afzal lived with his wife and young son in a small house close to the edge of Qaziwala: his older brother, six younger brothers and three younger sisters lived nearby. Afzal's parents owned no agricultural land and said that they could not afford to educate all their sons. But they tried hard to encourage Afzal to attend school. Afzal went to the Begawala madrasah up to Fifth Class and an aided inter-college close to Qaziwala for a year. But in the face of his family's poverty and his own disinterest in his studies, Afzal left school at the beginning of Seventh Class. He said that he had learnt very little and referred to himself as illiterate. Sitting outside his family's three-roomed mud house, Afzal told Craig that he now regretted leaving school:

I wish I had studied harder: it is sorry thing. I think education is very important. Education enables people to understand everything and would also help with their work. I was once in Shimla and I had taken food and bought some things in a stall there. The bill came to Rs. 150 but it was written in English. I had notes of Rs. 500, Rs. 100, Rs. 50 and Rs. 20, but I didn't know how much money I had to give. So I just gave the shopkeeper the Rs. 500 note and the shopkeeper gave me the change. I really felt it [*mujhe ehsās huā*]. I had put the shopkeeper to trouble when all the time I had the correct change. If I had been educated, I could have given him the correct money.

Like Afzal, many uneducated men referred to the relative competence of educated young men, and some spoke dejectedly of the combination of poverty, bad luck and personal disinterest that had conspired to prevent them from staying in school. A few uneducated Muslim young men said that as uneducated people they are "no better than animals," "like buffaloes" or "people leaning against a wall."

But uneducated young men, like their educated peers, were engaged in a quest for respect that often involved shifting between different positions and styles. For example, Afzal frequently questioned the idea that he is inevitably 'inferior' to educated people, and he spoke of his skills as a person engaged in carpentry work. He bragged about the strength he had developed as a carpenter, showed off his biceps and recounted with glee his alleged superiority in physical combat. Afzal:

Fifteen days ago, we started a fight! There were fifty men against just my brother and me. My brother and I managed to beat the fifty men! We are very strong [tāqatvar]. The two of us together can be compared to fifty men in strength. Our hands are very strong [showing us his hands]. Because of the nature of my work, I can do physical exercise for 24 hours. I can put 1 quintal [220 pounds] weight on my feet and then put in screws, and do other strenuous work of this type. Every night I sleep from midnight until 3 AM and in the morning I run from Qaziwala to Ravli to Bijnor and on to Hameedpur before returning to Qaziwala [a total of 20 miles]. After the run, I do exercises. I never feel sleepy during the day.

We questioned the details of Afzal's story of physical heroism, but he stuck by his words: "Yes, we wrestled fifty men!" "Yes, I run 20 miles a day!" Afzal took out a cigarette at this point and lit up. He squinted through the smoke at Craig and surmised that "as an educated person" Craig would be incapable of such feats of strength and endurance. Warming to the theme, Afzal contrasted his power and daring with the feebleness and timidity of educated people in Qaziwala. Stuck inside, "bent over their pen and paper," he said that the educated—"those book insects" (kitābi kīrā)—lose strength and vitality, become incapable of long periods of hard work (mehnat) and are unable to defend themselves or their families. He also said that the educated are unable to lift heavy weights, run long distances or consume oily or spicy foods. Consistent with his vision of macho masculinity, Afzal proudly recalled how he had used his strength to terrorize teachers in school: he remembered damaging teachers' chairs, placing a nail pointing upwards on the teacher's seat and shouting during classes. He said that he was never afraid during the beatings that followed, unlike many others in the class. Afzal concluded that "the educated are weak and the uneducated are strong."

Several other uneducated Muslim young men ridiculed peers who had spent long periods in formal education. They referred to the educated in unflattering terms, alluded to a tendency among the educated to spend time lost in thought rather than attending to worldly matters (duniyādārī) and spoke of the educated man's lack of experience (anu-bhāv) and practical knowledge: the "foolishness of the educated." As in Afzal's case, many uneducated Muslim young men affirmed a type of rural machismo based on the strength and experience built up within labor. These men commonly said that the educated are incapable of the sustained manual work required to be effective farmers.

In developing these themes, uneducated young men discussed moral discourses of their relationship to the environment that differed from the narratives of the educated young men. Like the educated, uneducated Muslim young men claimed that schooling changes people's relationship to surrounding nature. But the uneducated perceived this change to *undermine* rather than *affirm* a young man's moral stature and masculinity. For example, an uneducated young man told Craig:

Look at us! We sometimes have to do dungwork and so we get covered with dung. Sometimes we do work with earth and so we get covered in earth. Sometimes we become black and sometimes we become green. We work hard all day in the fields [*jangal*]. It is also very cold. All day and all night we spend time in water. If you [Craig] worked all day in the fields, your cheeks would become like an apple, you would become black and you would dry out. You sit in the town under a fan and in the air from a cooler. You loll about on a double bed. If we lived in as much comfort, then we would also become handsome like you. But if we didn't work in the fields then where would the grain come from?

Uneducated young men who had migrated to work as artisans in Delhi also occasionally ridiculed the failure of educated people to make money. These men said that their own exclusion from secondary school had allowed them to earn substantial amounts from a young age. These uneducated men returned to the village wearing expensive clothes and taunted their 'impoverished' educated peers.

In contrast to Afzal, indeed, we heard several young men and some of their parental generation claim that illiteracy has not disadvantaged them in their daily life. They maintained that they can negotiate urban settings with ease, are unabashed by their lack of schooling and are confident in their dealings with others. Those holding this view emphasized their common sense, practical wisdom and capacity to improvise (*jugār*) in settings requiring them to decipher written texts or make rapid calculations. In addition, some Muslim young men contested the notion that literacy and numeracy are only available in schools or madrasahs. They said that they had developed a type of 'oral arithmetic' (*munh-zabānī hisāb*) and had learnt to read road signs through hard work (*mehnat*), experience (*anu-bhāv*) or games (*khel*). Certainly, these views were less common among the uneducated than ideas of formal education as progress, but they constituted an important feature of village discourse.

Educated young men attempted to counter the taunts of the uneducated by pointing out that very few educated young men in Qaziwala had become manual wage laborers. If the educated had not been able to acquire salaried employment, at least they had been able to avoid entering the types of work regarded as least attractive in the village at large. But as uneducated Muslim young men observed, the ability of the educated to avoid manual wage labor reflects the greater wealth of their households more than the capacity of local educational systems to provide skills, knowledge and confidence relevant for entering 'better' employment. Moreover, many uneducated Muslim young men were working in the same types of employment as the educated, and they were frequently more successful than the educated in this work. There were several educated Muslim young men working as unpaid apprentices alongside a well-paid but uneducated peer of a similar age.

In response to the threat posed by men such as Afzal to their standing and self-esteem, educated young men working in farming and artisanal work often fell back on the argument that their education allowed them to perform their tasks more effectively than the uneducated. Like the Jats, some educated Muslim young men stressed their capacity to practice a 'scientific' agriculture that the uneducated would fail to understand. Similarly, educated young men working as artisans claimed to have established expansive social networks in school that left them better placed than unschooled men to advance careers in craft. Our observations in the village suggested that these claims lacked substance, but they were important in generating among the educated a sense of their distinction.

The optimism and relative absence of resentment evident among educated Muslim young men suggests that they were mostly successful in shoring up their sense of themselves as distinctively 'qualified' and thereby countering the threat posed by uneducated critics. Their determination to invest heavily in the future education of their children also points to their confidence in the benefits of education. But these men had failed to convince other members

of rural society of the value of prolonged mainstream schooling. The failure
of school-educated Muslim young men to obtain employment better paid or
more prestigious than that conducted by many uneducated young men had
persuaded Muslim parents to alter their views of the benefits of mainstream
schooling. Muslim parents increasingly referred to the impossibility of Muslims' obtaining government employment and the uselessness, in this context,
of investing large sums in secular education. For example, a woman in her early
forties explained her recent decision not to encourage her sons to attend school
by noting:

There is no point in Muslims studying Hindi. We have to spend so much [on education]
and even then we don't get a salaried job. All the salaried jobs go to Hindus. In the village there are now five or six young men who have degrees, and only one has obtained a
salaried job, so what is the point in studying?

In discussing their decision-making in relation to educating sons in the early
2000s, a Muslim man in his mid-forties told us:

Muslims don't need Hindi and English. They just need Urdu and knowledge of *Qu'rān
Sharīf*. For them, that is a lot. Even if Muslims do study English and Hindi, they won't
get service.

These opinions were not new; we argued in Chapter Two that Muslim parents'
perception of the irrelevance of prolonged mainstream schooling for their sons
was important in limiting the expansion of education among Muslims in Qaziwala in the 1980s and 1990s. But narratives of mainstream schooling as 'useless'
(*bekār*) had become more common in the village in the early 2000s. In the face
of competing demands upon their meager resources, and a hostile employment market, many Muslim parents planned futures for their children outside
mainstream schooling.

   In addition, Muslim boys were increasingly deciding to leave formal education before Eighth Class in the light of the failure of educated Muslim men to
find government employment or private service work in the 1990s and early
2000s. Asif provides an example of this trend. In his early thirties in 2001, Asif
was the second son of a Muslim Sheikh farming family owning 12 acres of land.
His father, Ashraf, was one of the first men in Qaziwala to obtain an Eighth
Class pass, having attended a secondary school in the nearby village of Dharm-

nagri in the early 1940s. Ashraf was a fervent champion of the transformative potential of education. He told us:

If people were educated, they would make their environment different from others. Their thoughts and living conditions would be different. Because people are uneducated, their minds fill up with filth and they are not capable of good thoughts. There is information about wonderful things and human hearts also strive to do good, but the ability to change things only comes through education.

Asif's elder brother, Tausif, obtained the first BA in the village in the mid-1980s. But Tausif struggled for over ten years searching for a government job. Observing the difficulties faced by his elder brother, Asif decided that he should leave school after Sixth Class. Despite recriminations from his father, Asif said that he could see no point in continuing with his studies when his BA-educated brother could find neither government work nor satisfactory private employment. Asif petitioned relatives for starting capital and set up a small carpentry workshop in Bijnor. By 2001, Asif was making a large profit and did not regret his decision to leave school. At the same time, however, Asif planned to send his own children to mainstream schools "for as long as possible."

Asif's case reminds us that Muslims were not straightforwardly 'rejecting' prolonged mainstream schooling as a mode of social mobility in the early 2000s. The rise of a class of educated un/under-employed young men and the energetic attempts of some uneducated young men to question the value of education had generated ambivalent feelings in Qaziwala regarding the purposes of formal education. Parents in the early 2000s often differed markedly in their perceptions of the benefits of mainstream schools, and the same people expressed different views on separate occasions, even within the same conversation. While such ambivalence is a common feature of people's discussions of education in numerous contexts, the rise of educated un/under-employment had lent a particular force to villagers' sense of uncertainty.

The Social Dangers of 'Acting Islamic'

Political changes in the 1990s and early 2000s complicated the employment strategies and cultural styles of Muslim young men. Educated Muslim men often pursued opportunities to obtain artisanal or religious employment while dressing and acting in a manner that connoted a shared Islamic educated identity. In projecting this style, they risked antagonizing the predominantly Hindu state officialdom and influential local employment brokers within markets for salaried work. An Islamic young male demeanor hampered young men's efforts to secure salaried employment or find new opportunities for skilled work outside Muslim circles. Moreover, by projecting an Islamic cultural style, young men ran the risk of police harassment, including threats, unlawful arrest and murder. Police harassment of Muslims is a well-documented feature of north India (Brass 1997), and many Muslims who had worked in urban areas complained about state brutality linked to institutionalized communalism within the police force.

The aftermath of the attacks on America on 11 September 2001 further politicized the process of looking for employment for young men who cultivated Islamic identities in rural Bijnor district. Rising communal tensions related to two sets of processes. First, the BJP-led coalition government of UP at the time used the pretext of a global Islamic terrorist threat to circulate fears of a 'Muslim danger' and to intensify its long-running verbal attacks on madrasahs. Sections of the Western and Indian media found common cause in depicting educated Muslims as fundamentalist, violent zealots and in accusing madrasahs of propagating militant Islam. The *Daru'l `Ulūm* seminary was a particular focus of national and international media concern, and senior officials at this institution fielded hostile questions from visiting journalists and investigators in the autumn of 2001. Such politically-motivated harassment appeared to strengthen the hand of the police force in Bijnor district. On 15 October 2001, police shootings in Bijnor led to the deaths of three Muslim young men, one of whom was from Qaziwala.[1] Fearing police intimidation, no one from Qaziwala was willing

---

[1]The police stopped a van on one of the main roads into Bijnor, apparently because they believed that it contained firearms. We heard different stories about how events unfolded: in one, the Superintendent of Police was said to have instructed the police via radio to kill the men; in another, the story was linked to gun-smuggling in which the police were themselves implicated. Whatever the immediate cause or sequence of events, the outcome was that the police shot two men close to the van and then pursued and shot another man who ran into the surrounding countryside. Such incidents—commonly euphemized as 'encounters'—have become a common means through which the police are alleged to eliminate criminals or opponents.

to visit the police station in Bijnor to identify the body of the murdered young man.

Second, in response to the US-led bombing of Afghanistan, on 16 October 2001 the *Daru'l `Ulūm* seminary issued a *fatwā* advising Muslims to avoid products manufactured by US or British companies. *Daru'l `Ulūm* provided an extensive list of consumer goods forbidden under the terms of the *fatwā*; Muslims were told they could drink Tata tea but not Lipton, use Godrej toothpaste but not Colgate, and smoke 365 Black cigarettes but not Gold Flake, for example. In a message circulated via pamphlets and on its website, *Daru'l `Ulūm* told people that:

All the Muslims must boycott the USA and Britain in every possible way and discard completely the products of these countries, because if they [Muslims] do not do so it will be tantamount to co-operating with their oppressive and cruel activities and such co-operation is totally prohibited in the light of Islamic Law.

The political assertion of the Hindu Right could not prevent educated Muslim men from seeking education and work in madrasahs. The educated Muslim men were unconcerned by the possibility of exposure to attack by religious communal or state forces as *maulwīs* or madrasah students. They argued that madrasahs would do nothing to incite such attacks and that madrasahs could protect staff and students from the risk of state intimidation. Young men ridiculed the suggestion that their participation in madrasah learning might lead them to absorb terrorist doctrine. A young *maulwī* at Begawala madrasah summarized the views of the majority of educated Muslim young men in Qaziwala when he explained that:

The people in the media are saying that madrasahs are teaching about terrorism. This is completely wrong. . . . There is nothing about terrorism in our religion, and nothing is taught about terrorism in our madrasah.

Educated Muslims depicted madrasahs and the *Daru'l `Ulūm* seminary as spaces of order, learning and civility, and other Muslim young men concurred. Our experience of visiting madrasahs in Bijnor district and the two trips we made to *Daru'l `Ulūm* strongly endorse this view of madrasahs (cf. Sikand 2005).

While communal tensions were not radically altering Muslim young men's assessments of becoming Islamic teachers or clerics, they were discouraging some educated Muslims from migrating to Delhi to perform artisanal work. Several educated Muslim young men returned to Qaziwala complaining of police harassment of Muslims in Delhi even *before* the attacks on America in September 2001. Many educated Muslim young men said that the Delhi police had been intimidating Muslim young men for as long as they could remember, but that police harassment increased markedly after August 2000, when the Delhi government introduced a program formally designed to reduce the large-scale emission of industrial pollutants (Tarlo 2003). But the reports of Muslim young men returning to Qaizwala in the autumn of 2000 strongly suggested that some sections of the Delhi police force used the program as a cover for intimidating Muslim young men, vandalizing Muslim property and even destroying whole businesses. For example, one educated young man doing embroidery work in Delhi told us that:

Two people cannot stand together. If they do, the police will beat them. This happened to me once. It was during *Ramzān*. I had read some prayers and went outside at about 9:30 PM. A policeman grabbed me and said that it is forbidden to wander around at night. He told me that if he catches me wandering around at night again he would throw me in jail. He wrote down my name, address and occupation.

Similarly, in January 2001, another educated Muslim young man who had been working as an embroiderer in Delhi told us:

Things in Delhi have become very bad. People who had put machines in private houses would wake up to find a sign on the door that meant that their house would be demolished. They then bring along equipment to demolish the house, and the house shakes and falls over. They are cutting houses down to this height [he signaled a height of about two feet from the ground]. People can do nothing.

State harassment affected both educated and uneducated Muslims, but several young men told us that, because educated young men are typically more confident on the street and make greater efforts to wear prayer caps, *keffiyeh* and *kurtā-pājāmā*, they are a particular target for the police.

These considerations help explain a reluctance among educated Muslim young men to enter politics. The frustrations of un/under-employment had not provoked educated Muslim young men to formulate identities as local politicians and work as intermediaries between rural people and the state. Notwithstanding the attempts of Mulayam Singh Yadav to attract Muslim voters,

Muslim young men educated in schools and madrasahs said that they lacked a political figure capable of inspiring them to engage in party- or movement-based politics. The continued strength of norms of seniority within local Muslim politics also strongly discouraged Muslim young men from trying to assume intermediary roles between the state and rural society. In Qaziwala the *pradhān, ex-pradhān,* and one of the richest landowners in the village, all in their fifties or sixties, were the three key intermediaries between rural people and government agencies. These men had developed close relationships with state officials in Bijnor and with influential religious figures in the district, and their village courtyards served as reception areas for visiting bigwigs. Families sought to maintain good relations with these men in the hope of receiving their support in negotiations with state officials.

Mohsin was the only educated Muslim young man in Qaziwala to play a role comparable to that of new politicians in Nangal. A *maulwī* in a Bijnor madrasah, Mohsin had five years of mainstream schooling and extensive experience of madrasah education. Building on his reputation as an educated person, Mohsin became *vice-pradhān* in the village *panchāyat* in 1998. In this role, Mohsin had improved the access of the poor in Qaziwala to development resources. He lobbied the *pradhān* to ensure that poor households received scholarship money and interviewed poor families to verify that they had received government resources. Mohsin seemed to work hard for the poor, repeatedly insisting that he did not acquire illegal money from his post and that he avoided giving or receiving bribes. Beyond his *panchāyat* work, in the mid-1990s, Mohsin and his wife collected money from friends and established a madrasah in Qaziwala, the *Talīmul Banat wal Mastūrāt* (School for Older Girls and Women), with a view to improving women's educational opportunities. Between 1996 and 2003, when they closed the madrasah, Mohsin and his wife provided lessons in *Qu'rān Sharīf* and Urdu in their rural home.

Mohsin did much for the village, but his work should be read in context. Educated Muslim young men usually appeared disinterested in circulating political ideas in the village, and many had migrated outside Bijnor district. As the Sachar Report (Sachar 2006) would lead us to expect, educated Muslim young men regarded the government as a threat to their futures and stressed their *disengagement* from party-based, district-level and *panchāyat* politics.

In sum, Hindu political mobilization in the 1990s and early 2000s in Bijnor district was both powerfully influencing the capacity of educated Muslim
young men to migrate in search of work and complicating their attempts to obtain government jobs, private white-collar employment and political influence.
Many Muslim young men felt that their best strategy was to concentrate their
efforts on small-scale artisanal work in the local area or on acquiring work as a
religious teacher, both of which could be achieved without confronting government opposition or seeking the assistance of Hindus.

Conclusions

There are clearly some similarities between the strategies of educated Muslim young men and those of their educated peers among the Jats and new politicians in Nangal. Educated Muslim young men had typically responded to
their exclusion from government employment in the early 1990s and 2000s by
reaffirming the value of education. Like the young men we discussed in Chapter Four and Chapter Five, educated Muslim young men in Qaziwala typically
possessed economic resources and social connections that allowed them to negotiate educated un/under-employment fairly effectively. Some had fallen back
on farming. Many others were able to draw on social networks that linked them
to co-religionists in urban areas in order to enter artisanal occupations. Still
others found it possible to shift the weight of their educational effort to place
greater emphasis on madrasah education and thereby obtain work as teachers
or clerics.

But we advance this story of 'Muslim success' with caution. First, educated
Muslim men constituted only a tiny proportion of the overall cohort of young
Muslim men in Qaziwala. Many of their uneducated peers questioned the resources and moral authority of the educated and dwelt on the 'weakness' of the
educated and their disconnection from the realities of village life. A second set
of threats was external and involved the heightening of religious communal
tension in Bijnor district and Delhi before and after the attacks on America in
2001. By increasing the risks attached to projecting an educated Islamic identity,
rising communal tension appeared to be making it more difficult for educated
Muslim young men to develop the cultural styles required to negotiate entry

into artisanal work and discouraged them from seeking Hindu-dominated white-collar work, private service or local political careers. In the context of Hindu assertion in 2001, the majority of educated Muslim young men were pursuing a strategy of withdrawal which served, in turn, to reinforce exclusion and strengthen closed circles of distinction.

The chapter therefore shows how power and culture mediate people's access to the entitlements that education allegedly provides (cf. Sen 1999). The capacity of educated Muslims to devise effective responses to their exclusion from white-collar work depends crucially on their social capital—especially networks of trust based on religion and kinship—and, usually, on their economic capital, in the form of agricultural land. The next chapter considers young men who lack even the moderate levels of economic backing and social support available to educated Muslims in Qaziwala.

7

Down and Out in Nangal and Qaziwala: The Cultural Politics of Resentment

These young people, whose social identity and self-image have
been undermined by a social system and an educational system
that have fobbed them off with worthless paper, can find no other
way of restoring their personal and social integrity than by a total
refusal.... [A whole generation] finding it has been taken for a
ride, is inclined to extend to all institutions the mixture of revolt
and resentment it feels toward the educational system

Bourdieu 1984: 144

Where are they now: the beautiful village and the shade of the
    banyan, *pīpal* and *nīm* trees?
Where are they now: the peaceful neighborhood, fun among friends,
    cheap *dāl* and *rotī*?
Where are they now: children's games, harmony among friends, oil
    from the oil-cake?
Where are they now: the village grandmother and king and queen of
    fairy-tales?
Where are they now: a mother like Parwati, the cream of the milk
    and all good in the world?[1]

(Poem written by a Jat young man from a village
close to Nangal, recited April 2002)

---

[1] *Sundar-sā gānv; vat, pīpal aur nīm kī chhānv, ab rahī kahan ...*
Shāntī bastī, yāron mein mastī, dāl-rotī sastī, ab rahī kahan ...
Bachchon ke khel, dostī mein mel, khālī mein tel, ab rahī kahan ...
Ganvwālī nānī, rājā aur rānī, pariyon kī kahānī, ab rahī kahan ...
Parwātī-sī māi, dūdh mein malāī, jag mein bhalāī, ab rahī kahan ...

Many young men in rural Bijnor district have responded to educated un/
under-employment by cultivating an image of disillusionment. They claimed
to be 'wanderers,' 'useless men' or people engaged only in '*timepass*.' This reaction was particularly common among educated Chamar young men, especially
those from poorer backgrounds, who distanced themselves from the cultural
styles of the new politicians. These Chamar men lacked the money, guile and
confidence to enter the types of fallback work obtained by *naye netās*, for example as contractors or political intermediaries. Chamars also lacked the links
into private salaried employment that were available to Jats or the land required
to enter farming. They suffered, too, from their exclusion from the urban networks that rural Muslims in north India possess. Economically impoverished
and socially isolated, these Chamars were often angry and resentful, and some
had even come to challenge the notion that education improves people's lives.

There are references to such disillusionment in recent scholarly work on India (e.g. Jeffrey 2001; Osella and Osella 2007), but few detailed studies of young
men's practices. A notable exception is Heuzé's (1996) account of social change
in Chhattisgarh. Heuzé described young men engaged in a culture of 'waiting'
oriented around an image of disillusionment and self-conscious 'unemployment':

By remaining together in doing nothing, by refusing to participate in the domestic economy and to work in the fields, by dressing in city attire—college dress—and frequenting
the main streets of Batipur and Bharu and the tea stalls located on the main road from
Chandankiari to the mining basin, the educated unemployed assert themselves by drawing attention to the injustice meted out to them. [Heuzé 1996: 105]

Anandhi et al. (2002) make a similar point in a recent analysis of Dalit political action in rural Tamil Nadu, south India. They argue that Dalit young men
increasingly refuse to enter agricultural work. Instead, educated Dalits, who
defined themselves as 'unemployed,' spend time wandering the village, starting
quarrels and displaying consumer goods. Anandhi et al. (2002: 379) therefore
identify a "new spatial politics" where "the ability to roam the *mudaliar* [upper
caste] streets by displaying acts of violence is a new embodiment of masculinity, which challenges upper caste privileges." There are marked differences
between the Tamil Nadu context, where Dalits entered education much earlier

than they did in most parts of north India, as there also are between Heuzé's study area and our own. But we will highlight some similarities between young men's strategies in western UP, Chhattisgarh, and Tamil Nadu as well as showing how our material provides new perspectives on the cultural politics of resentment among the educated un/under-employed.

The chapter is divided into a further five sections. First, we introduce a Chamar young man named Amarpal. We then build on this case study to outline Chamar young men's employment strategies. In the next section we point to a tendency among these men to imagine themselves as 'wanderers' engaged only in *timepass*. The penultimate section examines how far these cultures of resentment traverse distinctions of class, caste and religious community by describing the practices of Rauf, a Muslim young man, and Chandu, a Jat. The conclusion links our discussion to wider themes of the book.

Introducing Amarpal

When we first met Amarpal in March 2001, he was standing outside his family's small brick house in a busy Chamar section of Nangal. Dressed in plain fawn trousers and slip-on plastic shoes, he was leaning against a gully wall chatting to two friends. He was eager to talk and led us into one of the family's dimly lit rooms, which contained two rope beds and a stack of old textbooks. Sitting on a broken rope bed beneath a faded poster of a Bollywood film star, Amarpal described his long struggle with feelings of resentment and hopelessness. Speaking in a plain style of Hindi strikingly different from the rhetorical exuberance of Nangal's new politicians, Amarpal told us:

My problem is that I have yet to find work. I am unemployed. For this reason I have lost the will to live [*jīne ki tamannā*]. There seems to be no good [in the world].

Married for two years, childless and in his late twenties in 2001, Amarpal belonged to a landless family in Nangal and had one younger brother and three younger sisters. His parents and younger brother worked as agricultural laborers on the farm of a nearby Jat and supplemented this income with occasional work in local brick-kilns. Amarpal's parents, Chottey and Gomti, who were both uneducated, had encouraged their sons to stay in formal education for "as long as possible." Amarpal's father, Chottey, told us that he wanted education to "change the environment (*māhaul*) of the home" in addition to improving his sons' employment prospects. Amarpal started school in the Nangal Junior Primary School and then attended Nangal Junior High School. He moved on to an aided inter-college near Nangal and ended his studies at a government degree college in Bijnor. By 2001, Amarpal had a BA, MA and BCom and was studying for an MCom. He also had a technical diploma from the government Industrial Training Institute in Bijnor.

A few un/under-employed Chamars referred excitedly to their involvement in the competition for government jobs. Like many Jats, these men boasted of their knowledge of corruption (*bhrashtāchār*) and appeared to relish the feeling of being participants in the quest for secure work. But most educated Chamar young men talked of their frustration in the face of repeated failure. After ten or more years of competing for government employment, Amarpal's anger focused on the importance of bribe money (*rishvat*) in obtaining a job. Recalling his attempt to secure a position on a government Basic Teaching Certificate (BTC) training program, Amarpal told us:

I did the exam very well and had taken four to six weeks of tuition. My mind is good and my tutor said that my 'number' would certainly come [I would certainly be successful]. But my number did not come. Another boy—some fool—was successful. He beat me because he paid a bribe of Rs. 71,000.

Amarpal recalled visiting a BTC training camp shortly afterwards. He said that the trainees laughed at his anecdote: "They told me I would have to pay at least Rs. 50,000 or Rs. 70,000 to obtain a position on the course." Such stories of corruption ran through many of our discussions with educated Chamar young men. They emphasized that their ignorance regarding the extent and nature of bribery frequently led to their embarrassment or even humiliation. Amarpal recalled two popular village phrases, "The world's drums are all pretence, money talks" and "throw money and watch the spectacle."

Aside from the money required for a bribe, Amarpal said that without social contacts in state bureaucracies he was highly unlikely to obtain government work. Amarpal stressed the social isolation of the poor and the difficulty of obtaining knowledge (*jānkārī*) about recruitment processes and corruption. For example, discussing his efforts to find a trustworthy broker (*dalāl*) who could assist him in finding a government job, Amarpal told us:

One broker was a distant relative from another village. He told me that he would get me salaried employment but that it would cost Rs. 4,000. I trusted him and handed over the money. From that day to this, I have not caught sight of his face. Another time a driver came here and said he could get me a job as a [government] driver in Moradabad. . . . With great difficulty, we managed to give him Rs. 2,000. The driver did not arrange salaried employment for me and he did not return the money. The main problem is that we don't have any knowledge about all this.

Amarpal regarded reservations in government employment for SCs as useless:

Reservations only benefit Scheduled Caste people who have money and social contacts. It is not of any benefit to the poor because the poor don't have Rs. 50,000, Rs. 70,000, Rs. 100,000 to spare for a bribe. And without a bribe there is no position.

Amarpal and other educated Chamar young men also said that educational credentials no longer provide advantage in the market for government jobs. Chamars said that a BA is 'worthless.' At other moments, young men dwelt on the increasing irrelevance of their own ability (qābiliyat), talent (hunar) and suitability (yogya) for government work. A Chamar young man working as a private teacher in the Ambedkar Junior High School told us:

First you have to run around for training and then you have to do the same to find service. And, without a bribe and social contact, you won't get a service job. I should tell you that I have been successful in ten or eleven interviews and I don't know how many written tests, but I haven't yet been selected. On one occasion I sat through an interview answering every question quickly and correctly. Well, my only mistake was that I had written my full name in the place where I was supposed to write 'candidate.'

Educated Chamar young men also referred bitterly to the ubiquity of flattery (chāplūsī, khushāmad, jī-jī huzūrī) within competition for government work. They said that it is necessary to cajole, sweet-talk or compliment higher caste government officials in order to obtain a valued post. Some young men perceived the ability to praise an official while laughing behind one's hand at the bigwig's stupidity as a marker of a person's educated status. But most educated Chamar young men resented having to kowtow to upper caste officials and said that such flattery was at odds with their sense of themselves as educated people: dignified, independent and confident. Some Chamar young men also identified a contradiction between flattering the upper castes and Ambedkar's dictum: "Do not bow down before others." One educated Chamar young man complained loudly, "We have to put our hands together [in supplication] when we should be punching these men in the face!"

Educated Chamars' resentment tended to be more intense than that of Muslim and Jat young men. Feelings of exclusion from circuits of power, knowledge and influence 'up above' (ūpar) were stronger among Chamars than among most Jats. Chamars frequently perceived their inability to find government work to be a condensed symbol of their wider exclusion from sources of money and political advantage. Educated Chamar young men's sense of facing caste discrimination in the competition for government work sharpened their feelings of indignation and anger. Moreover, a long period of receiving reservations in government employment and the movement of a relatively large number of educated Chamar men into salaried work in the 1970s and 1980s had instilled in some educated Chamars a belief in their entitlement to government work.

Chamars' Search for Fallback Work

In spite of failing to obtain secure salaried employment, Amarpal often referred to the value of education. For example, Amarpal broke off from discussing his marriage to note:

My wife is illiterate. She doesn't like education. She thinks that I should earn Rs. 50 a day. Because I don't earn that much, she thinks of my education as being useless. Education doesn't have any meaning for her, she just needs money. I am educated and so I want to raise the *standard* of the house. There are certain things that I think need to be done. But my wife doesn't listen to me. She does everything a different way. Illiterate people think that whatever way they do things is right.

Paralleling *netās'* discourses, Amarpal referred to the contemporary irrelevance of caste as a social marker and the much greater importance of education as a sign of social distinction. He asked how Jats could claim to be superior when they frequently behave in a filthy and depraved manner. He continued by denigrating Brahmins:

Take the example of Ram Kumar Pandit or Suresh Pandit [two Brahmins in Nangal Jat]. Inside they are not Brahmins. When they are in front of us, they behave as if they are Brahmins, but they go for 10 or 12 days at a time without washing or praying. And even so people say that they are of a higher caste [*svarn*]!

Amarpal maintained that his educated status prevented him from under-taking any form of 'hand work' (*hāth kā kām*). Like the Jats, educated Chamar young men associated 'being educated' with new forms of youth masculinity in which they would be removed from manual labor. Amarpal asserted:

I am educated and so I feel that I should do pen work [*pen chalāne kā kām*], even if it means earning only Rs. 40 or 50 a day. I'll get more doing manual wage labor—Rs. 50 or 60—but I won't do that type of work.

Amarpal said that as an educated person he should not only avoid manual wage labor and farming but also traditional forms of skilled artisanal work, such as tailoring, shoe repair or masonry. Chamar young men mocked the few educated Chamars who had become skilled artisans by shouting '*nāī*' (barber) or '*darzī*' (tailor). The terms '*nāī*' and '*darzī*' referred to specific occupations and particular lower castes, often also Muslim. The taunts therefore emphasized educated young men's remove from salaried employment by linking them to former low caste village-based craft activities (*dastkārī*). These taunts also had a communal overtone. Chamar young men frequently displayed anti-Muslim sentiments during interviews, asserting that Muslims were averse to educating their children, had large families and entered 'dirty' manual work *because they were Muslims*. The move of large numbers of Muslims in rural Bijnor district into tailoring, embroidery and metalwork therefore increased Chamars' aver-sion to such occupations. Some Chamar parents had tried to persuade their sons to ignore other people's jeers. One Chamar woman told an educated boy: "What's the matter? They will call you '*nāī*' and '*darzī*' today, but tomorrow they will call you 'Master'!" These arguments had failed to sway young men: just five young men, 5 percent of educated Chamar young men aged between twenty and thirty-four, had entered artisanal work in 2001.

Amarpal's immediate neighbor, Hemraj, was one of the few educated Chamars who were performing craft activity. Hemraj left formal education af-ter Eighth Class and traveled to the nearby town of Haldaur to take on an ap-prenticeship as a tailor. Having observed other young men's attempts to obtain government work, Hemraj decided not to seek salaried employment: "What's the point, when even MAs wander the village without work?" After four years, he had accumulated enough experience of tailoring to start his own business on the main road into Nangal. He worked cheerfully, beside his brother, sitting at their two Singer sewing machines in their workshop. Hemraj told us:

This is the work I enjoy. Some boys begin learning a craft, but then leave after a while. Some boys don't feel satisfied as tailors [*man nahīn kartā*]. But even now I feel content in this work.

Amarpal's younger brother, Jagbir, followed a different route. Jagbir said that he had little enthusiasm for school work and failed his Tenth Class examinations. When he observed his brother struggling to find government employment, Jagbir decided that he should leave school: "I thought: 'what good will education do?' My brother is BA pass and even he doesn't benefit [from schooling]!" In 2001, Jagbir earned between Rs. 50 and Rs. 60 a day doing manual wage labor in the village. Jagbir said that he finds this employment tiring and demeaning. But he also enjoyed the opportunity to spend long periods with friends that laboring work afforded.

Given his determination to avoid manual occupations of the type conducted by his brother and Hemraj, Amarpal was aware of four 'options' open to him in the employment sphere. First, he could refuse to work. Amarpal said that he spent about two years after completing his high school examinations wandering about the village, chatting to friends and only very occasionally undertaking paid employment. Unlike rich households, however, and the Dalits described by Anandhi et al. (2002), Amarpal's parents lacked the funds to support him in continuing idleness. The poverty of most Chamar households made it difficult for them to support a son who repudiated paid employment.

Amarpal's second option was to acquire further educational qualifications. As we observed in Chapter Four, it was relatively inexpensive for young men to accumulate qualifications in local degree colleges and they could combine their study with attempts to find permanent government employment. Moreover, by remaining in formal education, Amarpal had been able to project an image of himself as someone for whom salaried work was "just around the corner." But Amarpal also recognized the ultimate futility of this strategy:

This is India's greatest difficulty [*mushkil*]. In India we are encouraged to acquire more and more education but there is no corresponding stimulus to create educated jobs.

Third, as Lipton (1977) predicted long ago, Amarpal could respond to the lack of rural employment opportunities by migrating in search of salaried work. Indeed, Amarpal had traveled to Mumbai in the early 1990s in pursuit of small parts in the Bollywood film industry. He spent a few months acting the role of a slave in a televised serial about colonialism in India. Without any personal recommendation, however, or social support in Bombay, this adventure turned sour. He returned to Nangal after suffering from loneliness and being robbed. Similarly, discussing the difficulties he faced in running a tailoring business, Hemraj told us:

I also went there [to Delhi] once. There's a factory at the Delhi Badarpur border. But I returned after eight days. I didn't feel at home there [*man nahīn lagā*]. The water there didn't agree with me. I became ill and so I came back. . . . I was alone in Delhi and that is why I didn't feel at home.

Jagbir also spoke of his emotional attachment to village life and fear of urban areas. He maintained that:

There is more love among people in the village. If you go to a house in town, you receive tea. But if you start going to the same house every day, the people in that house will think, "You are coming every day, so I won't give you tea." In the village, if someone is going to a house every day, they will be given tea straight away [*ek dam*].

A few *uneducated* Chamar young men, roughly 4 percent of those aged between twenty and thirty-four, migrated to work as construction laborers in Dehra Dun, typically for a period of between five and fifteen years. These men had established a small but trusted network of friends and kin who assisted aspiring builders and masons in finding work in Dehra Dun, and they referred to city life as sociable, relatively devoid of caste prejudice and offering possibilities for greater earnings than the village. But most Chamar young men lacked sources of urban support and tended to speak of urban areas as treacherous and unwelcoming. Only three young men, 3 percent of educated Chamar young men aged between twenty and thirty-four in 2001, were in paid employment outside Bijnor district.

Amarpal's fourth option, the one he had pursued with most vigor, was to engage in local forms of small-scale entrepreneurship or clerical employment while living at home. Shortly after completing his course at the Industrial Training Institute, Amarpal opened a television and radio repair shop in Nangal. Perhaps because of the association between electrical goods and 'modern' lifestyles, Amarpal said that he felt comfortable repairing televisions and radios. The business provided little money, however, and involved spending long periods outside the home. Citing his desire to spend more time with his wife, he abandoned the repair shop and opened a small business running three-wheeled vehicles between Nangal and a local town. Lacking financial backing and facing stiff competition from other operators, however, this enterprise lasted just a few months. Amarpal then obtained a series of poorly paid administrative and sales jobs in or around Bijnor town: as a supervisor in a private dairy, rural-urban milk trader, accountant at a private finance company and sales assistant in a garage. He described these jobs as demoralizing and repetitive, and he criticized the unscrupulous, immoral and 'corrupt' (*bhrasht*) behavior of many of his colleagues.

Although only seven young men, 7 percent of the educated, listed their primary occupation as 'business' employment, many others had attempted to start small enterprises, usually within Nangal. Educated Chamars running these businesses stressed that the absence of institutional credit and the frequent need for them to assist their families with medical and dowry expenses prevented their obtaining starting capital for their ventures or making effective business plans. Educated Chamar young men also maintained that they lacked experience of profitable business activity and the social contacts that would allow them to develop an entrepreneurial culture.

Only six Chamar young men, 6 percent of the educated, indicated that their primary employment was private service (*private naukrī*), but many other men had moved through an assortment of private-sector jobs in the informal economy similar to those undertaken by Amarpal. These posts were usually non-manual in nature, involving sales, teaching, administration or basic accountancy. But educated Chamar young men also seemed to put aside their aversion to 'hand work' by accepting jobs as cleaners and sweepers in urban areas, occupations regarded as low caste. Some Chamar young men referred to such work as "light salaried work" (*halkī naukrī*) or "laboring-type salaried work" (*mazdūrī kism ki naukrī*). But the possibility that cleaning or sweeping employment held out of capturing similar work in a government office or factory led most educated Chamar young men to ignore references to these jobs as 'unclean' or 'uneducated.' Two of the educated Chamar men in Nangal who had obtained government employment had secured jobs as cleaners: one, Jaibir (Chapter Five), polishing shoes in the local police station and one sorting and cleaning files in a bank.

Although the work within the informal economy conducted by Chamars and Jats sometimes overlapped, the positions in private service obtained by Chamars were typically less prestigious and secure than the 'semi-bourgeois' jobs obtained by wealthier Jat young men. Jats excluded from government employment had usually been able to obtain positions that offered some measure of permanence and paid over Rs. 2,000 a month. By contrast, the jobs performed by educated Chamars usually offered salaries of between Rs. 900 and Rs. 1,500 a month. Laboring work in Nangal therefore offered slightly higher pay and more reliable employment than most types of private service conducted by Chamar young men.

Chamars argued that their lack of social contacts and knowledge largely explained their exclusion from the types of "good private employment" (*achchhī private naukrī*) obtained by many educated rich Jat young men. As we noted in Chapter Three, young men's ability to perform urban styles of accomplished masculinity—to demonstrate, in Bourdieu's (1984) terms, "affinities of habitus"—was often crucial in obtaining secure private service. Amarpal conveyed this idea when referring to an interview in Lucknow for a clerical post in a large Indian manufacturing firm. He said that the interview had been progressing well, until an interviewer told him enigmatically, "You have come to Lucknow." Amarpal guessed that this was his moment to offer a bribe and brought out a Rs. 50 note. People commonly offered such sums to government officials as a tip. In this case, the interviewers were expecting at least Rs. 50,000. Lacking an understanding of the institutional culture of the recruitment process and tangibly failing in his actions and appearance to impress the panel, Amarpal left the interview in a dejected mood and having failed to secure the post (cf. Gupta 1995).

It is likely that educated Chamar young men's relative exclusion from urban social networks and their frequent inability to master styles of confident upper caste masculinity also prevented them from developing successful criminal careers. We heard of only one educated Chamar young man who had engaged in illegal activity, and he was from one of the very few Chamar households possessing a substantial amount of land. Indeed, perhaps the only area where educated Chamar young men had been quite successful in obtaining lucrative 'fallback work' was as contractors (*thekedār*) for government development programs, which we identified in Chapter Five as a staple form of temporary work for *naye netās*. But jobs as a contractor were scarce, intermittently available and unpredictable.

Like Jat parents, Chamars were commonly willing to allow their sons to experiment with small business work and private service during their twenties. Chamar parents expected their sons to spend their early manhood moving between jobs (*ghūm rahe hain*). By shifting between 'service-type' employment, parents could advertise their sons as people on the verge of secure salaried work. Indeed, Chamar parents' lack of knowledge of employment markets allowed some unscrupulous parents to fudge the employment status of their sons, for example by pretending that a privately employed administrator had a permanent job in a government bureaucracy. Such a tactic offered advantages in parents' efforts to arrange a son's marriage and obtain a higher dowry from the bride's family.

Just as Jat parents often sought to persuade their sons to enter agricultural work after a period 'wandering about,' Chamar parents frequently urged their newly married sons to swallow their pride and enter wage labor in the village. Sixty-eight percent of educated Chamar young men were in local manual wage labor in 2001, mostly employed by local Jats. Amarpal and many other Chamar young men steadfastly refused to resign themselves to manual wage labor, however. In response to Amarpal's apparent obstinacy, his mother, Gomti, said that he had become selfish and forgotten his family responsibilities: "I wish I had never sent him to school." Gomti also complained that Amarpal's wife, Munni, had corrupted her son and distracted him from the need to earn money. At the same time, Amarpal's father-in-law said that if Amarpal refused to enter manual laboring work he would arrange for Munni to divorce him. For much of 2001, Munni's father compelled her to live in her natal home. Amarpal said that his father-in-law had taken this extreme measure in order to persuade him to enter manual laboring work. According to Gomti, this decision followed accusations that Amarpal had been beating his wife. Whatever the truth, Amarpal perceived himself to have run out of options. He said that if he entered manual laboring work he would feel ashamed, but his continued refusal might entail losing his wife and angering his family.

As in Amarpal's case, the apparent aimlessness and anomie of educated un/

under-employed Chamar young men in Nangal had contributed to the pro-liferation of parental narratives casting young men as a moral danger. Instead of celebrating the civilizing power of the educated, many Chamar parents said that the depraved behavior of educated young men was "ruining the atmo-sphere of the village." Chamar parents often connected the idleness of young men to the corrupting role of a young wife, and we heard several stories to this effect. The following example, presented by Savitri, a Chamar woman in her mid-forties, typified these narratives. Savitri told us:

My son Devpal is very well educated, but even so he couldn't get a job. He is BA. He works with spades in the field. When I see him I feel great sadness. He is so well-edu-cated and he is working in the fields. But what to do? He has shot himself in the foot [literally: buried a hatchet in his foot (*usne to apne pair khud kulhārī mārī hai*)]. When I see him, my heart is always sad. I used to do hard laboring work: beating rice and grinding wheat. I used to earn Rs. 4 or Rs. 5 a day. It was very difficult to educate my son. Now he is doing laboring work, so why shouldn't I feel sad? All our hard work has been destroyed. Devpal had the chance to obtain salaried employment, very good salaried employment. Someone came to see us seeking to establish an engagement between Dev-pal and his daughter. The man said that the marriage would be in one year, after Devpal had been installed in a salaried job [which the prospective father-in-law would arrange]. At that moment, there were two possible marriages for Devpal: the family of the person offering salaried employment or another person who had a beautiful daughter. Devpal had wanted to get married to the beautiful young woman and didn't want to wait for a year before getting married. He became possessed by this girl. He said that if he couldn't get married he would die. He even carried a bullet around in his pocket. When he was ready to die, what could I do but arrange for him to be married to the beautiful one?

At this point another woman broke in, "Yes, she is very beautiful, I have seen her." Savitri replied bitterly:

What is that beauty going to do [for us]? She may be beautiful but she doesn't know how to behave. The beautiful wife even beats her husband!

Gomti's reference to her son's being 'possessed' by a young woman who subse-quently beats and therefore humiliates him illustrates a broader feature of par-ents' narratives of young male failure, which commonly focused on the weak-ness of young educated men's bodies, their susceptibility to bad influences and humiliation and young men's disorientation in time and space.

Timepass Cultures

Like most educated Chamar young men in Nangal, Amarpal showed minimal interest in stories of Dalit heroism and he avoided active roles within local
politics or social associations. Amarpal claimed that the BSP had reduced corruption and improved the flow of development resources into the village, but
that genuine improvements in Chamars' position could occur only through
a radical redistribution of resources in society. Amarpal's detachment from
formal politics and cultures of Ambedkarism reflected a wider view among
educated un/under-employed Chamars—most of whom were uninterested in
the arguments of Chamar *netās*, which they felt bore little relation to their own
hardships. Indeed, many educated Chamar young men mocked the exuberance
of men like Brijpal and used the term '*netā*' sarcastically to emphasize the gap
between the vaunting ambitions of village politicos and 'real *netās*' in Lucknow
and Delhi.

Whilst rejecting the arguments of *netās*, educated Chamar young men did
not advocate the forms of direct social action occasionally discussed by older
Chamars in Nangal: burning upper caste fields or destroying the houses of the
rich, for example. Amarpal said that his sense of hopelessness was sometimes
so intense that he felt like attacking successful Jats in the village or harming
himself. But he typically went on to observe that as an educated person such
actions would bring shame on his family: "I can't even commit suicide, because
people would ask why an educated person killed himself!" Amarpal was also
opposed to drinking alcohol or taking drugs as means of coping with frustration and he spoke angrily of the immorality of young men who wandered the
village drunk. Unlike the Dalits described by Anandhi et al. (2002) few educated
Chamar young men drank heavily. Instead, Amarpal and many of his peers devoted energy into developing cultural styles in which they depicted themselves
as 'lost' and 'good for nothing.' Amarpal referred to himself as someone who
had "lost his way in life" (*bhatak ho gaya*). On another occasion, he told us:

I believe that educated people are useless [*bekār*]. Educated people are trapped. They are
restricted in the work that they can do. Uneducated men are free; they can do whatever
they like: labor, farming, whatever. And if an illiterate man does something wrong, they
receive less of a punishment. People say that the person is illiterate and therefore lacks

understanding: they are seen as innocent. And if an educated person does something wrong, they do not receive a lesser punishment. People in society say, "That man is educated and even so he does bad things." So I think that in today's world, given the nature of unemployment, it is right to be illiterate.

Amarpal also referred to the opportunity costs associated with spending a long period in formal education:

Educated people cannot do labor or agricultural work—they feel ashamed and they haven't acquired the habit [ādat] of doing farming work. If you take one person who has been a farmer since childhood and another who becomes a farmer after twenty-five years of education, there is clearly a difference between them.

Paralleling the narratives of uneducated Chamar and Muslim young men, educated Chamars sometimes argued that education had made them weak (kamzor). They referred to the burden of expectations placed on them as 'educated people' and occasionally regretted going to school.

The themes of educated people's entrapment and desperation were repeated in many other interviews with educated Chamar young men (cf. Heuzé 1996). Like Amarpal, a few Chamars were so jaundiced by their inability to find suitable work that they rarely or only half-heartedly expressed their sense of educated distinction. Appropriating parental narratives of young male aimlessness, these men often characterized themselves as useless, empty, wandering and unemployed. In making these statements, they were not claiming that they were incapable of performing useful work or that they lacked employment: many of them would refer to themselves as 'unemployed' while engaged in wage labor. Rather, they used these terms to signal the disjuncture between their present occupational status and their educated standing and to signal their own sense that "something better must be just round the corner." These statements often emerged during angry and heartfelt outbursts regarding the nature of poverty. Yet at other moments, educated Chamars joked about their predicament and made semi-humorous references to their status as wanderers (ghūmnewale or ghūmte phirte ādmī). Humor, joking and spirited banter were important elements of young men's reaction to a sense of personal crisis.

Notions of lost time pervaded ideas of Chamar male 'uselessness.' Chamar young men occasionally discussed their activity, work and leisure, as forms of 'timepass,' which highlighted young men's sense of the provisional status of their current work but was also linked to their frustration at the many years wasted in applying for government jobs. Whereas Jat young men used '*timepass*' as a label for particularly 'meaningless' study or work, Chamars seemed to deploy the term to refer to a whole style of life and disposition toward the future.

In emphasizing their standing as 'wandering men,' or men engaged only in *timepass*, Amarpal and his Chamar peers challenged higher caste assumptions that Chamars are suited only for manual labor and should be subject to forms of spatial segregation. Chamar efforts to perform a vision of themselves as 'wandering men'—by hanging around on street corners or roaming the village—disconcerted many Jats, who frequently referred to Chamars becoming over-confident. But educated Chamar young men such as Amarpal lacked the economic resources necessary to sustain cultural styles centered on educated unemployment, for most Chamar young men could not afford to remain un-employed or engaged in private clerical work. In addition, the efforts of edu-cated Chamar young men to stress their wandering status served to reinforce male control over public space in Nangal. By emphasizing their standing as people "mooching about the village," educated Chamars fuelled moral narra-tives among parents that cast educated young men as a public sexual threat. The increasing number of un/under-employed young men standing around the bus stop and chatting by shops in the center of the village was a common source of consternation among Chamar parents. Chamars spoke of how these men were making it more difficult for young women to travel safely to and from school.

These observations throw further light on the public reception of *netās*' discourses discussed in Chapter Four. Rather than creating a shared feeling of purpose and direction among educated young men, *netās*' steadfast optimism tended to alienate or disinterest their educated un/under-employed peers. It is therefore possible to identify a bifurcated response to educated un/under-employment among Chamars: some young men among the richer sections of the caste developed explicitly political styles whilst the majority demonstrated a sense of anger and resentment.

We nevertheless encountered pragmatism among educated Chamars that neither accorded with the tenacious politics of the *netās* nor with the melan-cholic disposition of '*timepass*' Chamars. For example, while disinterested in local forms of politicking, Hemraj displayed only mild resentment regarding his exclusion from secure salaried work and he did not cultivate an image as a 'useless man' or 'wanderer.' Hemraj was much more concerned about his father's ill health and the employment prospects of his siblings than finding creative means for expressing his disillusionment. Similarly, Amarpal's younger brother, Jagbir, although keen to distinguish himself from uneducated peers, said that there was little point in proudly refusing to do manual wage labor. As one of Jagbir's educated Chamar friends put it:

When you don't have money and have a wife and children to support, you have to do laboring work. Some people don't like labor because they have studied a lot, but without money there is nothing . . . It is just no use being ashamed.

Rather than fashioning images of themselves as people "waiting for better work" in the manner of Amarpal, Jagbir and some other educated Chamar young men sought practical means of reducing the ignominy and hardship of their laboring occupations. Jagbir discussed how he and his friends steal off into the fields to play cards, joke, chat or read. They did not imagine these acts as a means of developing a distinctive 'educated' style of being a manual laborer. They argued that if they tried to develop such a culture, Jat employers would complain of their haughtiness and refuse them work. Instead, Jagbir spoke of his activities as a laborer as piecemeal efforts to 'have fun' or "improvise with available resources" (jugār).

More commonly, however, Chamar responses to educated un/under-employment either tended toward an optimistic drive for transformation or resigned feelings of hopelessness. We examined the impact of naye netās' ideas on rural society in Chapter Five. The practices of young Chamar disillusionment also shaped parental opinion and strategies. Several Chamar parents said that they now believed it best to educate boys only up to Eighth Class and then send them for vocational training or an apprenticeship. These parents argued that there is little point in investing money in formal education beyond Eighth Class given the virtual impossibility of obtaining government employment. A poor Chamar man told us:

It's not like there's no point in study. You should study up to Eighth Class or Tenth Class. After that you should learn some technical work. From that a man can earn at least Rs. 2,000 to Rs. 2,500 per month.

Another poor Chamar man maintained that

Children should be educated up to Eighth Class and put into the *mechanic line*. They shouldn't be educated beyond this. Get them educated to BA or MA and then they don't get salaried work and can't do laboring work either. They become useless. They feel ashamed doing laboring work.

In Chapter Six we suggested that the combination of educated Muslim young men's failure to obtain white-collar work and the narratives of uneducated Muslims about the weakness of the educated had persuaded some Muslim parents to downgrade their expectations of mainstream schooling. Paralleling this process, widespread resentment among educated un/under-employed Chamars had provoked some parents to reconsider the benefits of education. While school education among Chamars between 1990 and 2001 in the cohorts aged 8–12 and 13–17 increased markedly, the proportion of young men aged 18–22 in formal education declined: from 22 percent in 1990 to 11 percent in 2001. The total number of Chamar men of all ages in higher education fell from ten in 1990 to three in 2001. The decrease in the number of Chamar young men studying into their late teens and twenties may reflect increasing pressures on the household economy, but this hardly squares with the large *increase* in school education within the younger cohorts of Chamar boys and among girls. It seems more likely that the widespread failure among Chamars to obtain service employment in the 1990s encouraged members of this caste to re-evaluate their approach to formal education for boys. Consistent with this interpretation, among Jats, who have been more successful in obtaining government work or appropriate fallback employment during the 1990s, enrollment in formal education within the 18–22 cohort *increased* between 1990 and 2001. A new Chamar strategy focused on concentrating resources in primary and early secondary schooling to obtain key skills and some measure of educated distinction for their sons.

Muslim and Jat Resentment

Most educated un/under-employed Jat and Muslim young men were upbeat about their prospects, but some exhibited a markedly different reaction to their circumstances, as the case of Rauf suggests. Rauf was 30 in 2001, the eldest son in a moderately wealthy Muslim household possessing five acres of land. He was married to a distant cousin and had two infant children. Rauf had two younger sisters and two younger brothers. He was educated at a private primary school and Begawala madrasah and then at an aided inter-college close to Qaziwala. Rauf failed his Twelfth Class examinations twice. Rauf's parents, Faruq and Anwari, could not afford to enroll him as a non-attending student, and Faruq required Rauf's assistance on the farm at this time. His parents therefore decided to remove Rauf from school. Rauf attended two government job interviews in the late 1990s, and he told us how he had failed to obtain a position on both occasions. Rauf helped his younger brother, Nadim, establish a small car repair shop in Bijnor, but this business failed because of a lack of customers. In 2001, Rauf was working as a farmer in Qaziwala.

Rauf's sense of resentment arose in part out of a feeling that his school education failed to provide useful skills and knowledge. He complained that teachers in the schools he had attended were "running a tuition racket" (*tuition kā chakkar*) and refused to teach in class. Rauf deeply resented the lack of facilities in rural schools and he spoke of the better infrastructure available within urban, English-medium institutions. Faruq and Anwari could not afford to give Rauf a managerial role on the farm and often called on him to assist with the sowing, weeding and harvesting of crops. Rauf complained about the grueling and dirty nature of agricultural work and that as a farmer he is compelled to liaise with corrupt officials. Rauf spent much of his time trying to avoid agricultural work. He channeled his energy instead into racing pigeons in the village. He enjoyed betting on pigeon races and discussing the relative strengths of different birds. His parents were appalled at his hobby, however. Anwari attributed Rauf's errant behavior to his wife's corrupting influence, and the deteriorating relationship between mother and son had resulted in Rauf establishing a separate stove (*chulhā*) within their household compound. Equally frustrated by his son's apparent waywardness, Faruq had set Rauf's share of the household's harvest at just 8 percent. In the spring of 2001, Rauf responded by stopping work on the household farm. He supported himself and his family using money given to him by his father-in-law, who sympathized with Rauf's circumstances.

The disillusionment displayed by Rauf was more common among educated

un/under-employed Jat young men. The case of Hukum Singh and his family is
instructive. Hukum Singh owned about 9 acres of agricultural land in 2001 and
had five sons and two daughters. He had an Eighth Class pass and had formerly
worked as a government bus conductor. In the late 1960s, he sold a quarter of his
agricultural land to fund his sons' education. Three of his five sons had become
doctors. But the eldest son, Pyush, stole money from his parents and left home
after Eighth Class. During the next ten years, Pyush built up a rural criminal
network and 'wandered' between Nangal and Bijnor. In the late 1990s, Pyush
decided he should lead a 'civilized' life. He obtained work as a government elec-
tricity worker in a local town and lived at home with his parents in 2001. His
mother, Manju, said that her family could afford to buy a bride for Pyush in the
area north of Bijnor, but that villagers would then taunt her for having failed to
arrange Pyush's marriage in the 'right' way. Pyush said that he did not want to
bring dishonor on the family by marrying a bought bride. Manju was bitterly
disappointed by Pyush's dissolute past. Hukum was also furious with him, and
he recounted how he had been forced to leave his own job in the State transport
department to hunt for Pyush when he ran away from home. Hukum described
Pyush as "my enemy from birth" (*janam kā dushman*). "But for him, our family
could have touched the sky!"

Chandu was Hukum and Manju's fourth son. He was thirty-two and unmarried in 2001. Chandu obtained good results in his Eighth Class examinations in
Nangal Junior High School, and his peers remembered him as a lively pupil "full
of jokes." After Eighth Class, he studied at one of the better provisioned aided
inter-colleges in Bijnor, where he also achieved high grades. Keen on pursuing
a career in agricultural science, Chandu successfully completed the entrance
examinations for Pantnagar Agricultural College (PAC), about 65 miles north-
west of Bijnor. Chandu and his mother said that he developed a reputation as
a 'hard man' at Pantnagar. Chandu remembered, "Everyone respected me and I
never had any trouble." Chandu also developed a drug habit. Mid-way through
his career there, Chandu applied for a lucrative post as a government agricultural advisor. As the family tells the story, an enemy of the family, who worked
as the village postman, intercepted and destroyed the letter offering Chandu
the position. By the time that Chandu discovered this, the government had
appointed someone else in his place. Hukum said that, after Chandu received

news of this loss, he 'became useless.' In 2001, Chandu slept each night in sugar cane fields surrounding the village and only traveled to the family home in the village when he needed food, often in the middle of the night.

When Craig and Chhaya first met Chandu, he was sprawled in the doorway of his family home singing a song from a Bollywood film. He was dressed in fawn pants torn at the knee, and trainers through which two toes poked out. His pants were sodden up to his calves and he was drunk. Chandu did not recognize Chhaya, who had been a classmate at Nangal Junior High School. Chandu walked unsteadily to a rope bed and said that he wanted to talk. During the discussion that followed, Chandu frequently stopped to retch over the side of the bed. He spoke in a loud, declamatory style, saying that it was pointless for people to go around chasing white-collar employment. In his view, rural people had developed a craze for salaried jobs without reflecting properly on the purpose of employment. Chandu told us:

The villagers' *mentality* is that if you get salaried work after being educated then you are fine, and if you don't, they think that your education is useless. Why do people do salaried work? People get married, have children and pay for their children's education: people's responsibilities and expenses increase. And how do people pay for all this? They get salaried work!

In spite of referring to his own 'uselessness,' Chandu said that as an 'educated person' he is the bearer of important skills and knowledge. He contrasted his manly acceptance of his exclusion from government work with the emotional outbursts of women and uneducated people. Chandu also boasted that, as an educated person, he possesses detailed knowledge of north Indian politics, assists friends in securing government jobs and monitors the careers of Pantnagar graduates in local newspapers. Consistent with young male narratives of educated distinction, Chandu claimed to take drugs in moderation and stressed his prudent approach to caffeine consumption: "I never drink more than one cup of tea a day." Central to Chandu's discussions of himself as an educated person was a vision of his cultural versatility. He referred to his ability to move between the world of student politics in Pantnagar and rural cultivation in Nangal and he claimed to possess an in-depth knowledge of social and political matters outside India. Chandu referred to details of the US invasion of Afghanistan, talked about the difference between research in India and Scotland and scattered English words in his sentences. Chandu also stressed that as an educated person from Scotland, Craig was one of the few people who could really understand him: "If you [Craig] lived in the village, people would think you were mad too!"

Having listened to Chandu's explanation of his refusal to seek salaried work, Manju fumed:

Go, don't do salaried work, stay in farming, but don't stay like this. Get married! Have children! Become a householder! How can you stay in such a dirty condition? Look at your filthy shoes. You don't meet anyone, you don't talk to anyone. The idea of brother and sister has no meaning for you. And you don't take any notice of the villagers and neighbors either!

When Chandu responded by ridiculing his mother's lack of education, she snapped back quickly:

Yes, I'm not very intelligent, not very educated! Yes, that's true, not very *educated* at all. [Crying] But I gave birth to you and your brothers. I have spent so much money getting you all educated. We used to have more land and now we have just 50 *bīghas* [10 acres]. The land went in order to get you educated.

On another occasion, she pleaded with Chandu:

If you are going to carry on living like this, you should start living as a holy man [*sādhū*]. If you are not going to marry or think about anyone else, then become a *sādhū*: at least then you will obtain the name of god. What sort of life is it that you are living? You just get intoxicated and lie around!

Chandu mumbled something at this point about his mother not understanding the pressures that young men are under. This comment incensed Manju who exploded:

Why do you talk only of your struggles? What do you know about the insults that we receive? We are forced to listen to what people from our own family say about us, but you know nothing about worldly goings on [*duniyādārī*].

Chandu had refused financial help from his brothers, turned down opportunities to discuss his position and ridiculed his parents when they scolded him. Manju said, "He does whatever his heart desires, nothing else." Chandu told us that his life was 'useless' and that he intended just to "live out his time":

We are all just doing *timepass* in this world. God created us and will call us back again. No-one stays in the world permanently. Those who have come will have to go. I have lived for 30–35 years and I will probably live for another 30–35 years. I will spend the rest of my life in the same manner as I am living now. There is no more excellent way to spend one's life than the way that I am living. I am enjoying it [*mazā ātā hai*].

The cases of Rauf and Chandu show how the experience of un/under-employment had led to profound despair among some Muslim and Jat young men. By 2001, six educated un/under-employed Jat young men, five of whom were unmarried, and three Muslims aged between 20 and 34 had responded to exclusion from government work by cultivating an image as 'wanderers' or '*timepass* men.' Conversations with other educated Jat and Muslim young men suggested that this cultural style had become much more common between the late 1980s and early 2000s. Lacking the enthusiasm and resilience of men like Sonu (Chapter Four) and Zamir (Chapter Five), and disillusioned with the process of competing for government work, some Jat and Muslim young men preferred to label themselves 'unemployed' (*berozgār*) or 'useless' (*bekār*) than seek fallback work or develop a managerial role on family farms. Like many Chamars, these young men used the term *timepass* to signal their detachment from the responsibilities and challenges commonly associated with young male adulthood. The mood and practices of disillusioned Muslims are likely to have exacerbated the ambivalence toward education that we characterized as a feature of parents' narratives in Chapter Six, and the actions of men like Chandu may have been tempering Jat parents' general enthusiasm for education.

Like Chamars, Jat and Muslim parents reacted to the emergence of self-consciously disillusioned young men in part by circulating moral narratives of young men as a danger. One Jat woman told us:

All day the boys just wander all over the place. They just sit around chatting and playing [cards] by the shops near the temple. They don't stick to any work and they don't go to the fields either.

As in the Chamar case, Jat and Muslim observations of young male waywardness often referred to the corrupting influence of a daughter-in-law and cohered into broader moral narratives. Parents frequently said that young men are 'by nature' (*fitrat, sva-bhāv*) lazy, suggestible and weak and therefore likely to remonstrate with parents, shirk paid employment and come under the influence of 'bad elements,' such as strong-willed wives. In these narratives, parents often contrasted their sons' and daughters-in-law's natures with those of their daughters, whom they perceived to be in essence obedient, diligent and conscientious. That many parents prioritized their sons' educational needs over those of daughters, and sacrificed a great deal to educate their sons, exacerbated their anger at young male misdemeanors.

Chamar and Muslim parents who remonstrated with their sons usually did so without having personal experience of formal schooling and seeking government work. By contrast, many Jat fathers had experienced educated un/under-employment. These men tended to be more sympathetic to young men's idleness but also sharper in their criticism of precisely how young Jats used their free time. For example, Bedpal, Sonu's father (Chapter Four), said that when he was a young man searching for government work, those around him were revolutionaries (*krāntīkarnewāle*), with passion in their hearts and agitation (*manthan*) on their minds. He then said that contemporary educated un/under-employed young men have an 'inferiority complex' (*hīn bhāvnā*) that renders them politically inconsequential and apathetic. Bedpal argued that the furious competition for government work prevents young men from expressing political ambitions, weakens their bodies and leaves them 'entangled' (*uljhnā*) in their own affairs. Bedpal also criticized the tendency among some Jat young men to imagine themselves as engaged only in *timepass*.

Unlike Chamars, most Jat and Muslim young men expressing resentment were farmers, and some of these men adopted everyday forms of resistance geared toward displaying their anger and frustration at agricultural work (Scott 1985). These acts included performing farming work late or refusing to work with their hands. Alongside other popular pastimes, such as cards, cricket and *karem* (a traditional board game), rearing pigeons was a particularly popular means for educated Jat and Muslim young men to communicate resentment and escape from the anxieties of searching for secure salaried work. Chamars did not engage in pigeon racing, largely because they could not afford to do so. But many Jats and Muslims had built curved bamboo perches that towered over their houses and spent hours watching and exercising their pigeons. They spoke of their deep passion for pigeon rearing, boasted of their ability to recognize their own birds at a distance and hand-fed their birds with seed. The competitive urge to breed winning birds and the desire to gamble money on pigeon races appeared to be less important to educated young men than the desire to nurture and protect their pigeons. Jat and Muslim parents were unwilling to entertain the possibility that pigeon rearing might prepare their sons for civilized male adulthood, in spite of a tradition of Muslim male involvement in pigeon rearing in the Mughal courts of north India. Parents complained instead that pigeon rearing and racing had contributed to a deterioration in their sons' employment prospects and that pigeons consume scarce economic resources and do not generate income, but cause fighting, swearing and gambling in the village. In addition, Jat parents commonly regarded pigeon racing as a Muslim pastime wholly inappropriate for Jats.

Read alongside Chamar practices, Jat cultures of resentment were reordering to a limited extent the relationship between caste and space in Nangal. Cultures of resentment sometimes brought disillusioned Jats into Nangal's main street, where they ostentatiously 'hung about,' chatted or raced pigeons and occasionally came into conflict with Chamars. But more commonly, Jats frequented spaces remote from village affairs. They were scattered around the edge of the villages or mainly confined to their family courtyards. Two educated Jat young men lived with a *sādhū* under a large tree outside the village, two slept in their parents' tube-well shed in the fields and another spent most of his waking hours in a pigeon-loft with his birds. Given a propensity for disillusioned Chamars to gather in the center of the village, rising disillusionment had partially reversed, or at least unsettled, the relationship between space and caste in the village.

Cultures of alcoholism and drug use have existed among Jats in Bijnor and adjacent districts since the nineteenth century, partly due to Jats' contact with alcohol within the army (Stokes 1986). There was nevertheless widespread agreement among villagers that the consumption of alcohol, cannabis and opium had increased sharply among Jat men since the early 1980s, due to rising frustration and to young men's greater contact with urban cultures, and the village's two liquor stores were popular and highly profitable.

Villagers also claimed that rising educated un/under-employment had moved some Jat young men to suicide (*ātmaghāta*) and that this was a new phenomenon. Between 1985 and 2001, we were told, three educated Jat young men committed suicide. In two cases, the increased pressure of obtaining educational credentials and secure employment appears to have been an important factor. Suicide had become an important topic of conversations among Jat parents, and some spoke of the need to hide dangerous chemical fertilizers and pesticides from young men who might use these substances to end their lives. In contrast, we did not encounter frequent references to a rise in alcoholism or suicide among Muslim or Chamar young men. Muslim parents and young men agreed that alcohol consumption and suicide are un-Islamic and, like Chamar young men, they regarded drinking alcohol and ending one's life as 'uneducated' behavior.

The similarities in the strategies of educated Chamar young men and those of a more limited set of Muslims and Jats provide some evidence of a public culture of resentment among educated un/under-employed young men in rural Bijnor district. Ideas of being trapped by one's educated standing and enduringly dispirited by the search for government work or appropriate fallback employment traversed boundaries of class, caste and community. But disillusionment was much more common among Chamars than among Jats and Muslims. The intensity with which educated Chamar young men experienced exclusion from salaried employment, their inability to obtain fallback work and the financial obstacles that Chamars faced in maintaining a vision of themselves as wandering men had fostered a broader crisis of masculinity and deeper disillusionment with education than we observed among Jats and Muslims.

Conclusions

Many educated un/under-employed young men have reacted to their predicament by referring to themselves as 'wandering' 'timepass' or 'useless' men. Poor educated Chamar young men were especially likely to display this cultural style. These men lacked the charisma and political interests of naye netās, the agricultural land owned by Jats and the urban social contacts possessed by educated Muslims. Outside a small circle of new politicians, educated Chamars felt frustrated by their exclusion from government employment and were deeply reluctant to 'settle down' to manual wage labor. We have therefore identified three broad species of response to un/under-employment among Chamars: a first in which young men work as political intermediaries, a second centered on *'timepass'* cultural styles and a third in which young men demonstrate prag-matic responses to un/under-employment outside the sphere of politics, typi-cally by entering daily waged labor.

One educated Muslim young man in Qaziwala and several Jats in Nangal also cultivated images as disconsolate men. Whereas Chamar parents usually lacked the resources required to keep their sons in idleness, Muslim and Jat parents who had been able to fund extended periods of education for their sons also had the money necessary to finance *timepass* cultures. Indeed, in several cases a 'wandering' son had lived side-by-side with his parents in an atmosphere of mutual distrust and resentment for many years. Young men's resources therefore shaped their capacity to build and sustain cultures of self-conscious 'unemployment.'

The rise of a cohort of *timepass* young men generated parental narratives that constructed young men as either hyper-masculine—a sexual threat to vil-lage women, for example—or lacking in masculinity, for example as susceptible to the 'evil influences' of their wives. The high profile of disillusioned educated young men in Nangal and Qaziwala had also spurred many parents to rethink their approach to boys' and young men's education. Chamars and Muslims, in particular, were increasingly concentrating their efforts on ensuring that their sons received basic educational skills and withdrawing them from school after Eighth Class.

These conclusions bear on the work of Heuzé (1996) in Chhattisgarh and Anandhi et al. (2002) in Tamil Nadu on educated unemployed young men. As in these cases, the idea of being 'unemployed' and embodied cultures of wan-dering had become means through which lower caste men challenge higher caste privileges. At the same time, and perhaps because of the relative 'newness' of educational opportunities in western UP, Chamars in rural Bijnor district seemed much less inclined to reject visions of 'civilized comportment' than did Dalits in Tamil Nadu. Our material also points to the ambivalence of educated un/under-employed young people's masculinities. Conventional images of the disenchanted educated unemployed young man—such as Chandu's reputation as a 'hard man' in an urban college—coexisted with cultural practices that are more difficult to position within literature on contemporary South Asian mas-culinities, such as young men's gentle attention to pigeon rearing.

This chapter has also exposed parents' eagerness to express their *own struggles* to obtain power, resources and respect in the context of processes of widespread un/under-employment. As the exchange between Chandu and Manju illustrated, parents were often angered by a tendency among young men to concentrate on the hardships of youth un/under-employment without appreciating the sacrifices that their parents had made. Educated un/under-employment had led to the emergence of new struggles between parents and young men to express and circulate visions of their own suffering and acquire the sympathy and support of other family members. Notions of what constitutes 'educated' and 'uneducated' behavior were key 'word weapons' in these ongoing inter-generational feuds.

8

Conclusions

In the early 2000s in rural Bijnor district large numbers of young men were emerging from school or university with few prospects of obtaining secure 'educated' work. A generation of young men born in the 1970s and '80s, usually much better educated than their parents and groomed to expect salaried employment, spent their twenties searching in vain for government jobs. Educated young men were differentially equipped to negotiate un/under-employment, however. The differing histories of class, caste and community did not determine educated young men's strategies; young men's approaches to un/under-employment were diverse because they had varied aims in life, individual personalities and agendas, and responded to specific opportunities and constraints in divergent ways. But the economic, social and cultural resources that young men can command—which are a function in large part of their caste, class and religious backgrounds—powerfully influence their responses to economic uncertainties.

We have identified four main 'clusters' of practice among young men, three of which overlap with caste/religious community, while the fourth transcends these boundaries. First, educated un/under-employed young men among the Jats were relatively successful in maintaining an image of themselves as 'educated' people. These young men had used their inherited economic, social and cultural resources, to obtain 'fallback' employment in service, business or agriculture. Jat young men's capacity to utilize their educational credentials successfully depended upon their ability to bribe government officials, build social networks with well-placed people outside the village and emphasize cultural affinities with upper caste Hindus.

A second set of Chamar young men had responded to their exclusion from secure salaried work by entering politics. Widespread un/under-employment among Chamars combined with new forms of party political support for this caste in UP had generated a class of self-styled 'new politicians' or *naye netās* in rural areas who acted as intermediaries between rural society and government bureaucracies and circulated political discourse at the local level.

A third response to educated un/under-employment was to pursue respect outside the search for secular white-collar work. In rural Bijnor district, this strategy was especially common among Muslims, who used social links in urban areas to enter Muslim-run craft workshops or religious work. At the same time, rising religious communal tensions were threatening educated Muslim young men's employment strategies.

A final set of young men, from Jat, Muslim, as well as Chamar households, reacted to educated un/under-employment by cultivating an image as 'wanderers' or 'useless' men. Without the resources of the Jats and social links of new politicians and Muslims, educated Chamar young men, in particular, often internalized parental narratives criticizing their behavior and spoke of themselves as engaged only in '*timepass*' lives.

The strategies of these sets of educated young men must be examined relationally. For example, the emergence of a cohort of Chamar *netās* intent on challenging the power of middle castes intensified Jat young men's search for new marks of distinction. Similarly, the popularity of skilled craft work as a source of fallback employment among Muslims heightened Chamars' aversion to careers as artisans. Educated un/under-employed young men's quest for work and dignity therefore occurred in terrains constituted in part by the actions and resources of the other 'players' (Bourdieu 1984).

This chapter explores the broader implications of this account of youth cultures, education and inequality in north India with reference to the social reproduction of class, caste and religious inequalities in UP, discussions of plural modernities within and beyond South Asia and debates about education within development academia. What ties these three discussions together is a concern with moving beyond binary choices presented within much contemporary social science—is north India becoming more democratic? Are rural UP youth imitating western modernity? Does education transform society?—to emphasize ambivalent, contradictory and partial social change.

Reproducing Difference?

There is a widespread consensus among political scientists that a 'Dalit revolution' has taken place in north India (Pai 2000; Varshney 2000; Jaffrelot 2003). In this view, the rise of the BSP in UP politics combined with mobilization from below has resulted in a shift in the balance of power at the local level. A 'rural elite'—comprised of either Hindu upper castes or locally dominant intermediate castes—is increasingly being forced to share power with Dalits. Jaffrelot (2003) has argued with particular force that in rural north India there is an ongoing transformation in local power relations.

Our account provides some support for this argument. A small set of confident, articulate and socially skillful 'new politicians' had emerged among Chamars in Nangal and was improving poor people's access to state services, politicizing the Chamar population and circulating visions of social improvement through education. The rise of these *naye netās* points to the potential for formal political change combined with increased educational access to improve the prospects of marginalized communities. At a more everyday level, Chamar young men who had developed cultural styles as 'wanderers' or '*timepass* men' were undermining historical relationships between caste and space in Nangal. The aesthetic nature of the challenge to higher castes presented by new politicians and *timepass* men reflects the dangers associated with directly antagonizing dominant rural classes (Scott 1985) and the need to protect a core of self-esteem by acting in an 'educated' manner.

But most Chamars in Nangal remained dependent on Jats. Chamars were confined to poorly paid manual labor, owned little or no land and typically lacked a sense of collective strength and political power. The entrenched nature of Chamar deprivation prevented new politicians from generating a popular movement for social change. Most Dalits were disillusioned with the BSP and the idea of political transformation through the capture of state power. Our evidence therefore supports other recent studies of the continued vulnerability and subordination of Dalit castes in rural UP (Lieten and Srivastava 1999; Lerche 1999; Jeffrey 2001).

Jaffrelot might counter that he is describing only a partial transformation in the relationship between caste and power. But he goes on to argue that a full 'political revolution' will work itself out over the next few decades (Jaffrelot 2003: 364). Such linear conceptions of social transformation are problematic. Indeed, some of the processes of social change we have discussed in this book point in the other direction: toward, for example, a deepening mood of pessimism and hopelessness among Dalits and a retreat from Dalit investment in higher education.

We highlight this aspect of our research mindful of how debates about social mobility and revolution have been politicized on the ground. Some Jats in Nangal advanced arguments similar to those of Jaffrelot about lower caste 'revolution' (*krānti*) to justify their own oppressive practices. They also used discourses of Dalit revolution to position Jats as economically impoverished. This formed part of a wider move among Jats to demonstrate their alleged social and economic deprivation in order to obtain OBC status.

Jaffrelot employs the term '*silent* revolution' to signal the relatively calm nature of the social transformation he identifies, a calmness he links to divisions within the lower caste movement and to the gradual form that the revolution is allegedly taking. But we would do well to reflect on the theoretical work that the adjective 'silent' performs. Distinct from ideas of silent political revolt, we have suggested that, in as far as Dalits were mobilizing for political change, they were doing so in a loud and articulate manner and their activity generated similarly noisy 'counter-resistance' on the ground. Indeed, the process of 'raising voice' had itself become an object of discourse in grassroots processes of Dalit mobilization. In rural Bijnor district, new politicians' cultural practices were oriented around the development of an ideology of voice, in which they presented themselves as distinctively equipped to speak and in which the ability to vocalize ideas was connected to moral notions of educated success.

The disjuncture between our account of Dalit politics and that of Jaffrelot (2003) largely reflects differences of method. Jaffrelot's analysis of 'silent revolution' is compiled mainly from archival evidence, election figures and interviews with key politicians. This perspective is important for understanding large-scale processes of political change. But Jaffrelot's history of lower caste politics does not engage closely with the views of 'ordinary' Dalits and links between national level policy changes and everyday practice. In drawing attention to these issues in western UP our work contributes to a history of political anthropological work in north India (e.g. Bailey 1957; Khare 1984; Robinson 1988).

Recent accounts of Dalit revolution have also tended to downplay elite counter-resistance. It is possible to identify two strands of recent research into the everyday dominance of upper and middle castes in rural UP and neighboring states. The first, of which Mendelsohn (1993) provides an example, dovetails with Jaffrelot (2003) by proposing that there has been a marked decline in the dominance of higher castes in rural north India (see also Gupta 1998; Pai 2000). A second strand, represented in the work of Lerche (1995, 1999), suggests that dominance relationships in north India have only been slightly moderated.

There are some parallels between our account of Jat social action in rural Bijnor district and the strand of work represented by Mendelsohn (1993). As in Mendelsohn's case study village in Rajasthan, Jats in Nangal no longer paid other castes to perform particular services in line with the *jajmānī* system of caste. Moreover, in Nangal the dominant caste was becoming rapidly differentiated economically and they increasingly looked outside the village for new social and economic opportunities.

Contra Mendelsohn, however, Jats continued to dominate Chamars in Nangal by controlling landownership, investing in education themselves and maintaining exclusionary social networks. Social change in this part of rural UP is best characterized as a shift from a period of *direct dominance*, in which power was exerted primarily through control over land and labor, to *mediated dominance*, in which access to social networks and cultural capital are increasingly significant. Mendelsohn's (1993) claim that dominant castes have ceased to act in a coordinated and collective manner to defend social advantages is also questionable (see Béteille 1992). Whilst Jats and other powerful caste groups in UP do not pursue social goals with reference to the type of 'caste councils' described by Srinivas (1955) in his classic essay on dominant castes, kinship links continue to be crucial to the strategies of powerful middle and upper castes in contemporary north India, particularly in the spheres of education and employment. Rather than declining in significance, caste solidarities have changed form; caste was more often expressed through relatively 'informal' networks than overtly within formal associations.

A spatial perspective illuminates the importance of dominance and caste in rural north India (Jeffrey 2001). Jat young men and their parents in rural Bijnor district had used their superior resources to nurture and sustain a dense nexus of power that connected their rural homes to government offices in Bijnor, private schools outside the district and more expansive networks of consumer good distribution and political mobilization. Through such networks, Jats had largely co-opted the local state, circumvented the deterioration of rural government schools and found new ways to signal their social distinction. Muslims and Chamars fashioned their own networks in the face of economic uncertainty, for example by acting as intermediaries between rural people and the state or migrating to urban centers. But these 'subaltern' networks had not substantially altered the overall balance of power in rural Bijnor district or interrupted the process through which Jat young men reproduce their advantage.

In addition to offering a counterpoint to recent accounts of Dalit social revolution, our discussion of young men's strategies challenges discussions of Muslim social and economic change in north India that posit too stark a contrast between 'Muslim strategies' and those of other social groups. Educated un/under-employed Muslim young men, like their Chamar and Jat peers, invested in visions of progress through education. Like the Chamars and Jats, educated Muslim young men were keen to obtain government employment, acquire a 'modern' identity and lead civilized, prosperous and respectable lives. Muslims' anxieties and strategies represent ordinary struggles for respect.

Where Muslim strategies *did* vary from those of Chamars and Jats, these differences relate primarily to the structural conditions in which Muslims were living, and not the working out of a distinctively 'Muslim mindset' (cf. Jeffery and Jeffery 2006). Muslims in rural Bijnor district remain poorly placed relative to Chamars and Jats in the search for mainstream schooling, government jobs and regional political influence (cf. Sachar 2006). Indeed, the rise of the BJP in formal politics further threatened and marginalized Muslim households and encouraged religious communal prejudice in the 1990s and early 2000s. In the context of their exclusion from government schooling, Muslims in rural Bijnor district had invested in a form of parallel madrasah education. Simi-

larly, the few Muslim young men who had obtained mainstream schooling responded to their exclusion from local forms of white-collar employment by
looking for alternative work. We have also pointed to how the single category
of 'rural Muslims' obscures marked variations in the resources and standing of
rural households and in the strategies of individual young men. Our emphasis
on the perpetuation of social inequalities based upon caste and religion arises,
then, not out of a dogmatic adherence to notions of reproduction, but through
analysis of the dialectical relationship between young men's diverse strategies
and the broader political forces shaping their lives.

Grounding Modernities

The overwhelming majority of Muslim young men and many Chamars
had abandoned formal education before completing Eighth Class, and some
of these men had formulated critiques of formal schooling. These uneducated
men frequently referred instead to visions of social progress based on a type of
muscular masculinity. In addition, madrasah-educated young men articulated
ideas of appropriate Islamic masculinity which emphasized withdrawal from
the pursuit of worldly goods and schooling qualifications. Uneducated and madrasah-educated young men's cultural assertions represent important 'alternative modernities' (Gaonkar 2001): they express beliefs about how to live distinctively in the contemporary era that are at odds with the opinions of the most
powerful in rural society and of mainstream government and development organizations. These men also identified spaces outside school—such as the fields,
home and street—where people can obtain useful skills and knowledge.

But the predominant response of school-educated Jat, Chamar and Muslim young men to un/under-employment has been to reaffirm their belief in
formal school education as a basis for social betterment. Young men imagined
that education defines what it means to be civilized, moral and up-to-date.
Young men claimed that they are distinct from previous generations because
they possess skills, knowledge and embodied capacities unavailable to their
predecessors. Notions of education and illiteracy acted as a grand narrative for
organizing other forms of cultural capital.

The redeployment of binary concepts such as developed/underdeveloped,

global/local, modern/traditional are central to the efforts of subordinate social groups to mark, claim or defend social distinction in a number of settings
(e.g. Weiss 2002; Cole 2005). That educated young men seized on the educa-
tion/illiteracy binary in rural Bijnor district is perhaps partly attributable to
the distinctive association of education with technological competence. The
Hindi term for educated, *parhe likhe* (literally: reading-writing), encapsulates
the close connection in young men's minds between prolonged participation
in school and forms of embodied technological acuity. In Nangal and Qaziwala
educated young men imagined the 'educated' to be in possession of a suite of
internalized orientations to action (*uthnā baithnā*) that will slowly transform
their behavior, their family's standing and the broader village environment.
Educated young men also claimed that the educated are distinctively able to
move deftly between technologies coded as 'traditional' and those imagined
as 'modern,' and the emphasis of the educated on their capacity to improvise
(*jugār*) encapsulates their sense of cosmopolitan skill.

Education is also attractive to many young men because it provides an
achieved model of success distinct from *ascribed* ideas of social value. Educated
Chamar and Muslim young men argued that education rather than caste or
religion is the most appropriate basis for social recognition and respect in a
'modern' age. But, even as they criticized caste as an ordering concept, educated Chamars and Muslims invoked new hierarchical principles of difference
based on school qualifications and an educated demeanor. This complicates
efforts to map narratives of education onto notions of either 'hegemonic' or
'oppositional' masculinity. Young men's discussions of educated manhood in
Nangal and Qaziwala approximate 'hegemonic masculinities' elsewhere in the
world in that they represent a form of symbolic violence (Bourdieu 1984) and
are crafted through reference to the bodies and practices of women and inferior
men (Connell 1987, 2005). But young men's constructions of this ideal masculinity are often characterized by mischievousness, humor and self-conscious
irony. Moreover, young men in rural Bijnor district were able to deploy a vision
of educated masculinity in socially subversive ways: for example, to challenge
dominant castes' right to authority or to invoke traditions of low caste protest.

Spatial tropes featured prominently in the performance of educated masculinities, particularly ideas of nature, culture, dirt and cleanliness. Most Jat

and Chamar young men argued that educated people—in essence genteel, civilized and clean—should undertake 'pen work' and distance themselves from intimate contact with the dirt and soil (*dhūl mittī*) of rural areas. By contrast, Muslim young men argued that the educated could enter skilled manual employment involving work with cloth, wood or metal and even that *dhūl mittī* work was acceptable, if it was conducted as a form of self-employment. These environmental subjectivities were overdetermined; they reflected histories of gender, caste and class prejudice against manual work and the circulation of relatively 'new' visions of appropriate labor promoted by the Indian state, development organizations and private educational institutions.

Concepts of the educated person—and their elaboration in the strategies of young men—were also caught up in shifting understandings of temporal change. In different ways, Jats, new politicians and educated Muslim young men produced linear narratives of progress through time. Educated Jats sometimes claimed to be in a stage of transition between 'the rural' and 'the urban' and 'traditional' and 'modern,' and therefore "on the road to development." New politicians articulated an equally linear vision of transition based upon increasing Dalit awareness of their subjugation, their 'empowerment' through education, and collective social mobility through formal Dalit politics. Drawing on their experiences of urban north India, educated Muslim young men also occasionally presented themselves as people en route to development. In contrast, many Chamar young men among the educated un/under-employed emphasized their detachment from linear time. Attention to multiple narratives of time therefore points to how young men oriented themselves to visions of 'educated' accomplishment. Rather than constituting a single apprehension of 'the modern,' notions of education as civilization were incorporated in diverse, shifting and ambivalent efforts to communicate distinction from the past.

Narratives of time and modernity were also becoming politicized. Influenced by the BSP and development narratives circulating in north India, new politicians were critical of *timepass* cultures which they connected to a defeatist attitude inconsistent with the responsibilities of educated Chamars. From a rather different perspective, educated Jats argued that Chamar young men's narratives of '*timepass*' signaled their failure to appreciate the 'true value' of education. Furthermore, inter-generational tensions over the actions and futures of educated un/under-employed young men often surfaced in debates over how young men should use time-space. Parents chastised sons who thought only in terms of *timepass*, urged them to employ their time productively and tried to assist them in imagining and planning for meaningful futures.

In developing distinctive ideas and configurations of space and time, young men were not under the thrall of dominant ideas moving down from above, as Althusser (1971) suggested. Rather, educated young people actively created positions that might appear, at first glance, to be imitations of dominant discourse. Indeed, young men reshaped received ideas about 'education' and 'illiteracy' in response to new opportunities. For example, Jats identified differences between the 'qualified' and 'truly educated,' Chamar new politicians argued that Dalit male heroes epitomized education, and many educated Muslim young men spoke of the links between education and artisanal work. To write of young men being hegemonized would also be to imply that the internalization of an educated style was markedly at odds with young men's interests. But there was a considerable amount of what Gramsci (1971) calls 'good sense' in young men's decision to invest in notions of progress through education. Narratives of education as civilization allowed Jats to defend their privileges and Chamars and Muslims to contest their social subordination, for example.

The characteristic response of educated young men in Bijnor district to their exclusion from government work—to stress their 'modern' status as 'educated people'—presents a contrast with the types of 'neo-traditional' cultural styles described, for example, by Demerath (1999) in Papua New Guinea and Levinson (1999) in Mexico. Yet we must also enter some caveats. Some educated Muslim and Chamar young men drew on symbols understood to be traditional, such as notions of a history of Dalit political resistance among Chamars, and urbane styles of moral comportment (*adab*) among Muslims. Moreover, many of the Muslim and Chamar young men who left school before Eighth Class circulated critiques of education. But there are, nevertheless, important differences between educated young men's enthusiasm for mainstream education and white-collar employment and the several accounts of cultures of underemployment that emphasize educated young people's move to embrace lifestyles coded as 'traditional' (e.g. Demerath 1999; Levinson 1999).

Similarities of method and theoretical approach also offer a basis for contrasting our conclusions with those of Willis (1977), who studied the strategies of working class young men in a UK school in the 1970s. Like Willis, we have identified multiple responses among marginalized young people to the threat or experience of un/under-employment. Paralleling the working class 'lads' in Willis's study, some young men in rural Bijnor district responded to the prospect of unemployment by abandoning formal education before high school. But a growing proportion of Muslim and Chamar young men reacted by continuing in school up to Eighth Class and valuing formal education and white-collar work. Willis argued that a tendency for large numbers of working class men to reject middle class work was necessary for the smooth reproduction of society in the 1970s in the UK and he predicted that working class young men's acceptance of middle class ideas of mobility would lead to widespread unrest:

The transition from school to work of working class kids who had readily absorbed the rubric of self-development, satisfaction and interest in work would be a terrifying battle. Armies of kids equipped with their 'self-concepts' would be fighting to enter the few meaningful jobs available, and masses of employers would be struggling to press them into meaningless work. [Willis 1977: 177]

The UP case material suggests that, even in a situation where a significant number of educated young men from marginalized groups do accept ideas of education as progress, they remain politically weak. Despite the efforts of *naye netās*, educated un/under-employed young men in rural Bijnor district were poorly organized and, indeed, divided along the lines of caste and religion. In addition, rather than trying to challenge state power, as Willis (1977) and Bourdieu (1984) argued they might, young men excluded from secure government jobs in rural Bijnor district more commonly strove to colonize the state.

Educated un/under-employed young men's move to embrace progress through education related to the efforts of state agencies, educational institutions and the media to promote visions of transformation through education and development. Ideas of education as progress were especially influential among Chamars, whose enthusiasm for entry into formal education arose, in part, out of a vision of bourgeois mobility presented by the BSP. Such narratives of progress were less pronounced in the contexts in which Demerath (1999) and Willis (1977) were working.

The tendency for young men to stress their educated standing might also be explained with reference to the struggles that young men from marginalized social groups had experienced to acquire school qualifications. Large numbers of Chamar and Muslim young men in Nangal and Qaziwala spoke of the difficulty of passing school examinations in the face of teacher apathy. These men were often the first in their families to obtain schooling and had watched their parents make considerable sacrifices for their education. In such a context, it is unsurprising that young men in rural Bijnor district continued to place value on formal education, even in the face of poor occupational outcomes.

Degrees Without Freedom? Rethinking Education

Finally, our work provides a basis for re-evaluating the common emphasis on education as a 'social good' within development studies. Drèze and Sen (1995) argued that elementary education is crucial to processes of human development in the global south. They claimed that formal education has an intrinsic importance, in that education is a value 'in itself' and possesses instrumental significance. In recent presentations in Scotland and India, Sen reiterated these points by underlining how education can assist people in getting jobs and gainful employment, enhance their understanding of legal rights, improve women's security, open up political opportunities, tackle health problems and increase the dignity of the marginalized.[1]

Sen's emphasis on education as a development driver serves a key political function in certain institutional contexts, for example in persuading multilateral organizations and national governments to recognize the role that schooling sometimes plays in promoting development goals. Building on Sen, the World Bank states that:

Education is development. It creates choices and opportunities for people, reduces the twin burdens of poverty and diseases, and gives a stronger voice in society. For nations

[1]The full text of Sen's speech in Kolkata is available on the web at http://www. humansecurity-chs.org/activities/outreach/Kolkata.pdf, last accessed 12 April 2006. The full text of his speech in Edinburgh, Scotland, in 2003 is available at http:// www.cis.ksu. edu/~ab/Miscellany/basiced.html, last accessed 14 March 2006.

it creates a dynamic workforce and well-informed citizens able to compete and cooperate globally—opening doors to economic and social prosperity. [http://web.worldbank.org/WBSITE/EXTERNAL/TOPICS/EXTEDUCATION/, last accessed 5 March 2006].

Our book provides some support for these arguments. Formal education had provided young men with basic literacy and numeracy. This allowed them to assist their families in reading documents, letters and signs and improved their ability to negotiate with government officials, schoolteachers and doctors, for example. Formal qualifications—even if only an Eighth Class certificate—provided self-belief in many young men and encouraged the development of new networks of social support. For example, Chamar new politicians were developing narratives critical of higher castes, popularizing lower caste political parties and promoting education as a new, liberating, social identity. Education provided Muslims and Chamars with a basis for challenging upper-caste Hindu discourses and launching critiques of the schooling system itself. Importantly, most parents and young people also believed that education improves people's skills, knowledge and confidence. During the 1980s and 1990s, many parents invested a great deal of money and time in schooling their sons.

But the ability of young men to benefit from education depended crucially on money, social resources and cultural capital. This was especially true in the early 2000s, when the liberalization of the UP economy had created a highly segmented school system. The Jats were able to use their accumulated resources to monopolize access to non-state educational opportunities and privatized markets for jobs. They could 'up the ante' so that those following behind them in the educational contest acquired devalued credentials. In this context, educated Chamars and Muslims were enduringly excluded from the most prestigious qualifications and lucrative work.

These conclusions point to weaknesses in Sen's account of education as a route to prosperity and power. Sen tends to obscure the complicated process through which 'education' leads to secure work, new forms of political power and vibrant social institutions. Nor does Sen specify what other processes need to occur alongside education for poor people to experience an improvement in their lives. In certain contexts, education may not be the most appropriate point of entry for efforts at alleviating deprivation. Indeed, many of our Chamar and Muslim informants in rural Bijnor district had come to argue that their own 'development' depended on direct measures to reduce the privileges of the rich alongside initiatives to 'empower' the poor through education. In addition, Sen downplays the extent to which the experience of education may further marginalize young people from subordinate groups, for whom education commonly creates feelings of failure, anxiety and bewilderment.

In sum, formal education *can* provide valuable skills, knowledge and a sense of self-belief important in the efforts of young men in north India to negotiate a harsh economic landscape. But it tends to do so only *if* certain other conditions obtain. 'Social opportunity,' in Drèze and Sen's (1995) sense, is a contingent, not a necessary, outcome of prolonged participation in school. In this way, our account of education connects with other critiques of development theorizing that present a single social initiative—such as decentralization (Mohan and Stokke 2000) or participatory planning (Mosse 1995)—as a panacea for problems of deprivation and inequality.

Again, we are not arguing against education. To do so would only be to replace one problematic idea—that educational systems are in essence beneficial—with another: that education is intrinsically divisive and exclusionary. We must avoid suggesting that education offers a high road to the solution of problems of social inequality, whilst also being careful not to negate the life-enhancing potential of formal schooling. Paying attention to the voices of marginalized people is of paramount importance here: many of our subaltern informants increasingly recognize the ambivalent nature of education.

Bourdieu's notions of economic capital, social capital and cultural capital offer one means of addressing these tasks theoretically. Bourdieu's work is sensitive to how the efforts of subordinate people to capitalize on their education are played out within landscapes of power. Within these 'fields' of struggle, dominant groups often possess superior forms of cultural capital, as well as large stocks of economic wealth and social capital, which they can deploy to outmaneuver subordinate groups. More than Sen, Bourdieu therefore situates an analysis of education's potential with reference to politicized terrains of social competition. Bourdieu allows for the possibility that education may transform the prospects of some sections of erstwhile marginalized groups by highlighting the importance of educational qualifications (institutionalized cultural capital) and people's comportment, manners and taste (embodied cultural capital) in processes of social competition and transformation (Reed-Danahay 2005).

But Bourdieu is more concerned with theorizing reproduction than attending to resistance. Moreover, in failing to foreground the distinction between achieved forms of cultural capital, such as education, and ascribed forms, such as one's caste background, Bourdieu underestimates the iconic importance of education to marginalized populations. Many poor Chamars recognized that they were out-competed by higher castes in the search for secure employment and local political influence, but nevertheless valued education as a marker of civilization distinct from caste. Bourdieu's theoretical framework does not fully anticipate this possibility.

Rather more than Bourdieu, then, we have pointed to education as a *contradictory resource*: opening up certain opportunities to undermine established structures of power while also often drawing marginalized young people more tightly into structures and ideologies of dominance (Willis 1977; Levinson and Holland 1996; Jeffrey et al. 2005). Education could play a major role in improving the prospects of the rural poor in UP and there is a pressing need to examine precisely how this process of 'empowerment' might occur. But any such effort must recognize the role of the existing schooling system in reproducing inequality and the wider social and political context within which educational initiatives take place, themes well articulated in much educational research in the West (e.g. McLaren 1995; Giroux 2001) but less prominent in development debates. In particular, much more attention must be directed toward linking the educational system to the future employment prospects of highly differentiated populations. This effort requires culturally sensitive political economy approaches to processes of educational transformation, approaches grounded in awareness of the changing structures shaping social life (e.g. Corbridge and Harriss 2000; Chari 2004) and people's intimate relationship with the idea and practice of education (e.g. Parry 2005). The Amarpals and Zamirs of western UP will be ill-served by accounts that posit education as a catch-all solution to problems of poverty and those that deny the capacity of education to transform subaltern lives.

Bibliography

Bibliography

Agadjanian, Victor. 2004. "Men Doing 'Women's Work': Masculinity and Gender Relations among Street Vendors in Maputo, Mozambique," in *African Masculinities*, ed. Lahoucine Ouzgane and Robert Morrell. Oxford: Palgrave Macmillan.

Agarwal, Bina, Jane Humphries, and Ingrid Robeyns. 2006. *Amartya Sen's Work and Ideas: A Gender Perspective*. London: Routledge.

Ahluwalia, Montek, S. 2001. "State Level Performance Under Economic Reforms in India." Working Paper No. 96, Center for Research on Economic Development and Policy Reform, Stanford University.

Aitken, Stuart C. 2001. *Geographies of Young People: The Morally Contested Spaces of Identity*. London: Routledge.

Althusser, Louis. 1971. *Lenin and Philosophy* (trans. Ben Brewster). London: New Left Books.

Anandhi, S., J. Jeyaranjan, and R. Krishnan. 2002. "Work, Caste and Competing Masculinities: Notes from a Tamil Village," *Economic and Political Weekly*, 37, 24, pp. 4403–14.

Appadurai, Arjun. 1996. *Modernity at Large: Cultural Dimensions of Globalization*. Minneapolis: Minnesota University Press.

Ara, Arjumand. 2003. "Madrasas and Making of Muslim Identity in India," *Economic and Political Weekly*, 38, 1, pp. 45–54.

Arnold, David. 1994. *Public Health and Public Power: Medicine and Hegemony in Colonial India*. Cambridge: Cambridge University Press.

Bailey, Frederick G. 1957. *Caste and the Economic Frontier: A Village in Highland Orissa*. Manchester: Manchester University Press.

Bakhtin, M. M. 1986. *Speech Genres and Other Late Essays*. Austin: University of Texas Press.

Bannerjee, Mukulika, and Daniel Miller. 2004. *The Sari*. Oxford: Berg.

Bara, J. 1997. "Western Education and the Rise of New Identity: Mundas and Oraons of Chotanagpur, 1839–1939," *Economic and Political Weekly*, 32, 15, pp. 785–90.

Bartky, S. L. 1988. *Foucault, Femininity, and the Modernization of Patriarchal Power*. Boston: Northeastern University Press.

Basu, A. 1994. "When Local Riots Are Not Merely Local: Bringing the State Back In, Bijnor 1988–92," *Economic and Political Weekly*, 29, 39, pp. 1456–1542.

Beck, Ulrich, and Elisabeth Beck-Gernsheim. 2002. *Individualization: Institutionalized Individualism and Its Social and Political Consequences*. London: Sage.

Bénéï, Veronique. 2005. "Serving the Nation: Gender and Family Values in Military Schools," in *Educational Regimes in Contemporary South Asia*, ed. Radhika Chopra and Patricia Jeffery. Delhi: Sage, pp. 141–60.

Bentall, Jim. 1995. "'Bharat versus India': Peasant Politics and Urban-Rural Relations in North-West India." PhD dissertation, Cambridge, UK: University of Cambridge.

Bentall, Jim, and Stuart E. Corbridge. 1996. "Urban-Rural Relations, Demand Politics and the 'New Agrarianism' in NW India: the Bharatiya Kisan Union," *Transactions of the Institute of British Geographers*, New Series, 2, 1, pp. 27–48.

Berry, Sara. 1985. *Fathers Work for Their Sons: Accumulation, Mobility and Class Formation in an Extended Yoruba Community*. Berkeley: University of California Press.

Béteille, André. 1992. *The Backward Classes in Contemporary India*. Delhi: Oxford University Press.

———. 2001. "Race and Caste," *The Hindu*, 10 March.

Bhalla, Sheila. 1997. "The Rise and Fall of Workforce Diversification Processes in Rural India," in *Growth, Employment and Poverty: Change and Continuity in Rural India*, ed. G. K. Chadha and A. N. Sharma. Delhi: Vikas, pp. 145–83.

Borman, Kathryn M. 1988. "Playing on the Job in Adolescent Work Settings," *Anthropology and Education Quarterly*, 19, 2, pp. 163–81.

Bourdieu, Pierre. 1977. *Outline of a Theory of Practice* (trans. Richard Nice). Cambridge: Cambridge University Press.

———. 1984. *Distinction: A Social Critique of the Judgement of Taste* (trans. Richard Nice). London: Routledge and Kegan Paul.

———. 1986. "The Forms of Capital," in *Handbook of Theory and Research in the Sociology of Education*, ed. J. G. Richardson. New York: Greenwood Press, pp. 241–58.

———. 2001. *Masculine Domination*. Stanford, CA: Stanford University Press.

Bourdieu, Pierre, and Jean-Claude Passeron. 1977, *Reproduction in Education, Society and Culture* (trans. Richard Nice). Beverly Hills, CA: Sage.

Bourgois, Philippe. 1995. *In Search of Respect: Selling Crack in El Barrio*. Cambridge: Cambridge University Press.

Bowles, Samuel, and Herbert Gintis. 1976. *Schooling in Capitalist America*. New York: Basic Books.

Brass, Paul R. 1985. *Caste, Faction and Party in Indian Politics: Volume I, Faction and Party*. Delhi: Chanakya Publications.

———. 1997. *Theft of an Idol: Text and Context in the Representation of Collective Violence*. Princeton, NJ: Princeton University Press.

Breman, Jan. 1985. *Of Peasants, Migrants, and Paupers: Rural Labour Circulation and Capitalist Production in West India*. Delhi: Oxford University Press.

Brown, Philip. 1995. "Cultural Capital and Social Exclusion: Some Observations on Recent Trends in Education, Employment, and the Labour Market," *Work, Employment and Society*, 9, 1, pp. 29–51.

Bucholtz, Mary. 2002. "Youth and Cultural Practice," *Annual Review of Anthropology*, 31, pp. 525–52.

Butler, Judith. 1990. *Gender and the Subversion of Identity*. New Haven, CT: Yale University Press.

———. 1991. "Imitation and gender insubordination," in *Inside/out: Lesbian Theories, Gay Theories*, ed. Diana Fuss. London: Routledge, pp. 13–31.

Byres Terence J. 1988. "Charan Singh (1902–1987): an Assessment," *Journal of Peasant Studies*, 15, 2, pp. 139–89.

CABE. 2004. http://www. education.nic.in/cabe/universalisation.pdf. Last accessed 22 January 2007.

Calhoun, Craig. 1993. "Habitus, Field and Capital: The Question of Historical Specificity," in *Bourdieu: Critical Perspectives*, ed. Craig Calhoun, Edward LiPuma and Moishe Postone. Cambridge: Polity, pp. 61–89.

Chakrabarty, Dipesh. 2002. *Habitations of Modernity: Essays in the Wake of Subaltern Studies*. Delhi: Permanent Black.

Chandrashekhar, C. P., and Jayati Ghosh. 2002. *The Market that Failed: A Decade of Neo liberal Economic Reforms in India*. Delhi: Manohar.

Chari, Sharad. 2004. *Fraternal Capital: Peasant-Workers, Self-made Men, and Globalization in Provincial India*. Stanford, CA: Stanford University Press.

Charsley, Simon. 1998. "Sanskritization: The Career of an Anthropological Theory," *Contributions to Indian Sociology*, 32, 2, pp. 527–49

Chatterjee, Partha. 2004. *The Politics of the Governed: Reflections on Popular Politics in Most of the World*. Delhi: Permanent Black.

Chopra, Radhika, and Patricia Jeffery (eds.). 2005. *Educational Regimes in Contemporary India*. Delhi: Sage.

Chopra, Radhika, Caroline Osella, and Filippo Osella (eds.). 2004. *South Asian Masculinities: Context of Change, Sites of Continuity*. Delhi: Kali for Women.

Chowdhry, Prem. 1994. *The Veiled Women: Shifting Gender Equations in Rural Haryana 1880–1990*. Delhi: Oxford University Press.

Cieslki, Mark, and Gary Pollock. 2002. *Young People in Risk Society: The Restructuring of Youth Identities and Transitions in Late Modernity*. Burlington: Ashgate.

Ciotti, Manuela. 2006. "'In the Past we were a bit "Chamar"': Education as a Self- and Community Engineering Process in Northern India," *Journal of the Royal Anthropological Association*, 12, 4, pp. 899–916.

Clifford, James. 1997. *Routes: Travel and Translation in the Late Twentieth Century*. Cambridge, MA: Harvard University Press.

Cole, Jennifer. 2005. "The Jaombilo of Tamative Madagascar (1992–2004): Reflections on Youth and Globalization," *Journal of Social History*, 38, 4, pp. 891–913.

Connell, Robert W. 1987. *Gender and Power*. Cambridge: Polity Press.

———. 2005. *Masculinities*. Berkeley: University of California Press.

Corbridge, Stuart. 1999. "The Militarization of All Hindudom: The Bharatiya Janata Party, the Bomb, and the Political Spaces of Hindu Nationalism," *Economy and Society*, 28, 2, pp. 222–25.

———. 2002. "Development as Freedom: The Spaces of Amartya Sen," *Progress in Development Studies*, 2, 3, pp. 183–217.

———. 2003. "Waiting in Line, or the Moral and Material Geographies of Queue Jumping." Mimeo.

Corbridge, Stuart, and John Harriss. 2000. *Reinventing India: Liberalization, Hindu Nationalism and Popular Democracy*. Cambridge: Polity Press.

Corbridge, Stuart, Glyn Williams, Manoj Srivastava, and René Véron. 2005. *Seeing the State: Governance and Governmentality in Rural North India*. Cambridge: Cambridge University Press.

Datta, Nonica. 1999a. *Forming an Identity: A Social History of the Jats*. Oxford: Oxford University Press.

———. 1999b. "Jats: Trading Caste Status for Empowerment," *Economic and Political Weekly*, 34, 45, p. 3172.

De Haan, Arjan. 2003. "Calcutta's Labour Migrants: Encounters with Modernity," *Contributions to Indian Sociology*, 37, 1–2, pp. 189–215.

Delhi Historians' Group. 2001. *Communalisation of Education: The History Textbooks Controversy*. Delhi: Delhi Historians Group.

Deliège, Robert. 2002. "Is There Still Untouchability in India?" Heidelberg Working Paper No. 5, South Asia Institute, University of Heidelberg.

Demerath, Peter. 1999. "The Cultural Production of Educational Utility in Pere Village, Papua New Guinea," *Comparative Education Review*, 43, 2, pp. 162–92.

———. 2003. "The Social Cost of Acting "Extra": Students' Moral Judgements of Self, Social Relations, and Academic Success in Papua New Guinea." Mimeo.

Dirks, Nick B. 1992. "Castes of Mind," *Representations*, 37, pp. 56–78.

———. 2003. *Castes of Mind: Colonialism and the Making of Modern India*. Delhi: Permanent Black.

Donner, Henrike. 2006. "Committed Mothers and Well-adjusted Children: Privatisation, Early-Years Education and Motherhood in Calcutta," *Modern Asian Studies*, 40, 2, pp. 371–95.

Dore, Robert. 1976. *The Diploma Disease: Education, Qualification and Development*. Berkeley: University of California Press.

Dreyfus, Hubert, and Paul Rabinow. 1992. "Can there be a Science of Existential Structure and Social Meaning?" in *Bourdieu: Critical Perspectives*, ed. C. Calhoun, E. LiPuma and M. Postone. New York: John Hopkins University Press, pp. 35–44.

Drèze, Jean, and Haris Gazdar. 1997. "Uttar Pradesh: the Burden of Inertia," in *Indian Development: Selected Regional Perspectives*, ed. Jean Drèze and Amartya Sen. Delhi: Oxford University Press, pp. 33–128.

Drèze, Jean, and Amartya Sen. 1995. *Economic Development and Social Opportunity*. Delhi: Oxford University Press.

———. 1997. *Indian Development: Selected Regional Perspectives*. Delhi: Oxford University Press.

Drèze, Jean, Peter Lanjouw and Naresh Sharma, 1999. "Economic Development 1957–93," in *Economic Development in Palanpur Over Five Decades*, ed. Peter Lanjouw and Nicholas H. Stern. Oxford: Oxford University Press.

Dube, Siddharth. 1998. *In the Land of Poverty: Memoirs of an Indian Family, 1947–1997*. London: Zed Books.

Duncan, Iain. 1997. "Agricultural Innovation and Political Change in North India: The Lok Dal in Uttar Pradesh," *Journal of Peasant Studies*, 24, 4, pp. 246–68.

———. 1999. "Dalits and Politics in Rural North India: The Bahujan Samaj Party in Uttar Pradesh," *Journal of Peasant Studies*, 27, 1, 35–60.

Dyson, Jane. 2007. "Respite and Rupees: The Impact of a New Market Opportunity on Everyday Lives of Children and Young People in the Indian Himalayas," in *Child hoods in South Asia*, ed. Deepak Kumar Behera. Delhi: Pearson Longman.

Engineer, Asghar Ali. 2001. "Muslims and Education," *Economic and Political Weekly*, 36, 34, pp. 3221–22.

Faust, David, and Richa Nagar. 2001. "English-medium Education, Social Fracturing and the Politics of Development in Postcolonial India," *Economic and Political Weekly*, 36, 30, pp. 2878–83.

Ferguson, James. 1999. *Expectations of Modernity: Myths and Meanings of Urban Life on the Zambian Copperbelt*. Berkeley: University of California Press.

Fernandes, Leela. 2006. *India's New Middle Class: Democratic Politics in an Era of Economic Reform*. Minneapolis: Minnesota University Press.

Fernandez Kelly, Patricia. 1994. "Towanda's Triumph: Social and Cultural Capital in the Transition to Adulthood in the Urban Ghetto," *International Journal of Urban and Regional Research*, 18, 1, pp. 88–111.

Foucault, Michel. 1977. *Discipline and Punish: The Birth of the Prison* (trans. Alan Sheridan). New York: Pantheon.

————. 1980. *Power/Knowledge: Selected Interviews and Other Writings* (ed. and trans. Colin Gordon). New York: Pantheon.

————. 1988. *Politics, Philosophy, Culture: Interviews and Other Writings, 1977–1984* (trans. Alan Sheridan and others). London: Routledge.

Frøystad, Kathinka. 2005. *Blended Boundaries: Caste, Class and Shifting Faces of 'Hinduness' in a North Indian City.* Delhi: Oxford University Press.

Furlong, Andy, and Fred Cartmel. 1997. *Young People and Social Change: Individualisation and Risk in the Age of High Modernity.* Buckingham: Open University Press.

Galanter, Marc. 1991. *Competing Equalities: Law and the Backward Classes in India.* Delhi: Oxford University Press.

Gaonkar, Dilip P. 2001. *Alter/Native Modernities.* Durham, NC: Duke University Press.

Geertz, Clifford. 1973. *The Interpretation of Cultures.* New York: Basic Books.

Giddens, Anthony. 1991. *Modernity and Self-Identity: Self and Society in the Late Modern Age.* Stanford, CA: Stanford University Press.

Gidwani, Vinay. 2001. "The Cultural Logic of Work: Explaining Labour Deployment and Piece-rate Contracts in Matar Taluka, Gujarat—parts I and II," *Journal of Development Studies*, 38, 2, pp. 57–74.

Gidwani, Vinay, and K. Sivaramakrishnan. 2003. "Circular Migration and Rural Cosmopolitanism in India," *Contributions to Indian Sociology*, 37, 1–2, pp. 339–67.

Giroux, Henry A. 1983. *Theory and Resistance in Education: A Pedagogy of Opposition.* London: Heinemann.

————. 2001. "Cultural Studies as Performative Politics," *Cultural Studies Critical Methodologies*, 1, 1, pp. 5–23.

Gooptu, Nandini. 1993. "Caste, Deprivation and Politics: the Untouchables in U.P. Towns in the Early Twentieth Century," in *Dalit Movements and the Meaning of Labour in India*, ed. Peter Robb. Oxford: Oxford University Press, pp. 277–98.

Gramsci, Antonio. 1971. *Selections from the Prison Notebooks* (ed. and trans. Q. Hoare and G. Nowell-Smith). London: Lawrence and Wishart.

Guha, Ranajit, and Gayatri C. Spivak. 1988. *Selected Subaltern Studies.* New York: Oxford University Press.

Gupta, Akhil. 1995. "Blurred Boundaries: the Discourse of Corruption, the Culture of Politics and the Imagined State," *American Ethnologist*, 22, 2, pp. 375–402.

————. 1997. "Agrarian Populism in the Development of a Modern Nation (India)," in *International Development and the Social Sciences: Essays on the History and Politics of Knowledge*, ed. Frederick Cooper and Randall Packard. Berkeley: University of California Press, pp. 320–44.

————. 1998. *Postcolonial Developments: Agriculture in the Making of Modern India.* Durham, NC, and London: Duke University Press.

Gupta, Dipankar. 1997. *Brotherhood and Rivalry*. Delhi: Oxford University Press.

Gutmann, Mathew C. 1996. *Meanings of Macho: Being a Man in Mexico City*. Berkeley, CA: University of California Press.

——. 2003. *Changing Men and Masculinities in Latin America*. Durham, NC: Duke University Press.

Hall, Stuart. 1985. "Signification, Representation, Ideology: Althusser and the Poststructuralist Debates," *Critical Studies in Mass Communication*, 2, pp. 91–114.

Hameed, Rumman. 2005. "Learning Processes within the Ustad-Shagird Relationship," in *Educational Regimes in Contemporary India*, ed. Radhika Chopra and Patricia Jeffery. Delhi: Sage, pp. 197–215.

Hansen, Thomas. B. 1996. "Recuperating Masculinity: Hindu Nationalism, Violence, and the Exorcism of the Muslim 'Other,'" *Critique of Anthropology*, 16, 2, pp. 137–72.

Harriss, John. 2002. *Depoliticizing Development: The World Bank and Social Capital*. London: Anthem.

Harriss-White, Barbara. 2003. *India Working: Essays on Society and Economy*. Cambridge: Cambridge University Press.

Harvey, David. 2005. *A Brief History of Neoliberalism*. Oxford: Oxford University Press.

Hasan, Zoya. 1998. *Quest for Power: Oppositional Movements and Post-Congress Politics in Uttar Pradesh*. Delhi: Oxford University Press.

Hebdige, Dick. 1979. *Subculture: The Meaning of Style*. London: Methuen.

Herzfeld, Michael. 2005. *Cultural Intimacy: Social Poetics in the Nation-State*. New York: Routledge.

Heuzé, Gerard. 1996. *Workers of Another World: Miners, the Countryside and Coalfields in Dhanbad*. Delhi: Oxford University Press.

Heyneman, Stephen P. 1980. "Investment in Indian Education: Uneconomic?" *World Development*, 8, pp. 145–63.

——. 2003. "The History and Problems in the Making of Education Policy at the World Bank," *International Journal of Educational Development*, 23, 3, pp. 315–37.

Hirschkind, Charles. 2003. "Hearing Modernity: Egypt, Islam, and the Pious Ear," in *Hearing Cultures: Sound, Listening, and Modernity*, ed. V. Erlmann. New York: Berg, pp. 131–51.

Hirschman, Albert. 1970. *Exit, Voice, and Loyalty: Responses to Decline in Firms, Organizations, and States*. Cambridge: Harvard University Press.

Hyams, Melissa S. 2000. "'Pay Attention in Class . . . [and] Don't Get Pregnant': A Discourse of Academic Success among Adolescent Latinas," *Environment and Planning A*, 32, 4, pp. 617–35.

Illich, Ivan. 1972. *Deschooling Society*. New York: Harrow.

Inden, Ronald. 1990. *Imagining India*. Oxford: Basil Blackwell.

Jaffrelot, Christophe. 1996. *The Hindu Nationalist Movement and Indian Politics*. London: Hurst and Co.

———. 2003. *India's Silent Revolution: The Rise of the Low Castes in North Indian Politics*. Delhi: Permanent Black.

———. 2005. *Dr. Ambedkar and Untouchability: Fighting the Caste System*. New York: Columbia University Press.

Jaoul, Nicholas. 2007. "Dalit Processions: Street Politics and Democratization in India," in *Staging Politics in Asia*, ed. Julia C. Strauss and Donal Cruise O'Brien. London: I. B. Tauris.

Jeffery, Patricia. 2000. "Identifying Differences: Gender Politics and Community in Rural Bijnor, UP," in *Invented Identities: The Interplay of Gender, Religion and Politics in India*, ed. J. Leslie and M. McGee. Delhi: Oxford University Press, pp. 286–309.

Jeffery, Patricia, and Roger Jeffery. 1996. *Don't Marry Me to a Plowman! Women's Everyday Lives in Rural North India*. Boulder, CO: Westview.

———. 1998. "Silver Bullet or Passing Fancy? Girls' Schooling and Population Policy," in *Feminist Visions of Development: Gender, Analysis and Policy*, ed. C. Jackson and R. Pearson. London: Routledge, pp. 238–58.

———. 2006. *Confronting Saffron Demography: Religion, Fertility, and Women's Status in India*. Delhi: Three Essays Collective.

Jeffery, Patricia, Roger Jeffery, and Craig Jeffrey. 2004. "Islamisation, Gentrification and Domestication: 'a Girls' Islamic Course' and Rural Muslims in Western Uttar Pradesh," *Modern Asian Studies*, 38, 1, pp. 1–52.

———. 2007. "Investing in the Future: Education in the Social and Cultural Reproduction of Muslims in UP," in *Living with Secularism: The Destiny of India's Muslims*, ed. Mushirul Hasan. Delhi: Manohar, pp. 63–89.

Jeffery, Roger, and A. Basu. 1996. *Girls' Schooling, Women's Autonomy and Fertility Change in South Asia*. Thousand Oaks, CA: Sage.

Jeffery, Roger, and Patricia Jeffery. 1994. "The Bijnor Riots, October 1990: Collapse of a Mythical Special Relationship?" *Economic and Political Weekly*, 29, 12, pp. 551–58.

———. 1997. *Population, Gender and Politics: Demographic Change in Rural North India*. Cambridge: Cambridge University Press.

Jeffery, Roger, Patricia Jeffery, and Craig Jeffrey. 2005. "Social Inequality and the Privatisation of Secondary Schooling in North India," in *Educational Regimes in Contemporary India*, ed. Radhika Chopra and Patricia Jeffery. Delhi: Sage, pp. 41–61.

———. 2006a. Patterns and Discourses of the Privatisation of Secondary Schooling in Bijnor, UP, *Education and Social Change in South Asia*, ed. Krishna Kumar and Joachim Oesterheld. Delhi: Orient Longman.

———. 2006b. "*Parhāī ka māhaul?* An Educational Environment in Bijnor, UP," in *The Meaning of the Local: Politics of Place in Urban India*, ed. Geert de Neve and Henrike Donner. London: Routledge, pp.116–40.

Jeffery, Roger, Patricia M. Jeffery, and Andrew Lyon. 1989. "Taking Dung-Work Seriously: Women's Work and Rural Development in North India," *Economic and Political Weekly*, 24, 17, WS 32–37.

Jeffery, Roger, Craig Jeffrey and Patricia Jeffery. 2001. "Social and Political Dominance in Western UP: a Response to Sudha Pai," *Contributions to Indian Sociology*, 35, 2, pp. 213–36.

Jeffery, Roger, and Jens Lerche (eds.). 2003. *Social and Political Change in Uttar Pradesh: European Perspectives*. Delhi: Manohar.

Jeffrey, Craig. 1999. "Reproducing Difference: The Accumulation Strategies of Richer Jat Farmers in Western Uttar Pradesh, India." PhD dissertation, Cambridge, UK: University of Cambridge.

———. 2000. "Democratisation without Representation? The Power and Political Strategies of a Rural Elite in North India," *Political Geography*, 19, pp. 1013–36.

———. 2001. "A Fist Is Stronger the Five Fingers: Caste and Dominance in Rural North India," *Transactions of the Institute of British Geographers*, 25, 2, pp. 1–30.

———. 2002. "Caste, Class and Clientelism: A Political Economy of Everyday Corruption in Rural North India," *Economic Geography*, 78, 1, pp. 21–42.

———. 2005. "When Schooling Fails: Young Men, Education and Low Caste Politics in North India," *Contributions to Indian Sociology*, 39, 1, pp. 1–38.

Jeffrey, Craig, and Jens Lerche. 2000. "Stating the Difference: State, Discourse and Class Reproduction in Uttar Pradesh, India," *Development and Change*, 31, 4, pp. 857–78.

Jeffrey, Craig, and Linda McDowell. 2004. "Youth in a Comparative Perspective: Global Change, Local Lives," *Youth and Society*, 36, 2, pp. 131–42.

Jha, Raghbendra. 2004. *The Political Economy of Recent Economic Growth in India*. Canberra: Australian National University ASARC Working Paper 2004/12.

Jones, Kenneth W. 1966. *The Arya Samaj in the Punjab: A Study of Social Reform and Religious Revivalism 1877–1902*. Berkeley: University of California Press.

Joshi, E. B. (ed.). 1965. *Uttar Pradesh District Gazetteer, Meerut*. Department of Uttar Pradesh District Gazetteers, Lucknow.

Katz, Cindi. 2004. *Growing Up Global: Economic Restructuring and Children's Everyday Lives*. Minnesota: Minnesota University Press.

Khare, Ravindra S. 1984. *The Untouchable as Himself: Ideology, Identity and Pragmatism among the Lucknow Chamars*. Cambridge: Cambridge University Press.

Kingdon, Geeta. 1997. "Private Schooling in India: Size, Nature, and Equity Effects," *Economic and Political Weekly*, 31, 51, pp. 3306–14.

Kingdon, Geeta, and Mohammad Muzammil. 2003. *The Political Economy of Education in India: Teacher Politics in Uttar Pradesh*. Oxford: Oxford University Press.

Klenk, Rebecca. 2003. "Difficult Work: Becoming Developed," in *Regional Modernities: The Cultural Politics of Development in India*, ed. K. Sivaramakrishnan and Arun Agrawal. Stanford, CA: Stanford University Press, pp. 99–121.

Krishna, Anirudh. 2002. *Active Social Capital: Tracing the Roots of Development and Democracy*. New York: Columbia University Press.

Kumar, Krishna. 1994. *Democracy and Education in India*. London: Sangam Books.

Kumar, Nita. 1998. "Lessons from Contemporary Schools," *Sociological Bulletin*, 47, 1, pp. 33–49.

———. 2000. *Lessons from Schools: The History of Education in Banaras*. New Delhi: Sage.

Lane, Jeremy F. 2000. *Pierre Bourdieu: A Critical Introduction*. London: Pluto.

Lave, Jean, and Etienne Wenger. 1991. *Situated Learning: Legitimate Peripheral Participation*. Cambridge: Cambridge University Press.

Leavitt, Stephen C. 1998. "The Bikhet Mystique: Masculine Identity and Patterns of Rebellion among Bumbts Adolescent Males," in *Adolescence in Pacific Island Societies*, ed. Gilbert Herdt and Stephen C. Leavitt. Pittsburgh: University of Pittsburgh Press, pp. 173–94.

Lefebvre, Henri. 1991. *The Production of Space*. Oxford: Blackwell.

Lelyveld, David. 1978. *Aligarh's First Generation: Muslim Solidarity in British India*. Princeton, NJ: Princeton University Press.

Lerche, Jens. 1995. "Is Bonded Labour a Bound Category? Reconceptualising Agrarian Conflict in India," *Journal of Peasant Studies*, 22, 3, pp. 484–515.

———. 1999. "Politics of the Poor: Agricultural Labourers and Political Transformations in Uttar Pradesh," in *Rural Labour Relations in India*, ed. Terence J. Byres, Karin Kapadia and Jens Lerche. London: Frank Cass, pp. 182–243.

Levinson, Bradley A. 1999. "Una Etapa Siempre Difícil: Concepts of Adolescence and Secondary Education in Mexico," *Comparative Education Review*, 43, 2, pp. 129–61.

Levinson, Bradley A., and Dorothy C. Holland. 1996. "The Cultural Production of the Educated Person: An Introduction," in *The Cultural Production of the Educated Person: Critical Ethnographies of Schooling and Local Practice*, ed. Bradley A. Levinson, Douglas E. Foley and Dorothy C. Holland. Albany: State University of New York Press, pp. 1–38.

Lewis, Oscar. 1965. *Village Life in Northern India*. New York: Random House.

Li, Tania. 2005. "Beyond 'the State' and Failed Schemes," *American Anthropologist*, 107, 3, pp. 383–94.

Liechty, Mark. 2004. *Suitably Modern: Making Middle Class Culture in a New Consumer Society*. Princeton, NJ: Princeton University Press.

Lieten, G. Kristoffel. 1996. "Panchayats in Western Uttar Pradesh: 'Namesake' Members," *Economic and Political Weekly*, 31, 39, pp. 2700–2705.

Lieten, G. K., and Ravi Srivastava. 1999. *Unequal Partners: Power Relations, Devolution and Development in Uttar Pradesh*. Delhi: Sage.

Lindsay, Lisa, and Stefan Miescher. 2003. *Men and Masculinities in Modern Africa*. Portsmouth, NH: Heinemann.

Lipton, Michael. 1977. *Why Poor People Stay Poor: A Study of Urban Bias in World Development*. London: Temple Smith.

Louie, Kam, and Morris Low. 2005. *Asian Masculinities: The Meaning and Practice of Manhood in China and Japan*. London: Routledge Curzon.

Lukose, Ritty. 2005. "Consuming Globalization: Youth and Gender in Kerala, India," *Journal of Social History*, 38, 4, pp. 915–35.

Lynch, Owen M. 1969. *The Politics of Untouchability; Social Mobility and Social Change in a City of India*. New York: Columbia University Press.

McDowell, Linda. 2003. *Redundant Masculinities? Employment Change and White Working Class Youth*. Oxford: Blackwell.

McGregor, Robert S. 1993. *The Oxford Hindi-English Dictionary*. Oxford: Oxford University Press.

McLaren, Peter. 1995. *Critical Pedagogy and Predatory Culture: Oppositional Politics in a Postmodern Era*. London: Routledge.

McRobbie, Angela. 1979. "Working-Class Girls and the Culture of Femininity," in *Women Take Issue,* ed. Centre for Contemporary Cultural Studies. London: Hutchison.

Madsen, Stig T. 1996. "Clan, Kinship and Panchayat Justice among the Jats of Western Uttar Pradesh," in *Social Conflict (Oxford in India Readings in Sociology and Social Anthropology)*, ed. N. Jayaram and Satish Saberwal. Delhi: Oxford University Press, pp. 402–12.

———. 1998. "The Decline of the BKU," paper presented at the European Conference of Modern Asian Studies, Charles University, Prague, September. Mimeo.

Madsen, Stig T., and Staffan Lindberg. 2003. "Modelling Institutional Fate: The Case of a Farmers' Movement in Uttar Pradesh," in *Social and Political Change in Uttar Pradesh. European Perspectives*, ed. Roger Jeffery and Jens Lerche. Manohar, Delhi, pp. 199–223.

Mandelbaum, David G. 1970. *Society in India* (2 volumes). Berkeley: University of California Press.

Massey, Doreen. 1994. *Space, Place and Gender*. Minneapolis: Minnesota University Press.

———. 2005. *For Space*. London: Sage.

Mendelsohn, Oliver. 1993. "The Transformation of Authority in Rural India," *Modern Asian Studies*, 27, 4, pp. 805–42.

Mendelsohn, Oliver, and Marieke Vicziany. 1998. *The Untouchables: Subordination, Poverty and the State in Modern India*. Cambridge: Cambridge University Press.

Metcalf, Barbara D. 1982. *Islamic Revival in British India: Deoband, 1860–1900*. Princeton, NJ: Princeton University Press.

Miles, Ann. 1998. "Women's Bodies, Women's Selves: Illness Narratives and the 'Andean' Body," *Body and Society*, 4, 3, pp. 1–19.

Miles, Rebecca. 2002. "Employment and Unemployment in Jordan: The Importance of the Gender System," *World Development*, 30, 3, pp. 413–27.

Mitchell, Timothy. 2004. *Intoxicated Identities: Alcohol's Power in Mexican History and Culture*. London and New York: Routledge.

Mohan, Giles, and Kristian Stokke. 2000. "Participatory Development and Empowerment: The Dangers of Localism," *Third World Quarterly*, 21, 2, pp. 247–68.

Mooij, Jos, and S. Mahendra Dev. 2002. "Social Sector Priorities: An Analysis of Budgets and Expenditures," Institute of Development Studies. *IDS Working Paper* 164, University of Sussex, Brighton, UK.

Mosse, David. 1995. "Authority, Gender and Knowledge: Theoretical Reflections on the Practice of Participatory Rural Appraisal," *Development and Change*, 25, 3, pp. 497–526.

———. 2003. "On Binaries and Boundaries," in *Regional Modernities: The Cultural Politics of Development in India*, ed. K. Sivaramakrishnan and Arun Agrawal. Stanford, CA: Stanford University Press, pp. 329–37.

Nambissan, Geeta B. 1996. "Equity in Education? Schooling of Dalit Children in India," *Economic and Political Weekly*, 31, 16 and 17, pp. 1011–19.

Nambissan, Geeta B., and M. Sedwal. 2002. "Education for All: The Situation of Dalit Children in India," in *India Education Report*, ed. R. Govinda. Delhi: Oxford University Press, pp. 72–86.

Nevill, H. H. 1922. *Meerut—A Gazetteer*. Lucknow: Government Branch Press.

Nieuwenhuys, Olga. 1994. *Children's Lifeworlds: Gender, Welfare and Labour in the Developing World*. London: Routledge.

Nilan, Pam, and Carles Feixa. 2006. *Global Youth? Hybrid Identities, Plural Worlds*. London: Routledge.

Omvedt, Gail. 1994. *Dalits and the Democratic Revolution: Dr. Ambedkar and the Dalit Movement in Colonial India*. Delhi: Sage.

Osella, Caroline, and Filippo Osella. 2002. "Contextualising Sexuality: Young Men in Kerala, South India," in *Coming of Age in South and Southeast Asia: Youth, Courtship and Sexuality*, eed. L. Rice Pranee and Lenore Manderson. Richmond, Surrey: Curzon.

Osella, Filippo, and Caroline Osella. 2000. *Social Mobility in Kerala: Modernity and Identity in Conflict*. London: Pluto Press.

———. 2003. "Migration and the Commoditisation of Ritual: Sacrifice, Spectacle and Contestations in Kerala, India," *Contributions to Indian Sociology*, 37, 1, pp. 21–22.

———. 2007. *Men and Masculinities in South India*. London: Anthem Press.

Oxfeld, Ellen. 1993. *Blood, Sweat and Mahjong: Family and Enterprise in an Overseas Chinese Community*. Ithaca, NY: Cornell University Press.

Pai, Sudha. 1998. "Pradhanis in New Panchayats, Field Notes from Meerut District," *Economic and Political Weekly*, 33, 18, pp. 1009–10.

———. 2000. "New Social and Political Movements of Dalits: A Study of Meerut District," *Contributions to Indian Sociology* 34, 2, pp. 189–220.

———. 2002. *Dalit Assertion and the Unfinished Democratic Revolution: The Bahujan Samaj Party in Uttar Pradesh*. Delhi: Sage.

Pai, Sudha, and Jagpal Singh. 1997. "Politicisation of Dalits and Most Backward Castes: Study of Social Conflict and Political Preferences in Four Villages of Meerut District," *Economic and Political Weekly*, 32, 23, pp. 1356–61.

Pandit, S. S. 1974. *A Critical Study of the Contribution of the Arya Samaj to Indian Education*. New Delhi: Arvadeshik Arya Pratinidhi Sabha.

Papanek, Hanna. 1979. "Family Status Production: The 'Work' and 'Non-work' of Women," *Signs*, 4, 4, pp. 775–81.

Parry, Jonathan P. 1999. "Two Cheers for Reservation: The Satnamis and the Steel Plant," in *Institutions and Inequalities*, ed. Ramachandran Guha and Jonathan P. Parry. Delhi: Oxford University Press, pp. 128–69.

———. 2005. "Changing Childhoods in Industrial Chhattisgarh," in *Educational Regimes in Contemporary India*, ed. Radhika Chopra and Patricia Jeffery. Delhi: Sage.

Pradhan M. C. 1966. *The Political System of the Jats of North India*. Bombay: Oxford University Press.

Prause, JoAnne, and C. David Dooley. 1997. "Effects of Underemployment on School-leavers' Self-esteem," *Journal of Adolescence*, 20, pp. 243–60.

The Probe Team. 1999. *Public Report on Basic Education in India*. Delhi: Oxford University Press.

Putnam, Robert, with Robert Leonardi and Raffaella Y. Nanetti. 1993. *Making Democracy Work: Civic Traditions in Modern Italy*. Princeton, NJ: Princeton University Press.

Raheja, Gloria G. 1988. *The Poison in the Gift: Ritual Prestation, and the Dominant Caste in a North Indian Village*. Chicago: University of Chicago Press.

Ramachandran, Vimala (ed.). 2004. *Gender and Social Equity in Primary Education. Hierarchies of Access*. Delhi: Sage.

Ramachandran, V. K., and M. Swaminathan. 2005. *Financial Liberalization and Rural Credit in India*. Delhi: Tukila.

Reay, Diane. 1995. "'They Employ Cleaners to Do That:' Habitus in the Primary School Classroom," *British Journal of the Sociology of Education*, 16, 3, pp. 353–71.

Reed-Danahay, Deborah. 2005. *Locating Bourdieu*. Bloomington, IN: Indiana University Press.

Registrar General & Census Commissioner of India. 2002. *Population in the Age Group 0–6 and Literates by Residence and Sex—India and States/Union Territories.* Delhi: Ministry of Home Affairs.

———. 2004. *Table C-14: Population in Five Year Age-group by Residence and Sex.* Delhi: Census Commissioner (Tabulations made available in electronic format).

Roberts, Ken, Colette Fagan, Klara Foti, Bohdan Jung, Sykia Kovatcheva, Adam Kurzynowski, and Ladislav Machacek. 1999. "Youth Unemployment in East-Central Europe," *Sociologica*, 29, 6, pp. 671–84.

Robinson, Marguerite. 1988. *Local Politics: The Law of the Fishes—Development Through Political Change in Medak District, Andhra Pradesh (South India).* Delhi: Oxford University Press.

Rutten, Mario. 1995. *Farms and Factories.* Delhi: Sage.

Sachar, Rajinder. 2006. *Social, Economic and Educational Status of the Muslim Community in India.* Delhi: Cabinet Secretariat, Government of India.

Sarkar, Sumit. 1996. "Indian Nationalism and the Politics of Hindutva," in *Contesting the Nation: Religion, Community, and the Politics of Democracy in India*, ed. David Ludden. Philadelphia: University of Pennsylvania Press, pp. 270–93.

Sawicki, Jana 1994. "Queering Foucault and the Subject of Feminism," in *The Cambridge Companion to Foucault*, ed. Gary Gutting. Cambridge: Cambridge University Press, pp. 379–400.

Scheper-Hughes, Nancy. 1995. "The Primacy of the Ethical: Propositions for a Militant Anthropology," *Current Anthropology*, 36, 3, pp. 409–40.

Scott, James. C. 1985. *Weapons of the Weak: Everyday Forms of Peasant Resistance.* New Haven, CT: Yale University Press.

Seabright, Paul. 2001. "The Road Upward," *New York Review of Books*, 48, 5, pp. 68–74.

Sen, Abhijit. 1997. "Structural Adjustment and Rural Poverty: Variables that Really Matter," in *Growth, Employment and Poverty: Change and Continuity in Rural India*, ed. G. K. Chadha and A. N. Sharma. Vikas: Delhi.

Sen, Amartya. 1999. *Development as Freedom.* Delhi: Oxford University Press.

Sharma, Rita, and Thomas T. Poleman. 1993. *The New Economics of India's Green Revolution: Income and Employment Diffusion in Uttar Pradesh.* Ithaca, NY: Cornell University Press.

Sharma, Ursula. 1980. *Women, Work and Property in North West India.* London: Tavistock.

Shukla, Shrilal. 1992 [1967]. *Raag Darbari.* (trans Gillian Wright) Delhi: Penguin.

Sikand, Yoginder. 2005. *Bastion of the Believers: Madrasas and Islamic Education in India.* Delhi: Penguin.

Singh, Jagpal. 1992. *Capitalism and Dependence: Agrarian Politics in Western Uttar Pradesh 1951–1991.* Delhi: Manohar.

Sivaramakrishnan, K., and A. Agrawal (eds.). 2003. *Regional Modernities: The Cultural Politics of Development in India*. Stanford, CA: Stanford University Press.

Skinner, Debra, and Dorothy Holland. 1996. "Schools and the Cultural Production of the Educated Person in a Nepalese Hill Community," in *The Cultural Production of the Educated Person: Critical Ethnographies of Schooling and Local Practice*, ed. Bradley A. Levinson, Douglas E. Foley and Dorothy C. Holland. Albany: State University of New York Press, pp. 272–300.

Spivak, Gayatri. 1988. "Can the Subaltern Speak?" in *Marxism and the interpretation of Culture*, ed. Cary Nelson and Larry Grossberg, Chicago: University of Illinois Press, pp. 271–313.

Srinivas, M. N. 1955. "The Social System of a Mysore Village," in *Village India*, ed. McKim Marriott. Chicago: University of Chicago Press.

———. 1989. *The Cohesive Role of Sanskritization and Other Essays*. Oxford: Oxford University Press.

Srivastava, Ravi. 1995. "India's Uneven Development and Its Implications for Political Processes: An Analysis of Some Recent Trends," in *Industry and Agriculture in India Since Independence*, ed. T. V. Sathyamurthy. Delhi: Oxford University Press, pp. 190–221.

Srivastava, Sanjay. 1998. *Constructing Post-Colonial India: National Character and the Doon School*. London: Routledge.

Stambach, Amy. 1998. "'Too Much Studying Makes Me Crazy': School-related Illness on Mount Kilimanjaro," *Comparative Education Review*, 42, 4, pp. 497–512.

Stokes, Eric. 1986. *The Peasant Armed: The Indian Revolt of 1857*. Oxford: Clarendon Press.

Sundar, Nandini. 2004. "Teaching to Hate: RSS' Pedagogical Programme," *Economic and Political Weekly*, 39, 16, pp. 1605–12.

Tarlo, Emma. 1996. *Clothing Matters: Dress and Identity in India*. London: Hurst and Co.

———. 2003. *Unsettling Memories: Narratives of the Emergency in Delhi*. Delhi: Permanent Black.

Ul Haq, Mahbub. 2003. *Human Development in South Asia 2003: The Employment Challenge*. Delhi. Oxford University Press.

Upadhya, Carol B. 1988. "From Kulak to Capitalist: The Emergence of a New Business Community in Coastal Andhra Pradesh, India." PhD dissertation, Yale University, New Haven.

Valentine, Gillian, Tracey Skelton, and D. Chambers (eds.). 1998. *Cool Places: An Introduction to Youth and Youth Cultures*. London: Routledge.

Varma, Pavan K. 1998. *The Great Indian Middle Class*. Delhi: Viking.

Varshney, Ashutosh. 2000. "Is India Becoming More Democratic?" *Journal of Asian Studies*, 59, 1, pp. 3–25.

Verma, Suman, and T. S. Saraswathi. 2002. "Adolescence in India: Street Urchins or Sili-
con Valley Millionaires?" in the *World's Youth: Adolescence in Eight Regions of the
Globe*, ed. Bradford B. Brown, Reed W. Larson and T. S. Saraswathi. Cambridge:
Cambridge University Press.

Visaria, Pravin. 2003. "Unemployment among Youth in India: Level, Nature and Policy
Implications." Mimeo.

Weiss, Brad. 2002. "Thug Realism: Inhabiting Fantasy in Urban Tanzania," *Cultural Anthropology*, 17, 1, pp. 93–124.

Williams, Raymond. 1977. *Marxism and Literature*. Oxford: Oxford University Press.

Willis, Paul. 1977. *Learning to Labour: How Working Class Kids Get Working Class Jobs*.
Farnborough: Saxon House.

———. 1982. "Cultural Production and Theories of Reproduction," in *Race, Class and
Education*, ed. L. Barton and S. Walker. London: Croome Helm, pp. 112–42.

Wolf, Eric R. 1956. "Aspects of Group Relations in a Complex Society: Mexico," *American
Anthropologist*, 58, 6, pp. 1065–78.

World Bank. 2002. *World Development Indicators*. Washington D C: World Bank.

Yon, D. 2000. "Urban Portraits of Identity: On the Problem of Knowing Culture and
Identity in Intercultural Studies," *Journal of Intercultural Studies*, 21, 2, pp. 143–57.

Index

In this index an "f" after a number indicates a separate reference on the next page, and an "ff" indicates separate references on the next two pages. A continuous discussion over two or more pages is indicated by a span of page numbers, e.g., "57–59." *Passim* is used for a cluster of references in close but not consecutive sequence.